"*A Therapist's Guide to Treating Eating Disorders in a Social Media Age* is a must-read for therapists. Shauna Frisbie takes the reader through an insightful journey about eating disorders. While the author pays attention to detail and research, the book also contains practical information. The emphasis on social media and its influence on eating disorders helps the reader navigate through the important issue of identity formation. The attributes of this book are many and stretch into both the professional and personal realm."

—**Loretta Bradley, Ph.D.,** Professor, Texas Tech University, Fellow, American Counseling Association, Former President of American Counseling Association

"This book is an essential read for therapists who treat eating disorders as well as therapists who work with adolescents. Dr. Frisbie eloquently weaves clinical experience and theory together to provide insight into how adolescents develop their personal identity through interactions facilitated by social media. The shift in how adolescents view themselves and the world profoundly impacts how identity is developed. All therapists need Dr. Frisbie's book as a guide through the new reality of identity development."

—**Beth Robinson, Ed.D.,** Professor of Psychology, Lubbock Christian University

A THERAPIST'S GUIDE TO TREATING EATING DISORDERS

IN A SOCIAL MEDIA AGE

A THERAPIST'S GUIDE TO TREATING EATING DISORDERS

IN A SOCIAL MEDIA AGE

SHAUNA FRISBIE

W. W. NORTON & COMPANY

Independent Publishers Since 1923

Note to Readers: Standards of clinical practice and protocol change over time, and no technique or recommendation is guaranteed to be safe or effective in all circumstances. This volume is intended as a general information resource for professionals practicing in the field of psychotherapy and mental health; it is not a substitute for appropriate training, peer review, and/or clinical supervision. Neither the publisher nor the author(s) can guarantee the complete accuracy, efficacy, or appropriateness of any particular recommendation in every respect. To protect client privacy, names, and details have been changed. Descriptions of images were likewise altered to protect confidentiality.

For information about permission to reproduce selections from this book, write to Permissions, W. W. Norton & Company, Inc., 500 Fifth Avenue, New York, NY 10110

For information about special discounts for bulk purchases, please contact W. W. Norton Special Sales at specialsales@wwnorton.com or 800-233-4830

Manufacturing by Sheridan Books
Book design by Anna Reich
Production manager: Katelyn MacKenzie

Library of Congress Cataloging-in-Publication Data

Names: Frisbie, Shauna, author.
Title: A therapist's guide to treating eating disorders in a social media age / Shauna Frisbie.
Description: First edition. | New York : W.W. Norton & Company, 2020. |
"A Norton professional book." | Includes bibliographical references and index.
Identifiers: LCCN 2019057966 | ISBN 9780393714456 (paperback) |
ISBN 9780393714463 (epub)
Subjects: LCSH: Eating disorders--Treatment. | Social media.
Classification: LCC RC552.E18 F75 2020 | DDC 616.85/26—dc23
LC record available at https://lccn.loc.gov/2019057966

W. W. Norton & Company, Inc., 500 Fifth Avenue, New York, N.Y. 10110
www.wwnorton.com

W. W. Norton & Company Ltd., 15 Carlisle Street, London W1D 3BS

2 3 4 5 6 7 8 9 0

To my mother, who made a calm, safe space for my early years, shared stories, and taught me to remember the ones that matter. And to my husband Gary, who makes possible the great relationship that we all deserve.

Contents

Acknowledgments

This book has been a work in progress for over ten years, the ideas growing slowly from my clinical experience with eating disorders. Thus, I must first acknowledge my clients who have shared their stories and their photographs. Their responses to photo therapy are the inspiration for this book.

Having an idea and turning into a book is a journey that would not be possible without the guidance of others. Thank you to W. W. Norton and Company for selecting this manuscript for publication. I am grateful to Deborah Malmud at Norton for taking an interest in my work and moving this project from proposal to reality. Words cannot express my gratitude for your feedback to the manuscript. I am also grateful to Mariah Eppes, project editor at Norton Professional Books, and the many competent individuals there who have edited, designed the cover, marketed, and generally smoothed this process. Thank you to Loretta Bradley, who was so generous with her time to read this book and to Latayne Scott for her willingness to read and edit.

Of course, no one can make it through life without their tribe, those people who make life worth living. Thank you to my friends, family, and friends who are really more family than friends—Tami Prichard, Christye Weld, and Kaylene Brown. Special thanks to Beth Robinson, colleague and true friend, whose giant whiteboard diagram structured my ideas for this book, who gives excellent advice and is ready for any adventure. I am blessed beyond measure by my family—Gary, who loves well and supports my endless array of projects. He is the best fit I can imagine in a husband and first-rate father to our next generation—Zane, Sonnet, and Nash. I love doing life with them all.

A THERAPIST'S GUIDE TO TREATING EATING DISORDERS

IN A SOCIAL MEDIA AGE

Chapter 1

EATING DISORDERS AND IDENTITY

In the social jungle of human existence, there is no feeling of being alive without a sense of identity.

—Erik Erikson

The phone rings, a text dings, and the task at hand is forgotten. We can turn off alerts from the myriad of social media platforms, but we still remain immersed, to varying degrees, in a technological maze that is always "on." Social media presence is now essential in obtaining and maintaining employment. From resumes and networking on LinkedIn to jobs relying on information obtained and transmitted via the Internet to idealized jobs as social media influencers, this generation is dependent on technology for their very livelihood. As the Internet became increasingly influential, a business essay titled *The Brand Called You*[1] introduced the idea that to succeed in the business world, people must view themselves as a brand to be marketed and promoted. The term "self-branding" was coined to describe the necessity of creating the "brand of You" to become a free agent in an increasingly competitive world of work.

This idea morphed into a personal mandate that we must create an online presence and following by distinguishing ourselves from others. In this scenario, the self is the created product and success is a matter of perception. If you want others to see you in a certain way, build a personal visibility campaign that promotes your brand. The impact of self-branding is a topic of considerable debate among mental health professionals, the technology sector, and those invested in making money from or protecting vulnerable segments of the population. Clearly, identity creation today is far more complex than in past generations.

All humans need space to think, to be, and to process without incessant distraction. This is especially true for adolescents and young adults for whom identity formation is one of the most consuming tasks at hand. But constant connection leaves little space without intrusion from others and may lead to feelings of isolation. The early days of the COVID-19 crisis brought an awareness of this dynamic into the mainstream media. When much of daily life unexpectedly moved online, many people found their days filled with online classes and meetings that left them feeling emotionally exhausted. Sudden changes in daily routines and the implementation of social distancing to prevent the spread of COVID-19 increased social isolation and led in a surge in social media usage. Yet, despite spending more time in online meetings and on social media, many people realized for the first time that they experience a sense of disconnection from others when they are physically isolated. Eating disorders and other mental health disorders thrive in conditions such as this. For those with body image disturbance, being on camera can heighten appearance concerns. Memes and other images on social media about gaining weight due to staying home all day, or conversely a push to use the time during lockdown for intense dieting or exercise, are especially triggering for those with weight and food concerns. Public health crises like the COVID-19 virus teach us that maintaining meaningful connections with support systems and learning to manage social media use are now survival skills.

As an eating disorder treatment specialist, I witness the effects of technology on many of my clients. Because they feel completely powerless in the face of this all-encompassing disease, sometimes a parent, partner, or friend frantically seeks help for their loved one who is struggling with an eating disorder. Other times, the person with the eating disorder will reach out for help when they no longer want to live life constrained by eating disorder symptoms. Seldom is the topic of social media brought up in initial conversations; however, I have learned over the years to inquire early on about technology use because it invariably becomes part of the picture of eating disorder pathology. Although there are no simple answers and no easy solutions for treating eating disorders in a social media age, this book offers strategies to address social media use in the eating disorder population.

Initially assessing social media behavior begins with normalizing technology use as an almost constant activity. General questions about social media use inquire about how clients access social media and which platforms they use.

- What devices do you use (computer, smartphone, tablet, smartwatch, or other devices)?
- Which do you use the most?
- Which social media platforms do you use?
- Which are your favorites?

We know that social media is a constant factor in in the lives of many of our clients. Learning more about their social media habits provides a context to assess excessive use and exposure to damaging images. While there are no right or wrong answers, these questions provide a basis on which to evaluate whether social media is contributing to client problems.

- How often do you go to your social media accounts?
- Some young people spend eight hours a day online. Compared with this, how much time do you spend on social media daily?
- How do you keep in touch with your friends (in person, social media, text, phone)?
- How many friends or followers do you have? Do you personally know all of them?
- What do you most often do on social media (look at others' profiles, posts or photos; post comments; post photos or videos you've taken)?
- What kind of photos or videos do you post?

Follow-up discussions to these last two questions can provide insight into what clients are viewing, how they are impacted by what they are viewing, and the images they may be creating and posting.

Assessing the positive aspects of technology can broaden client perspectives on social media use and further encourage open discussion of online behaviors.

- What do you think are positive aspects of social media?
- Which online activities are beneficial to you (connection with friends or making new friends; using social media for support through a difficult time)?
- Do you use social media to gain wellness or self-help information?
- Do you use media to deal with stress or strong emotions?

Indicators of problematic aspects of social media use include the following: comparison with others, excessive use that interferes with other activities or indicates dependence, behaviors that raise safety issues (sexting or revealing personal information), damaging influences due to certain content, or other negative outcomes from social media use (bullying). Answering yes to any of the following questions requires follow-up with psychoeducation and/or therapeutic interventions.

- Does social media use ever cause problems for you or have you ever had any bad experiences online?
- Does social media use cause you stress or bring up strong emotions that you have difficulty dealing with, and if so, how?
- How long are you awake in the morning before checking social media?
- How often are you on social media rather than going to sleep at night?
- Do you ever wake up at night due to alerts or notifications on your phone?
- Have you visited sites or followed people who promote extreme fitness or excessive food restriction? How about people who model excessive thinness?
- Do you have anonymous accounts or make posts using a false name?
- Have you ever posted something online that caused problems for you or someone else?
- Have you ever posted photos or other posts that you would not want your parents or future employers to see?

Formal assessment of problematic technology use can also be assessed with standardized assessment instruments. One such assessment tool, the 18-item Problematic and Risky Internet Use Screening Scale (PRIUSS-18)[2] specifically assesses social impairment, emotional impairment, and risky Internet use. Although this scale broadly assesses general Internet use, rather than targeting only social media use, the questions ask about behaviors similar to the ones included in the less formal interview format given above. This quick assessment can highlight problematic behaviors that can then be followed with more detailed questions to identify specific areas to address therapeutically.

Social media use can be especially problematic for individuals with eating disorders. According to the National Eating Disorder Association, an estimated

30 million Americans and 70 million people worldwide suffer from eating disorders.[3] These alarming numbers have spurred a growing body of research seeking answers to the underlying reasons for increasing rates around the world. Eating disorders have been linked with a wide range of factors, from family dysfunction and trauma exposure to genetics and personality traits. None of these alone fully explain why a young person adopts rigid rules for eating or not eating, binges uncontrollably, or engages in behaviors, such as purging, to compensate for food intake. Current research indicates that multiple factors impact the development of an eating disorder as the individual attempts to handle the experiences of adolescence and young adulthood. A common feature, however, is a deficit in identity. By focusing on something other than the frequently overwhelming experiences of these life stages, a young person is given a break from the arduous task of developing who they are in a continually shifting world.

Eating disorders are indeed complex issues. Often comorbid with other psychological disturbances, such as depression, anxiety, substance abuse, self-harm, and suicidal behavior, eating disorders have one of the highest mortality risks of all psychological diagnoses.[4] The difficulty of treating eating disorders is well-known in the therapy field, as these disorders are often chronic and treatment resistant. Among the most well-known treatment modalities are cognitive behavioral therapy, acceptance and commitment therapy, dialectical behavior therapy, emotionally-focused therapy, interpersonal psychotherapy, and internal family systems therapy. In recognizing the efficacy of each of these, this book specifically focuses on identity development in a social media age, a particularly salient target in those with eating disorders.

Rapid developmental and social processes occur from the beginning of adolescence, when the push for independence accelerates, to the late twenties; this span of ages also has the highest rates of eating disorders. During this time the question of "Who am I?" is central to normative development. The quest is intensified by rapid brain changes and a social milieu that encourages one to be constantly connected yet distinct from the crowd. Technologies such as the Internet and social media have expanded the contexts in which identities are developed. Whereas familial, local community, and religious influences were once primary information sources, today a constant stream of global culture, primarily transmitted through visual images, deluges young people. Western ideas and cultural norms regarding body weight and appearance now influence cultures worldwide. Previously, eating disorders were found only in westernized cultures such as the United Stated and much of Western Europe, but these disorders are now a growing problem in other parts of the world.[5] Eating disorders are no longer culturally bound, and global norms now shape identity.

IDENTITY DEVELOPMENT AND EATING DISORDERS

A necessary first step to understanding the relationship between identity and eating disorders is to clarify terminology. Scholars often use the terms self and identity interchangeably in describing them as mental constructs, social products, and forces for action.[6] While it is sometimes advantageous to make distinctions between the terms, a unified consensus is lacking across the diverse fields that have produced tens of thousands of scholarly articles with these keywords. Hence, I use the terms identity and sense of self interchangeably in this book to refer to what comes to mind when a person thinks of or describes who they are. I will explore this in more depth in subsequent chapters.

We speak of identity crises in which people lose a sense of who they are in response to life events, such as a loss, or to a developmental stage, like midlife. Identity deficits, on the other hand, occur when a person lacks enough identity to know who they are or to make important life decisions. As young people transition from childhood to adolescence and into early adulthood, the problems of living and identity can seem overwhelming. Kathryn Zerbe, a noted leader in the field of eating disorders, asserts "The individual who does not discover a stable sense of who she or he is during this developmental period is inclined to engage in forms of self-destructive behaviors that do violence to their changing bodies."[7] That an identity deficit is present in most, if not all, individuals diagnosed with eating disorders illustrates the developmental nature of eating disorders: eating disorders are artifacts of extreme difficulty in navigating the task of identity development.

Eating disorders occur most commonly between ages 12 and 25, when identity-making is a primary concern and identity deficits are common. The median age of onset for binge eating disorder is 21, and for anorexia nervosa and bulimia nervosa it is 18.[8] The tasks of these years can seem crushing, leading to feelings of helplessness and a preoccupation with controlling the body—core features of eating disorders.

Identity forms in the context of experiences and relationships.[9] The self is a product of social processes that influence what is valued in a culture, group, or time in history.[10] Thus, it could be said that our sense of who we are is molded both by the presence of others and our need to fit in with them. Their opinions shape our sense of self; one simply cannot exist without seeing oneself through the eyes of others. Belonging to the group is a social imperative, but also a challenging experience. The sheer number of roles an individual enacts when attempting to develop a coherent sense of self attests to the difficulty of this process.[11] Feedback comes from friends, more distant peers, parents, other family members, teachers, bosses, co-workers, and now also a barrage from strangers encountered through technology.

In times past, internal characteristics, such as character and intelligence, defined one's identity, but today, one's appearance and ownership of coveted goods define one's identity.[12] Consumerism is the natural outgrowth of this new focus, and products abound to help people meet the cultural standards of appearance and wealth. If identity is now based on these external factors, it can now be changed and manipulated at will to create an illusion to present to others. Appearance can be manipulated by applying camera filters and retouching, selecting camera angles, and even undergoing surgical procedures. Seeming to be a certain way and having status goods have become more important than being a person of honor or intelligence. One no longer must "be" a certain way; to "seem" it is enough.[13] In fact, social media provides a space to express identity via consumerism without the need to physically own or consume goods. One can now appropriate any number of digital images, brands, logos, and almost anything else onto a social media page in order to present the desired self-image.[14] For many, social media is now the single most influential factor in identity development.

Social media has not only generated a space for the creation of identity, but also the necessary audience. As social beings, humans have a need to be noticed, which is reflected in a burgeoning obsession with fame. If you ask young people today about their aspirations, it is not uncommon for them to confess that they want to be an Instagram influencer or a YouTube superstar. It is no longer enough to follow celebrities; anyone has the potential to become one if they can garner a following on social media; and having followers gives one a sense of self-importance. Online life has replaced the mall and park where groups of adolescents previously gathered, shifting the very nature of socializing and identity development. Social media posts are a platform to broadcast one's identity to those whose opinions and acceptance matter. Online feedback is an expected response, one that has important implications for identity. The massive amount of feedback is often anonymous, and in worst-case scenarios can be brutal. At best it provides affirmation, but at what cost? Affirmation of undesirable traits and affirmation based on a snapshot of behavior or on unhealthy appearance standards exact a heavy price. Without a doubt, these opinions have untold potential to shape one's sense of self.

In the early 1980s, as the millennial generation was entering this world, professionals in the eating disorder field began to identify impairments in identity development as precursors to eating disorder occurrence.[15] Maladaptive coping behaviors can eclipse normative development in the adolescent with an ill-formed or weak identity. This is especially true for females who may use thinness as a misguided attempt to meet the cultural demands of achievement while also adhering to female role and appearance expectations. If you have been taught that losing weight and being thin is a solution to most any problem, eating disorders are an unsurprising consequence.

These concerns are not unique to females. The growing number of males with eating disorders attests to the changing landscape of these devastating disorders, as males now make up 25% of all anorexia nervosa cases. In addition, males have a higher risk of dying because they are diagnosed later due to the stereotype that males don't suffer from eating disorders.[16] Disordered behaviors that don't meet clinical criteria for diagnosis, such as binge eating, purging, laxative abuse, and fasting for weight loss, are almost as common among males as females.[17] For both males and females, looking to the media for guidance leads to beliefs that appearance can be altered through hard work, manipulation, and even starvation. Underlying all this is the pervasive message that whatever you are, you're not good enough.

The development of an eating disorder is seen by some as an adaptive measure to compensate for perceived lack of responsiveness from early caregivers and the resulting identity deficit. From this perspective, eating disordered behaviors are attempts to attend to underlying unmet needs and developmental deficits, but these behaviors do not mitigate the underlying identity deficit.[18] Eating disorders are multifaceted; however, at a basic level the behaviors provide short-term relief from intolerable emotions, even if the emotions are not recognized by the sufferer. Anxiety, depression, excessive control, compulsive behaviors, and extreme perfectionism may emerge when trying to manage unrecognized emotional experiences. Determining who one is in relation to cultural expectations takes place outside of conscious awareness, diminishing the likelihood of effective coping strategies.

An eating disorder can define the self for some by providing an identity over which they feel they have control. It is not unusual for a client with an eating disorder to state that they would be no one without the eating disorder. Identity becomes warped when entangled in an eating disorder; the person comes to identify as an anorexic or bulimic and will strive to act in ways that fit with this identity. Separating the sense of self from the eating disorder is difficult because all thoughts are filtered through the mindset of the eating disorder identity. The eating disorder identity is foremost in one's mind, and behavioral decisions are often made at the unconscious level, meaning the person does not have insight into the underlying emotions and desires that drive their behaviors.

Eating disorder behaviors are ego syntonic: they fit with one's identity as they view it at the time. Individuals are more comfortable in identity-congruent behaviors and tend to interpret situations in ways that are congruent with the preferred identity.[19] An eating disordered identity leads one to believe that they would be lost without the eating disorder and often prevents them from desiring recovery. A central aspect of treatment involves relinquishing the eating disorder as the cornerstone of personal identity and building a new, fuller identity.[20] If this does not occur, the eating disorder may become chronic. The therapist's task is to assist the client in gaining awareness of the unconscious processes and of their true self, so they can begin to make decisions based on an authentic identity.

It is not enough to treat only the symptoms or thought patterns related to the eating disorder; separating the self from the eating disorder and creating healthy identity is vital for recovery. Full recovery has been shown to be associated with an improved sense of self,[21] making identity development a necessary component of eating disorder treatment. Given that eating disorders affect core issues of identity development, we need to understand how prevalent cultural images become integrated into identity. Most of these images are currently promulgated on social media, as these platforms have taken over other means of information acquisition.

TREATMENT OVERVIEW

Twenty plus years of treating eating disorders have given me great respect for the ongoing search for effective therapeutic models for these difficult conditions. Having received training in evidence-based models for working with this population, I have seen firsthand the positive changes these methods can impart and continue to implement these models with my clients; however, current models for addressing social media use are lacking. This book will equip trained therapists working with eating disorders to guide clients on their journey to development of a healthy sense of self in a social media age. Case illustrations will show how to implement photo therapy techniques in identity work, with emphasis on navigating visual images. Photo therapy should be viewed as one component in a comprehensive treatment model that addresses identity deficits, damaging behaviors, interpersonal relationships, and maladaptive thought patterns reflected in eating disorders, rather than a stand-alone treatment. True recovery from an eating disorder occurs when the healthy self is permitted to show up and is honored.

Chapter 2 looks at the dangers of social media to those with body dissatisfaction and/or eating disorders. Researchers are now beginning to look at how viewing images on social media and other online formats impacts those with body image and eating concerns. This chapter will introduce key components of a model for addressing social media use. Photo therapy techniques will be introduced for using client-selected images, whether of the client or others, to uncover the underlying messages that are impacting the client. Recommended photo therapy questions and activities given throughout the book are included in Appendix A.

One's self-narrative is crucial to identity: Chapters 3 and 4 examine the relationship of the narrative to identity work in relation to eating disorders and social media. The hallmark of identity formation in Millennials and Generation Z (Gen Z) is one in which visual input is a pervading force. Recognizing how culture influences identity development is key to working with this population. Chapter 3 explores identity development in more detail and introduces the case of Brandon, whose eating disorder, immersion in social media and video games, and identity confusion threaten to derail his future. Chapter 4 presents clinical treatment with Brandon, illustrating the necessity of narrative change. Family photographs are used to help him explore expectations in his family and how those expectations have impacted his sense of self. Brandon's own self-truths can emerge only if he allows himself room to explore and construct identity. This case study, as will others in subsequent chapters, illustrates the application of therapeutic techniques that use client-chosen photos to evoke insight and growth.

Chapter 5 explores photography on a deeper level, from the development of photographic processes that have reshaped culture to the ways that this technology impacts our ability to discern reality from fiction The case of Tia is presented to illustrate how the images one views and creates of others can impact identity. Chapter 6 follows the therapeutic work with Tia as she develops the ability to self-reflect on the behaviors, thoughts, and emotions that occur in response to the images she creates. She learns to monitor her use of images and gains insight into her inner longings. Tia acquires the capability to identify behavioral patterns that lead to and maintain food restriction as she explores her sense of self in relation to her emerging career as a photographer.

Chapter 7 moves further into the realm of social media by looking at the emergence of selfies, which were brought forth through the confluence of advancements in photography, the Internet, and social media platforms. Selfies have transformed the landscape of identity development by their widespread use and ease of sharing. Clients like Macy, introduced in Chapter 7, are lost in the overwhelming world of social media selfies. Without a good map or guidance in map-reading, Macy spends her days in an anxiety-induced haze. Bingeing provides only temporary relief from her rampant emotions. Chapter 8 follows up with Macy to demonstrate how to use client selfies in the therapeutic process. With self-awareness of her reactions to selfies that she gains in photo therapy exercises, Macy calms her anxiety and begins the work of identity formation.

In Chapter 9 the inborn desire to belong or feel part of a group is explored. Despite technology that enables and even requires constant connection, rates of loneliness in adolescents and young adults are skyrocketing. Sara is transitioning from middle to high school while in the throes of bulimia nervosa. She desperately wants to fit in and is unable to break the binge–purge cycle that replaced restriction as an attempt to gain a body she hoped would enable her access to a desired peer group. Near-constant use of Instagram and Snapchat exposes her to idealized images uploaded by others and produces anxiety over how others respond to images of her. Sara needs space to get in touch with her unique self and to differentiate herself from others. Chapter 10 illustrates identity development work with Sara using the images she is viewing on social media. Sara must balance the demands of social media for constant connection with her need for space to construct her own sense of self. She is highly reactive to images others post, and her social media feed is a reminder of what she is missing out on. The therapist's role in countering these typical responses to social media forms the core of this chapter.

Chapter 11 addresses potential issues that may arise when young people are damaged by others' images on social media. The potential for harm is heightened if these images depict the client, whether taken with or without consent. The case of Claire is introduced to illustrate one such scenario. Treatment with Claire, who engages in extreme exercise, body hatred, and perfectionism is presented in Chapter 12. This case highlights the need for trauma treatment when unresolved past trauma is present and demonstrates how photo therapy methods can be integrated into trauma processing to facilitate healing. The use of images can aid trauma processing in various ways, and several of these ways will be addressed in this chapter.

Chapter 13 integrates the material presented in previous chapters—healing narratives, neuroscience, and photo therapy—with the treatment of eating disorders. Mediating the effects of social media on those with eating disorders requires addressing the visual images that impact recovery. The therapeutic relationship is strengthened when the therapist meets the client where they are, and our clients are now online. When we bring this part of their lives into sessions, we demonstrate our openness to their experiences, and we will be rewarded with an unmediated front row seat into their everyday lives. As we facilitate the process of exploration through photo therapy, we guide the client toward self-compassion, self-reflection, self-awareness, self-differentiation, and self-realization. By encouraging these self-oriented processes, we provide a map to identity and we honor the unique person sitting in our office.

REFERENCES

1. Peters, T. (1997, August 31). The brand called you. *Fast Company*. Retrieved from https://www.fastcompany.com/28905/brand-called-you

2. Social Media and Adolescent Health Research Team (SMAHRT). (n.d.) Retrieved from http://smahrtrescearh.com/use-our-methods/

   Moreno, M.A., Jelenchick, L.A., & Christakis, D.A. (2013). Problematic internet use among older adolescents: A conceptual framework. *Computers in Human Behavior*, 29(4),1879-1887.

   Jelenchick, L.A., Eickhoff, J., Christakis, D.A., Brown, R.L., Zhang, C., Benson, M., & Moreno, M.A. (2014). The Problematic and Risky Internet Use Screening Scale (PRIUSS) for adolescents and young adults: Scale development and refinement. *Computers in Human Behavior*, 35, 171-178.

   Jelenchick, L.A., Eickhoff, J., Zhang, C., Kraninger, K., Christakis, D.A., & Moreno, M.A.

(2015). Screening for adolescent problematic internet use: Validation of the Problematic and Risky Internet Use Screening Scale (PRIUSS). *Academic Pediatrics*, 15, 658-665.

3. National Eating Disorder Association. (2019). Retrieved from https://www.nationaleating disorders.org/

4. Smink, F.R.E., van Hoeken, D, & Hoek, H.W. (2012). Epidemiology of eating disorders: Incidence, prevalence and mortality rates. *Current Psychiatry Reports*, 14:406–414. doi 10.1007/s11920-012-0282-y

5. Pike, K., & Dunne, P. E. (2015). The rise of eating disorders in Asia: A review. *Journal of Eating Disorders, 3*(33), 1–14.

6. Oyserman, D., Elmore, K., & Smith, G. (2012). Self, self-concept, and identity. In M. R. Leary & J. Price Tangney (Eds.), *Handbook of self and identity* (2nd ed., pp. 69–104). New York, NY: Guilford Press.

7. Zerbe, K. J. (2008). *Integrated treatment of eating disorders: Beyond the body betrayed* (p. 125). New York, NY: W. W. Norton & Company.

8. Hudson, J. I., Hiripi, E., Pope, H. G., Jr., & Kessler, R. C. (2007). The prevalence and correlates of eating disorders in the National Comorbidity Survey Replication. *Biological Psychiatry, 61*(3), 348–358.

Volpe, U., Tortorella, A., Machia, M., Monteleone, A. M., Albert, U., & Monteleone, P. (2016). Eating disorders: What age at onset? *Psychiatry Research, 238,* 225–27. doi:10.1016/j.psychres.2016.02.048.

9. Burkitt, I. (2008). *Social selves: Theories of self and society* (2nd ed.). London, UK: Sage.

10. Oyserman, D., Elmore, K., & Smith, G. (2012). Self, self-concept, and identity. In M. R. Leary & J. Price Tangney (Eds.), *Handbook of Self and Identity* (2nd ed., pp. 69–104). New York, NY: Guilford Press.

11. Gergen, K. J. (2011). The social construction of self. In S. Gallagher (Ed.), *The Oxford handbook of the self* (pp. 633–653). Oxford, UK: Oxford University Press.

12. Lasch, C. (1979). *The culture of narcissism.* New York, NY: Warner Books.

13. Bourdieu, P. (1984). *Distinction.* Cambridge, MA: Harvard University Press.

14. Doster, L. (2013). Millennial teens design and redesign themselves in online social networks. *Journal of Consumer Behavior, 12*(4), 267–279.

15. Bruch, H. (1982). Anorexia nervosa: Therapy and theory. *American Journal of Psychiatry, 139*(12), 1531–1538.

Casper, R. (1983). Some provisional ideas concerning psychological structure in anorexia nervosa and bulimia. In P. L. Darby, P. E. Garfinkel, D. M. Garner, & D. V. Coscina (Eds.), *Anorexia nervosa: Recent developments in research* (pp. 378–392). New York, NY: Alan R. Liss.

Schupak-Neuberg., E., & Nemeroff, C. J. (1993). Disturbances in identity and self-regulation in bulimia nervosa: Implications for a metaphorical perspective of "body as self". *International Journal of Eating Disorders, 13*(4), 335–347.

Stein, K. F., & Corte, C. (2007). Identity impairment and the eating disorders: Content and organization of the self-concept in women with anorexia nervosa and bulimia nervosa. *European Eating Disorders Review, 15*(1), 58–69.

16. Mond, J.M., Mitchison, D., & Hay, P. (2014). Prevalence and implications of eating disordered behavior in men. In L. Cohn & R. Lemberg (Eds.), *Current Findings on Males with Eating*

Disorders. Philadelphia, PA: Routledge.

17. Mitchison, D., Hay, P., Slewa-Younan, S., & Mond, J. (2014). The changing demographic profile of eating disorder behaviors in the community. *BMC Public Health, 14*(1). doi:10.1186/1471-2458-14-943.

18. Costin, C. (1999). *The eating disorder sourcebook: A comprehensive guide to the causes, treatments, and prevention of eating disorders* (2nd ed.). Los Angeles, CA: Lowell House.

19. Oyserman, D., Elmore, K., & Smith, G. (2012). Self, self-concept, and identity. In M. R. Leary & J. Price Tangney (Eds.), *Handbook of Self and Identity* (2nd ed., pp. 69–104). New York, NY: Guilford Press.

20. Zerbe, K. J. (1995). *The body betrayed: A deeper understanding of women, eating disorders, and treatment*. Carlsbad, CA: Gürze Books.

21. Bardone-Cone, A. M., Schaefer, L. M., Maldonado, C. R., Fitzsimmons, E. E., Harney, M. B., Lawson, M. A., Robinson, D. P., Tosh, A., & Smith. R. (2010). Aspects of self-concept and eating disorder recovery: What does the sense of self look like when an individual recovers from an eating disorder? *Journal of Social and Clinical Psychology, 29*(7), 821–846.

Chapter 2

OFF COURSE: A GENERATION LOST IN TECHNOLOGY

Distracted from distraction by distraction

—T.S. Eliot

The next time you are in a public place notice the other people around you. Odds are that many are seemingly unaware of their surroundings, with heads bent down to view the tiny screens that have become an extension of the immediate environment. According to the Pew Center *Teens, Social Media and Technology* research study in 2018, 95 percent of teens have access to a smartphone and 45 percent say they are online almost constantly.[1] The most popular apps are Instagram and the texting-with-photo-sharing app Snapchat.[2] Despite the traditional use of photographs as commemoration, Snapchat's paradoxical appeal seems to be its ephemeral design. In an age when phone memory storage is overloaded with images and all of life is documented, the fleeting nature of images that are visible to the recipient for only one to 10 seconds frees some people to post images that they believe will disappear quickly. These images are targeted to specific recipients rather than being posted on a more public site, such as Facebook.

Of Americans over age 18, Pew Center research noted that 88 percent of 18- to 29-year-olds and 78 percent of 30- to 49-year-olds use social media.[3] Freed from the mandatory educational time constraints of those under age 18, this age group's increased leisure time is often spent in online activity. Estimates of the average amount of time spent on the Internet and social media varies by age, with those in the 18- to 34-year-old age bracket spending the most time—an average of 7.5 hours a day. Approximately 30% of that time is spent on social media, which is no surprise to anyone who interacts with this age group.[4] We live in a media-drenched world where the hurricane of visual stimulation is continuously raging.

Technology has moved us to an age of constant connectivity and overexposure to visual stimuli. Bruce Hood, author of *The Self Illusion*,[5] believes that these technological advances are altering the very ways we communicate and ultimately the structure of the human brain, with consequences to the sense of self. Social media is the epitome of communication trends in which most information is no longer in written form. Not only are we now constantly connected but images have replaced text as the foundation of communication, leading to visual overload.

While we do not yet know the full impact of social media, we can look to emergent media in a previous era to predict the impact of digital technology. Coinciding with an increase in eating disorder rates, the years since 1950 have witnessed unprecedented acceleration in the average person's interaction with technological advances. Younger audiences are especially vulnerable to television programming that reinforces weight-based stigma by portraying higher weight individuals in a negative light and thinner individuals as happier and more successful.[6]

Exposure to magazines and television programs that promote a thin ideal body type increases body image concerns and eating disorder symptoms.[7] A classic study in Fiji found that disordered eating was significantly more prevalent after the introduction of television. In fact, television images that associate thinness with success and promote the belief that the body can, and should be, altered can reshape the very notion of female beauty.[8] Billion-dollar marketing campaigns, many targeting adolescents, show how desire itself (for a specific identity through appearance) can be both created and manipulated. In this case, identity is represented by an extremely slender body type, the standard for females in Westernized cultures but nonnormative for most women. Education regarding the cultural messages of the thin-body ideal is included in eating disorder treatment protocols, but the impact of social media exposure is only beginning to be incorporated. Social media use is unlikely to decline. Instead, we will likely continue to see new social apps, designed to ensnare fickle consumers.

Connectivity has resulted in an awareness of how others around the world live, what they own, and how they look. Millennials and Generation Z members, those born since the early 1980s, have been gifted with advances that seemed unimaginable just a few years ago. On the one hand, their lives are more convenient than ever: they can conduct almost any transaction and locate vast amounts of information on a handheld computer they carry in their pocket. On the other hand, there are now far more distractions and options. Simple lives with simple choices no longer exist, and overwhelming options and visual information leave many lost in technology that was designed to simplify life. The simple act of communicating with a friend is no longer done through a written letter, a phone call, or even an email. Young people are much more likely to snap a photo of themselves and send it via social media to share their mood than they are to put their feelings into words. In fact, most youths will tell you that this is the expected means to communicate personal information. When people view images and accept them as reality without reflection, there is no opportunity to explore the underlying meaning or unconscious thoughts and feelings an image evokes. Belonging to this visual generation is particularly challenging if you have an eating disorder.

The sexualized content of media also impacts body dissatisfaction. Explicit sexual content is readily available online, and it depicts virtually only one body type: the thin ideal. Despite most people's awareness that the images are electronically manipulated, the pervasive thin ideal continues to impact attitudes toward the female body and women's identities. These portrayals of perfect bodies and females as objects of male desire and dominance influence females in multiple ways. Most women cannot hope to live up to the standards and some attempt to make their body acceptable through any and all means possible, including starvation, cosmetic surgery, and extreme exercise. A society in which one is expected to be a complete package of appearance and success creates role confusion. To be sure, beliefs in women's abilities have changed, but the need for male approval is still deeply engrained in the messages vulnerable young females receive. No wonder so many girls fear becoming an adult but, ironically, at the same time pose in sexualized adult ways for approval. Males are also experiencing pressure to create an ideal appearance, most commonly through an unrealistically muscled body, hypermasculinity, or unbridled images of success.

SOCIAL MEDIA AND EATING DISORDERS

Whereas social media is not the sole reason for the increase in eating disorders, we are learning that social media use is a risk factor for eating disorders and that it makes recovery challenging in new ways. The Internet is the most frequently used form of media for young women in Western societies,[9] and the most commonly visited online sites are those social networking sites that are collectively termed social media.[10] Facebook, Instagram, Tumblr, and Snapchat are among the most popular, but new prototypes, such as the short-form video app Tik-Tok, appeal to young users. Recent literature indicates that social media use is a risk factor for body dissatisfaction, and it is this dissatisfaction that is a risk factor for developing, as well as maintaining, an eating disorder.[11]

Females diagnosed with eating disorders spend about the same amounts of time on the Internet (6 ½ hours per day) as those with no history of eating disorder symptoms however, distinct differences emerge regarding how this time is spent. Those with an eating disorder spend almost twice as much of their online time viewing information related to eating, weight, and body image, and they engage more often in social comparisons.[12] Photo-based activities, such as uploading and viewing others' photos, are particularly challenging for those struggling with body dissatisfaction.[13] For females, the ideal body size began shrinking in the 1960s when the British model Twiggy made the thin, waiflike body popular. Since then, ideal body size has continued to plunge to even more unrealistic and unattainable standards for thinness. This constant exposure to unrealistic models for comparison sets females up to feel inadequate when they cannot meet these impossible standards for body size.

On social media platforms based on images, social comparisons occur because visual media facilitates this comparing in ways that other formats cannot. Magazines depicting the ideal, thin body type have long been recognized as triggers for body dissatisfaction; however, they cannot compare with social media in term of convenience. Social media can be accessed anytime, from anywhere, on a smartphone with WiFi connection; and most young people are constantly connected. Further, appearance comparisons on social media are more damaging to body image than comparisons that occur in person.[14] Elevated exposure to photographs of self and friends on social media platforms such as Facebook, as opposed to other social media or Internet activities that are not photo-based, is a key factor in greater body dissatisfaction.[15] However, social media platforms such as Instagram rely more heavily on images than Facebook does, and how these newer image-based platforms affect body satisfaction remains to be seen. Most of my clients prefer sites other than Facebook, with Instagram and Snapchat as the current favorites. Social comparisons and aspirational images abound on social media, yet Internet use is often overlooked in therapy.

Social comparison is a sure way to unhappiness, and for those with eating disorders, it can be devastating. A good number of my clients have come to this conclusion and choose to completely remove themselves from social media to reduce the temptation for comparison. Some have gone so far as to remove the apps from their phones and have a trusted ally change the password. They have discovered firsthand what research is beginning to prove—negative affect and reductions in psychological health correlate with online behavior that focuses on eating, weight or body image.[16] Unfortunately, this solution does not typically last because they soon feel cut off from others and resume their use of social media. Before long, they are again immersed in a digital social world that inhibits a healthy sense of self.

As eating disorder therapists, we have an obligation to stay abreast of the changing culture in which our clients live. An understanding of how social media impacts identity development is vital. Eating disorders are developmental disorders that reside within a toxic culture. Within this culture, social media can provide opportunities to develop and hone social skills, as well as form an identity, if one is given the knowledge and skills to navigate what otherwise can be treacherous waters. We must address the online lives of our clients with eating disorders in ways that facilitate healthy identity formation. To do this, social media use should be assessed, and the culture of social media should be brought into discussions in therapy. The very images that our clients view or post can be used in therapy to help clients gain self-awareness and enhance identity development.

As social media now permeates our lives, it is imperative that therapists be well versed in how to exploit the potential benefits and mitigate the risks of technology use. Adoption and use of ever-newer social media platforms show no signs of abatement; they are now the primary means through which adolescents and young adults socialize and even build new relationships. Therapists can stay informed by remaining open-minded about social media and taking initiative to understand the common social media platforms and how young people socialize. The Common Sense Media website (https://www.commonsensemedia.org/) is a good source for information on various forms of popular media.

Digital culture is the new environment in which young people are going through the normal developmental phase of defining who they are. The culturally competent practitioner understands that social interactions that previously took place in school hallways and local hangouts now occur online. Young people need a balance between offline and online worlds. They need adults to discuss the dangers of the digital world with them without demonizing or using scare tactics. They need to be taught how to determine whether or not information they obtain online is based on scholarly research, how to guard their safety, and about the permanence of online postings. The always-on, 24/7 nature of social media can leave them exhausted, yet FOMO (fear of missing out) is a legitimate concern. Due to the growing interest in the effects of social media use, we are learning that technology use has benefits, but we have a right to be concerned about heavy usage. Providing a place to explore these aspects of social media is not only educationally beneficial; it can facilitate the relationship between therapist and client, which is the foundation of change.

The Internet is rampant with misinformation on diet and weight loss information, including the marketing of products to reshape the body. Triggering images that promote the thin ideal abound. Some of the most dangerous sites are those that promote eating disorders, generally known as "pro-ana" sites for pro-anorexia, "pro-mia" sites for pro-bulimia, and "thinspiration" sites. Users often state that these sites represent a lifestyle choice rather than a disorder and often document their weight loss with images as a way to encourage others in their weight loss goals. One of my clients showed me a self-portrait of herself posted on a site of this type. The photo shows her sitting on her scale with the weight clearly visible. An intense feeling of sadness came over me as I viewed the haunted look in her eyes. She talked of the accomplishment she felt in reaching her goal, and I could see the look of pride on her face as she commented on the jealousy it inspired among her peers. Yet there was something underneath that pride, a look of desperation. While her perception of her peers' reactions may not have been an accurate appraisal, it was her reality at the time. I have learned over my years of treating eating disorders that it is often only after full recovery that a person has an accurate view of the true state of their physical and emotional condition during the worst stage of the disorder. This young woman was not there yet.

Even without searching for pro eating-disorder sites, it's easy to land on one because the results of searches for information on or help with eating disorders can include pro eating-disorder sites. Those with body dissatisfaction are especially susceptible to the distorted messages these pro eating-disorder sites promote. Even viewing this type of information infrequently, accidently, or for only a few minutes is related to lower self-esteem, body dissatisfaction, and increases in dieting behavior, highlighting the fact that initial body dissatisfaction is not a prerequisite for responding to these sites in an unhealthy manner.[17]

Individuals with disordered eating and eating disorders spend more of their online time in food- and weight-related blogs and forums than those without weight concerns. Along with these detrimental behaviors, individuals often exhibit concomitant difficulties in their relationships to self and others. They are tempted to try to meet their needs for connection in online formats because anonymity and distance provoke less anxiety than face-to-face interactions. While the Internet can provide support in some ways, it does not necessarily fill emotional or social voids of individuals who have an eating disorder experience. Online treatment and support groups represent an emerging trend with the potential for providing services to those not able to access treatment in a traditional setting, but more research is needed on the effectiveness of these online interventions. Regardless of whether treatment takes place online or in a therapy office, it should guide these individuals in ascertaining how the Internet impacts their sense of self.

Eating disorder treatment does not solely target identity development, although most current treatment programs recognize and include components to address identity deficits. Symptom management must take precedence in cases where client health is endangered. In stable clients, individuals who focus on appearance and weight and experience body dissatisfaction benefit from endorsement of a more diversified sense of self concurrently with symptom management. Individuals with eating disorders usually view themselves negatively and have feelings of worthlessness and insignificance. They use the eating disorder to guard against experiencing negative emotions and feelings of vulnerability that arise in response to their belief that others will view them as they view themselves. They also tend to avoid close relationships, which trigger overwhelming emotions and subsequent eating disorder behaviors. Interventions that place rebuilding of the self at the center of recovery base self-worth on factors other than weight and appearance[18]—a challenging but necessary step toward growth in a social media age.

GUIDING THE IDENTITY JOURNEY IN A VISUAL CULTURE

In an ideal world, every child would grow up in an enriched environment consisting of loving touch and support, parents who model the ability to express feelings in healthy ways, and appropriate challenges to allow the development of self-confidence and a positive sense of self. Sense of self emanates from neural structures and connections in the brain that form over time. These structures develop in response to our experiences, with relational experiences being indispensable for construction and continual modification of the self.[19] Louis Cozolino's work is especially relevant in its attention to the brain networks responsible for the construction of the experience of self as well as for applications to therapy.[20]

While in-depth neuroscience discussions are beyond the scope of this book, knowledge of the brain-mind relationship gives insight into conceptions of self and identity. That there is a self is undeniable; however, the self is a process rather than a tangible object that can be observed. Over time, this has led to various concepts of what, exactly, constitutes the self. Antonio Damasio, a leading neuroscientist, considers the conscious mind to begin when the self is brought to mind. The conscious mind is aware of experiences, knows that these experiences belong to the mental owner, and reflects on the experiences. Selfhood and identity arise out of these mind processes, and these processes are only possible due to underlying neural circuits.[21]

The brain-mind relationship is not only incredibly complex, it is also the subject of much ongoing theorizing that will continue to influence the therapy field. Turning again to Damasio for a succinct explanation of the development of the neural networks that are the foundation to the development of a mind:

> *Minds emerge when the activity of small circuits is organized across large networks so as to compose momentary patterns. The patterns represent things and events located outside the brain, either in the body or in the external world, but some patterns also represent the brain's own processing of other patterns. . . . In brief, the brain maps the world around it and maps its own doings. These maps are experienced as images in our minds and the term image refers not just to the visual kind but to images of any sense origin such as auditory, visceral, tactile, and so forth.*[22]

Images reflect our internal and external experiences, but for the self to be present, there must be a subjectivity that is only possible when the images are made our own. Images are made salient through the awareness that they are part and parcel of oneself, that they belong to oneself and that they can be acted on by oneself. The feelings and emotions that arise out of this awareness give salience to images related to self. Simply stated, we perceive a multitude of sensory information, some of it originating internally. That which is related to self is marked on our maps as the symbolic representation of self. The neural networks that make the maps possible underlie the very notion of selfhood. Maps have symbolic importance to the concept of self. Just as we use maps to know where we are, to gain a physical sense of location, we also use mental maps to determine ourselves relative to others and to procure a sense of who we are— all in the form of images. No wonder we are drawn to images; the world as we know it is a collection of pictorial representations of our perceptions.

Appreciation of interpersonal neurobiology lays the groundwork for understanding how to initiate therapeutic change in the digital age. According to Cozolino, "Although psychotherapists do not generally think in 'neuroscientific' terms, stimulating neuroplasticity and neural integration is essentially what we do."[23] As the mind and the self are neural networks built from experiences, we now know that inadequate growth and integration within and between these networks are responsible for psychological difficulties. A primary task of psychotherapy is to create an enriched environment to support the development of neural maps for thriving in a rapidly changing environment.

To begin the difficult work of addressing deficits in self, a therapist must connect on a neural basis with the client. The brain is shaped by our relationships, making one's social milieu a dominate force in identity development. Relationship connections promote positive brain development through emotional attunement, affect regulation, and the co-construction of narratives.[24] Each of these actions interacts with the others, thereby creating an atmosphere of safety and potential healing. The therapist emotionally attunes to clients in ways that synchronize their brains, simulating the attunement of a competent caregiver to an infant, which is the basis of attachment in early life and a central component of a safe therapeutic relationship. After all, we never cease to be social creatures. Therapeutic attachment creates the space and lays the foundation for affect regulation and the cocreation of narratives. It is these attunement experiences that shape the neural networks necessary for building an identity-enhancing narrative. This book explores identity-enhancing treatment strategies based on neuroscientific research that supports the role of client narratives in neural integration and brain plasticity.

Narratives are a natural choice for addressing identity development. Stories or narratives are natural and implicit to the brain: our concept of self evolves from this implicit storytelling. As children we begin to organize our experiences into stories as our command of language emerges. The tendency to organize human experiences into a narrative configuration is present in all societies and cultures. Humans are natural storytellers. Our ancestors gathered to share stories of adventure, of their own ancestors, and of good and evil. There is an inborn need to tell stories, to organize and transmit our experiences to ourselves and to others.[25] As humans we are uniquely captivated by stories: the power of a narrative to elicit emotion in unparalleled. As we all know from reading or hearing an engaging story, a visual image is always constructed based on the story. In fact, we are disappointed when a movie created from our favorite book fails to represent the characters or setting the way we imagined them.

Narratives perform multiple functions that are crucial to self-identity. They transmit culture and unite families and even nations—all foundational elements of sense of self. Stories are constructed to make sense of our experiences: the self-narrative pulls the pieces of information together and provides an organizing framework for a coherent story of who we are.[26] For both the storyteller and audience, there is an element of remembering inherent in stories, as well as an opportunity to explore actions and emotions. A narrative in which one is both the narrator and the audience prompts self-organization and self-knowledge.[27] A narrative is a type of shorthand for the deeper processes of making sense of our humanness and of the world in which we live.

Through the story, feelings are expressed, whether intentionally or not, and emotions may be labeled, potentially leading to empowerment and emotion regulation. Sharing the narrative with a safe person can launch self-awareness and exploration. Co-construction of narratives within emotionally meaningful relationships integrates neural networks and facilitates change in the story of the self.[28] Narratives organize and provide a foundation for sense of self. They give the gift of a future through imagining a tomorrow of possibilities. Narratives can be edited when behaviors and emotions are explored, allowing for empowering possible selves to emerge, all in the safety of a therapeutic relationship. A more extensive look at identity and narratives will be explored throughout this book.

Consider for a moment the process of talk therapy in narrative work. In conversations between therapist and client, considerable attention may be focused on unraveling the meaning behind what the client recalls, observes, and experiences, whether conversations or behaviors. The client expresses their story in a safe space, created by the attuned therapist, and the therapist facilitates the reworking or enhancing of the client's story. In our digitally saturated culture, today more information is taken in visually than at any other time in history, so visual images have tremendous influence on client narratives. Sight is the most potent of our sensory functions,[29] thus the majority of our total sensory input enters through our eyes. Likewise, the mind specializes in images. As will be discussed in more detail in subsequent chapters, the mind has difficulty distinguishing the reality of visual images. Photographs have the capacity to emotionally engage us in ways that override our awareness of the fact that images do not always represent reality. This gives images incredible power to influence, especially if they are unconsciously accepted as the truth. We create and view so many images in the course of a normal day that we have become oblivious to the power this exposure has over us.

Visual narratives are a natural byproduct of the digital era. The advent of smartphones allows seamless uploading of images to social media as a means of writing the story of our lives, post by post. In the early days of Facebook, we took photos with a digital camera, then uploaded the images to a computer, and then posted them online. Smartphones now have a sophisticated camera and the ability to connect to the Internet via WiFi or cellular that allows instant uploading of images, thus one can create a visual narrative of one's life with unprecedented ease. The narrative may not be entirely accurate, however. We could argue that what is posted is a version carefully edited to convince ourselves or others of what we would like our lives or ourselves to be. Digital narratives are the preferred tool of storytelling among those whose main modes of communication are conducted via technology.

Narratives are often a part of eating disorder treatment; however, visual content has not been included because therapists usually consider use of imagery to be restricted to art therapy. Outpatient treatment for eating disorders requires a therapist with training specific to eating disorders, not necessarily to art therapy. Thus, art therapy may not be offered in the outpatient setting if a therapist either is not trained in or is uncomfortable using it. Another barrier to implementing art therapy in the outpatient setting may be the client's lack of familiarity with or comfort with creating art. In contrast, most of our clients today are comfortable with photographs, and many frequently post images of themselves and their experiences, making inclusion of this medium a valid choice. Visual content can no longer be excluded from therapy targeting eating disorders, regardless of the therapist's preferred theoretical model. As therapists, we would be remiss if we did not incorporate this part of storytelling into the narrative therapy process.

Given the pervasive nature of visual input and our reliance on digital means of documenting life and exploring identity, clients can benefit from exploring visual content in therapy to determine how the images reflect identity. We must be alert to how clients relate to the images they mindlessly interact with and be willing to explore the meanings clients make from viewing, creating, and posting images. The client's narrative is now expressed and processed through multiple means. It was my own clients who shifted my practice toward including photographic images in our work together when they began to spontaneously show phone images of themselves and others in session and later to talk about the ways that social media impacted them. They want to talk about their own reaction or another's comment in response to an image they have posted or their own internal responses to what others have posted. As these discussions became more frequent, it seemed expedient to process these experiences with them, not only as past experiences but also in the moment experiences; viewing the images in the session is more potent and allows for deeper processing of the experiences.

From my interest in photography theory, I knew that images on social media were affecting clients in ways they were unaware of, and the symbolic meanings of these images needed to be brought to light. The use of photography in therapeutic settings dates from the 1850s, the early days of photography itself. Various therapeutic uses of photography have been shown to be effective in addressing identity issues, facilitating the therapeutic relationship, improving communication problems, increasing insight, and treating trauma.[30] Due to its potential to facilitate identity work by accessing experiences on a deeper, unconscious level, I began to implement photo therapy techniques as an adjunct to the established eating disorder treatment protocols.

Photo therapy is not a therapeutic theory, but rather a set of techniques to facilitate emotional awareness and processing based on the use of images in the context of treatment by a trained mental health professional. Photo therapy can utilize various types of visual images including selfies, other photographs taken by the client, photographs of the client taken by others, family photographs, as well as images that are collected by or otherwise have relevance to a client. Based on a collaborative relationship between the therapist and client, photo therapy brings the visual content that the client interacts with outside the therapy room into the session, often discovering unconscious thoughts, feelings, and memories that may not have been reached through verbal inquiry alone. The emotional content associated with a chosen image bubbles forth as a resource for understanding one's life events and one's self.[31] Connecting visual content with conscious and unconscious meaning brings deeper insight to the client's narrative.

One element of the self that is particularly relevant to this type of therapy is the autobiographical self. Memories (especially those associated with strong emotions), value-laden experiences, and an anticipated future all represent the autobiographical self. The images a client brings to session often represent and express their autobiographical self. The autobiographical memory maintains the viewpoint of the narrator in one's story. Hence, it presides over self and identity and is central to deficits in identity, as are present with eating disorders. True recovery from an eating disorder requires attention to autobiographical self, to identity. Just as movies, television, and photographs have impacted the self in the last century, emerging digital technologies, most notably social media, continue to sway culture in ways that alter the individual brain processes responsible for mind and self.

REFERENCES

1. Anderson, M., & Jiang, J. (2018). Teens, social media, and technology. Retrieved from http://www.pewinternet.org/2018/05/31/teens-social-media-technology-2018/

2. Kosoff, M. (2016). Teen's favorite apps in 2016. Retrieved from http://www.businessinsider.com/teens-favorite-apps-in-2016-2016-1/#teens-are-shy-to-talk-about-how-much-time-they-spend-on-their-phones-but-its-a-lot-1

3. Smith, A., & Anderson, M. (2018). Social media use in 2018. Retrieved from http://www.pewinternet.org/2018/03/01/social-media-use-in-2018/

4. Among affluents, millennials spend the most time online. (October 19, 2016). Retrieved from https://www.emarketer.com/Article/Among-Affluents-Millennials-Spend-Most-Time-Online/1014618

5. Hood, B. (2012). *The Self Illusion: How the Social Brain Creates Identity.* New York, NY: Oxford University Press.

6. Eisenberg, M., Calrson-McGuire, A., Gollust, S.E., & Neumark-Sztainer, D.A. (2014). Content analysis of weight-stigmatization in popular television programming for adolescents. *International Journal of Eating Disorders, 48*(6), 759-766.

7. Grabe, S., Ward, L. M., & Hyde, J. S. (2008). The role of the media in body image concerns among women: A meta-analysis of experimental and correlational studies, *Psychological Bulletin, 134*(3), 460–476.

8. Becker, A. E., Burwell, R. A., Herzog, D. B., Hamburg, P., & Gilman, S. E. (2002). Eating behaviours and attitudes following prolonged exposure to television among ethnic Fijian adolescent girls. *The British Journal of Psychiatry, 180,* 509–514.

9. Bair, C. E., Kelly, N. R., Serdar, K. L., & Mazzeo, S. E. (2012). Does the Internet function like magazines? An exploration of image-focused media, eating pathology, and body dissatisfaction. *Eating Behaviors, 13*(4), 398–401. http://dx.doi. org/10.1016/j.eatbeh.2012.06.003

10. Tiggemann, M., & Slater, A. (2013). NetGirls: The Internet, Facebook, and body image concern in adolescent girls. *International Journal of Eating Disorders, 46*(6), 630–634. http://dx .doi.org/10.1002/eat.22141

11. Stice, E. (2002). Risk and maintenance factors for eating pathology: A meta-analytic review. *Psychological Bulletin, 128*(5), 825–848. doi:10.1037/0033-2909.128.5.825

12. Bachner-Melman, R., Zontag-Oren, E., Zohar, A. H., & Sher, H. (2018). Lives on the line: The online lives of girls and women with and without a lifetime eating disorder diagnosis. *Frontiers in Psychology.* doi:10.3389/fpsyg.2018.02128

13. Holland, G., & Tiggemann, M. (2016). A systematic review of the impact of the use of social networking sites on body image and disordered eating outcomes. *Body Image, 17,* 100–110. doi:10.1016/j.bodyim.2016.02.008

14. Fardouly, J., Pinkus, R. T., & Vartanian, L. R. (2017). The impact of appearance comparisons made through social media, traditional media, and in person in women's everyday lives. *Body Image, 20,* 30–39.

15. Meier, E. P., & Gray, J. (2014). Facebook photo activity associated with body image disturbance in adolescent girls. *Cyberpsychology, Behavior, and Social Networking, 17*(4), 199–206. doi:10.1089/cyber.2013.0305

16. Bachner-Melman, R., Zontag-Oren, E., Zohar, A. H., & Sher, H. (2018). Lives on the line: The online lives of girls and women with and without a lifetime eating disorder diagnosis. *Frontiers in Psychology.* doi:10.3389/fpsyg.2018.02128

17. Homewood, J., & Melkonian, M. (2015). "What factors account for internalisation of the content of pro-ana websites?" *Journal of Neurology Neurosurgery & Psychiatry, 86*(9). e3.

18. Williams, K., King, J., & Fox, J. R. (2016). Sense of self and anorexia nervosa: A grounded theory. *Psychology and Psychotherapy, 89*(2), 211–228.

19. Hood, B. (2012). *The self illusion: How the social brain creates identity.* New York, NY: Oxford University Press.

20. Cozolino, L. (2017). *The neuroscience of psychotherapy: Healing the social brain.* (3rd ed.) New York, NY: W. W. Norton & Company.

21. Damasio, A. (2010). *Self comes to mind: Constructing the conscious brain.* New York, NY: Vintage.

22. Damasio, A. (2010). *Self comes to mind: Constructing the conscious brain* (p. 19). New York, NY: Vintage.

23. Cozolino, L. (2017). *The neuroscience of psychotherapy: Healing the social* brain (3rd ed., pp. 28–29). New York, NY: W. W. Norton & Company.

24. Cozolino, L. (2017). *The neuroscience of psychotherapy: Healing the social brain.* (3rd ed.) New York, NY: W. W. Norton & Company.

25. Newman, R. F., & Baumeister, L. S. (1991). How stories make sense of personal experience:

Motives that shape autobiographical narratives. *Personality and Social Psychology Bulletin, 20*(6), 676–690.

26. Ziller, R. C. (2000). Self-counseling through re-authored photo-self-narratives. *Counseling Psychology Quarterly, 13*(3), 265–278.

27. Hermans, H. J. M., & Hermans-Jansen, E. (1995). *Self-narratives: The construction of meaning in psychotherapy.* New York, NY: Guilford Press.

28. Cozolino, L. (2017). *The neuroscience of psychotherapy: Healing the social brain.* (3rd ed.) New York, NY: W. W. Norton & Company.

29. Hultén, B., Broweus, N., & van Dijk, M. (2009). *Sensory marketing.* London, UK: Palgrave Macmillan.

30. Berman, L. (1993). *Beyond the smile: The therapeutic use of the photograph.* London, UK: Routledge.

   Lindfors, B. (2009). Written in the body. Working through traumatic memories by means of re-enactment phototherapy. *European Journal of Psychotherapy & Counselling, 11*(4), 397–408.

   DeCoster, V. A., & Dickerson, J. (2014). The therapeutic use of photography in clinical social work: Evidence-based practices. *Social Work in Mental Health, 12*(1), 1–19.

31. Weiser, J. (1999). *PhotoTherapy Techniques: Exploring the Secrets of Personal Snapshots and Family Albums.* Vancouver, BC: Judy Weiser and PhotoTherapy Centre Publishers.

   Halkola, U. (2013). A photograph as a therapeutic experience. In D. Lowenthal (Ed.). *Phototherapy and therapeutic photography in a digital age* (pp. 21–30). New York, NY: Routledge.

Chapter 3

IDENTITY FORMATION IN A
SOCIAL MEDIA AGE

We have, each of us, a life-story, an inner narrative—whose continuity, whose sense, is our lives. It might be said that each of us constructs and lives, a "narrative," and that this narrative is us, our identities.

—Oliver Sacks

Generation snowflake is a derogatory term used to describe the tendency to be fragile and easily offended of those who have lived their entire lives in the social media age. They are criticized for desiring to be unique or special, yet the very nature of identity development requires that a person differentiate themselves from others. A person's sense of self develops within a social context that, if one is to fit in, also requires conformity. As adolescents and young adults attempt to form their unique identity, they are caught between these opposing forces.

IDENTITY

The term *identity* is at once familiar and also fraught with imprecise definitions; most everyone has idea of the meaning, yet consensus is lacking. A lack of distinction between *self* and *identity* hampers clarity regarding the nature of identity, but this obscurity in no way reflects a lack of interest in these concepts. Google Scholar generates over four million citations when *self* or *identity* are included as key words. *Self*, the broadest term, is used in various ways by researchers and theorists to denote the broadest conceptualization of the individual and the social aspects of a person.[1] As a mental process originating in the mind of a person, the self is an organized set of processes that represent the whole of a person, including personhood and identity.[2] It is the integrative structure of the mind that creates the self, making sense of the countless internal and external experiences of an individual. Identity defines and differentiates one from others.

Many scholars consider identity to be nested under the broader concept of self. Multiple identities exist because a person has multiple characteristics and roles and belongs to multiple groups, and each of these relate to unique aspects of the self.[3] This idea of multiple identities is not intended to refer to the splitting of personality due to early trauma, as in dissociative identity disorder, but rather the idea of a unified identity that answers the question "Who am I?" Clients may state that they are a certain way with friends and very different with their parents, but in order to feel that they have an authentic identity, there must be threads that run through, and perhaps tie together, all aspects of a person. Identity reflects the traits, social relations, roles, and group membership of a person. It describes the sameness of a person from their past, through the present, and into the future.

Although *self* and *identity* can be differentiated in these ways, the terms are often used interchangeably by scholars, as they are throughout this book. *Identity* is more frequently used in reference to identity formation. At times, the term *self* is used to reflect concepts such as sense of self or autobiographical self. Self and identity share three key concepts that support this usage; they are: a mental representation, a social product, and a force for behavior.[4] Each concept offers insights for understanding identity formation in the social media age.

IDENTITY IS A MENTAL REPRESENTATION

Simply put, the self is a mental construct within the mind, making the brain the most critical body part for identity. The essence of who we are is created by and resides in the brain; without brain and mind there would be no self or identity. The brain processes all incoming information, as well as internal states, by creating mapped patterns that are experienced as images. These images are more than just sights, they are all types of live sensory input, recall of events, imagination, and internal states, such as emotions and body awareness. It is this mapping that constitutes the mind.[5]

Out of all this content in the mind, some images are more noteworthy to an individual than others. Images that evoke emotions and feelings are likely to be marked as having value to the individual. Images that relate to the self tend to have high emotional salience and give rise to the autobiographical self, the basis for identity.[6] As a mental representation that is held within the mind, identity provides a sense of continuity and an enduring sense of who one is.[7] The autobiographical self represents the mental life created by the brain as it attempts to make sense of the myriad of personal facts and experiences across a person's life. It provides a sense of "I" across past, present, and future. In doing so, the brain constructs a story of self, a narrative that guides interpretation and even actions.[8] We do not have an actual self so much as we engage in the process of making a self over time.

The autobiographical self is dependent on memory, as sense of self cannot exist without memories. As the brain experiences the world and creates a representation or image of the experience, neural architecture is shaped. The reactivation of these neural networks or maps is memory.[9] Autobiographical memories permit subjective time travel through emotionally weighted recollections of past events and emotional states. Whenever networks are triggered by related events or states, memories are brought into a dynamic process whereby the new content can modify the original memory.[10] Memories, in general, are not stable like photographs or videos; they are malleable and subject to reconstruction. The substance and emotional content of memories may be modified or rearranged any time the memories are recalled. Current experiences are interpreted through the lens of our memories, and present experiences may alter memories of the past in an ever-evolving creation of narratives in which new memories are integrated with older memories.

Autobiographical memories are crucial for constructing the self-narrative and are at the heart of personal identity. These memories are what make us who we are. By tying experiences together across time, the fragmented stories are woven together into a meaningful narrative, the basis of our identity. Identity slowly emerges from the earliest years. As the brain develops, so too does the sense of self. If the brain deteriorates, so too does the sense of self. The reason diseases that cause memory loss are devastating to those who suffer from and those who witness them is the ravaging of memory and the crumbing of sense of self. During adolescence, neural architecture is reorganized, and identity work accelerates. Elaborating the narrative of who one is comes to the forefront as brain development enlarges adolescents' perspective on self and others, creating a heightened desire to know oneself.

While there is likely no singular region in the brain where the construct of self is located, the prefrontal cortex (PFC) is activated by thoughts of self. Hyperactivation in the PFC is common in adolescence, an indication of the focus on self and identity during this time.[11] The impact of visual images, the primary content of social media, on the PFC during this period cannot be ignored. Enhanced medial PFC activation and connectivity between the PFC and the visual cortex occurs during self-referential processing of visual images, and these visual experiences shape the neural architecture underlying self in the PFC.[12] Further, visual input is the primary source for constructing a mental representation of the body. The implications of this process for memory and identity formation during this critical stage of development are clear. Self depends on the pictorial representations of images, and the digital revolution gives primacy to visual images in the process of identity formation. The rise in preoccupation with body and body dissatisfaction during these years illustrates the role of body awareness in identity formation. The mental processes that create the self are extremely susceptible to cultural and social influences that predominate in social media, especially during the critical stage of adolescence.

IDENTITY IS A SOCIAL PRODUCT

Of all mammals, humans spend the greatest proportion of their lives dependent on others for care and socialization. Human connections shape the neural architecture of the brain early in life and continue to influence brain function across the lifespan. Attachment relationships in the early years lay the groundwork for the neural connections that enable a coherent sense of self.[13] The mind itself arises and develops in social interactions, thus self is a social construction. Feedback from others and shared meaning is the basis of self-knowledge. In interactions with others, an individual learns values, attitudes, and roles that become internalized over time, so much so that the thoughts and feelings that subsequently arise are experienced as natural to the self.

Simply put, how others see us matters. Others' appraisals, whether supportive or undermining, are incorporated into the self-image. Becoming oneself requires that others acknowledge our selfhood. Of course, a healthy sense of self occurs in contexts in which a person's identity is endorsed and positively reinforced. Individuals who perceive that they are respected and admired internalize these positive appraisals, and they are more likely to positively interpret future social experiences. Contexts that support identity span the range from family dynamics and parenting practices to school and neighborhood, as well as larger cultural attitudes and societal practices at any given time. Much internalized learning is never questioned.

Midway through childhood, children begin to acquire an awareness of others' thought patterns. This lays the groundwork for self-understanding, as they develop beliefs about themselves from how others react to them.[14] Increased activation in the PFC during adolescence correlates with their heightened concern with what others think, which makes adolescents more susceptible to peer appraisals as they seek to define their identity.[15] Moment-to-moment situations arising from these contexts are seen as social inputs to identity. Thus, a person defines themselves based on what matters in their particular time and social context.[16] Social media is an identity-testing space where valued attributes are displayed and feedback is the norm.

Daniel Siegel suggests that the interactions between the brain, mind, and relationships are multidirectional. Not only does the brain influence the mind and relationships, the mind influences the brain and relationships, and relationships influence brain and mind.[17] These ongoing processes are continually shaping identity through underlying concepts: the mental representation of one's identity in the mind, the very structure of the brain, and how these play out in relationships. Identity is a product of social situations, but it is also a shaper of behavior, one's external reactions to their environment. The social media environment generates a novel space for the social interactions key to identity formation.

IDENTITY IS A FORCE FOR BEHAVIOR

Identity processes clearly function at both conscious and unconscious levels. Explicit memories allow conscious time travel to the past. Unconscious memories, in contrast, arise without awareness, but their impact on emotional states and behaviors is undeniable. Emotions are a driving force behind the formation of memories in our brain on both a conscious and unconscious level[18] and they drive behaviors regardless of the source.

Behaviors arising from conscious awareness of one's inner state or motivation to depict oneself in a certain light can lead to carefully chosen language or actions to communicate a desired identity. In today's social media age, there is ample opportunity to put information about oneself out into the social sphere to seek verification of identity. Symbols of identity are exhibited through appearance, possessions, and the experiences depicted in the images posted on social media. Appearance is a primary means communicating self to others, and in doing so an individual endeavors to know the self.[19] On social media a person can control the content and the amount of information with the goal of receiving verification of the desired identity. This is a conscious attempt to portray the self in a desirable way; however, unconscious processes are also at work in these same situations.

Many sophisticated mental processes occur outside of conscious awareness. Automatic processing of thoughts, feelings, and motives are the norm. In social psychology, a great deal of attention has been focused on trying to describe the mental process that transpire out-of-view. Historically, unconscious processes have been thought to result from repression, meant to protect an individual from disturbing or even traumatic information. More recent ideas propose that the unconscious is actively involved in learning, interpretation, and evaluating.[20] Identity resides in both the conscious and unconscious interpretations of the self, and both influence behavior, though in different ways. It is when unconscious processes remain out of awareness that the most identity confusion develops and extreme behaviors are most likely to occur. The case study of Brandon helps illustrate how identity confusion and extreme behaviors can be addressed in therapy.

IDENTITY DISRUPTED

Too embarrassed about his struggles with food and weight to reach out on his own, twenty-year-old Brandon came to my office for his first visit at his mother's insistence. Though I am now seeing more males in my practice than in past years, many continue to believe that eating disorders are a female problem, heightening the feelings of shame for males who struggle with eating disorders. The number of males who seek treatment for eating disorders now reflects estimates that they make up 10–25% of those with eating disorders. Subclinical eating disordered behaviors, such as fasting, binge eating, purging and laxative abuse, are almost as prevalent in males as they are in females. Males are less likely than their female counterparts to get help, however.[21]

Broad-shouldered and long-limbed, yet also somehow folded into himself, is how I remember Brandon. He slumped forward in my office waiting room, his shoulders internally rotated and forearms twisted to allow his palms to meet as they were shoved between his knees. When he stood, it is without reaching his full height or releasing the unnatural twist in his arms. It appeared that he desired more than anything to not be here, or at least not be noticed, but these nonverbals masked an intense desire to know himself and be known and appreciated for who he is.

Brandon, like many with eating disorders, exemplified his struggle with identity in characteristic ways. He wanted connection with others and tried to mold himself to be what he perceived they desire, yet he also desired autonomy and feared he was viewed as needy. His eating disorder behaviors were used to decrease the discomfort these difficulties engender. Hilde Bruch, one of the early pioneers in treating eating disorders, defined the therapeutic task as one that facilitates the "search for autonomy and self-directed identity by evoking awareness of impulses, feelings, and needs that originate within."[22]

Brandon's story holds clues to the origins of his identity struggle. When asked to describe himself, Brandon said he is a sensitive person, who is easily upset and is drawn to fantasy and artistic pursuits. He feels close to his mother and older sister but not to his father or older brother, who is the oldest of the three siblings in his family. Brandon believed himself to have been overweight for most of his life. Puberty hit around age 13, spurring Brandon to explore his sexual identity. In recognizing his attraction to males, he recalled earlier times in childhood when he felt drawn to male teachers or friends, but he quickly shut down those thoughts. Growing up in a family that did not discuss sexuality intensified his shame, and Brandon felt alienated from his father because he overtly disparaged gays. In many ways, Brandon felt estranged from everyone because he carried this secret that isolated him from family and peers. Gay males have higher rates of eating disorders than heterosexual males (15% compared to 5%). However, when population figures are considered, most males with eating disorders are heterosexual.[23] By early high school, Brandon began to restrict his food intake and to exercise excessively, attempting to gain the physical appearance that he hoped would garner acceptance from his father and others. With his peers he acted in outlandish ways to get noticed; at home he was quiet and withdrawn.

Adolescence is especially challenging due to the rapid physical, cognitive, and social changes that can unmoor even the most resilient and confident children. A further challenge for those with eating disorders is a difficulty with integrating past and present experiences into a coherent identity.[24] One clinically useful framework for understanding identity development is based on what occurs in earlier periods of a child's life. If parents support, tolerate, and encourage children in their desire to be separate and autonomous, children learn that their thoughts, emotions, and behaviors are acceptable. Children can be authentic because the full range of their emotions are accepted, and they can engage in activities and relationships that feel right to them. Winnicott used the term *impingement* to illustrate the effects of parental lack of attunement to a child's needs.[25] Children who do not receive parental affirmation are likely to struggle during adolescence.

Adolescence brings new challenges as teens seek to make sense of how they fit into the larger world. Changes in relational, sexual, intellectual, and status-seeking identities signal normal development during this stage. Yet conflict between these identities is prevalent because cognitive development permits awareness but not the ability to integrate incongruent identities. When too much time is spent trying to act in socially accepted ways and authentic parts are not tolerated, adolescents face the difficult task of choosing to be their true self or to enact a false self to gain love and approval. Choosing a false self can result in profound loss. Therapists can attest to the devastation in their client's lives from not receiving parental approval. It is in the disowning of the authentic self, the splitting of self into acceptable and unacceptable, that leads to a lack of wholeness and a withering of the self.[26] When the false self is dominant, validation comes from outside sources and self-worth is dependent on the everchanging whims of others. Confusion and conflict arise in determining which attributes and behaviors represent the true self and which represent the false self.[27]

Brandon's false self was desperate for the approval he did not get at home or with peers. No longer interested in art, Brandon feigned interest in what his peers were interested in when he was with them and what his father and brother were interested in when he was home. He had no identity outside of his physical appearance and earning good grades so that he could get into a good college and win his father's approval. As a result, Brandon sought the coping mechanism of anorexia. Anorexia was a function of Brandon's false self. Brandon was unable to discriminate between the expectation and needs of others and himself.[28] By the end of high school, Brandon had managed to shrink his body to a weight that was 25 pounds below normal for his height and was preparing to attend a prestigious university on the east coast. He met the criteria for anorexia, but no treatment was sought at that time. In many ways, Brandon's life experiences had primed him to seek unhealthy ways to alleviate the emotional turmoil of adolescence. He had little ability to recognize, express, or regulate emotions and no sense of identity.

Obviously, extremes of parental acceptance or rejection of a child's true self are not the norm. Basic socialization processes involve rejection of some behaviors that do not fit with social acceptability. Tolerating all behaviors does little to prepare children for fitting in to the larger world. In fact, minor violations create manageable levels of stress that are necessary to promote development.[29] As in most things, a balance of socialization and support practices creates an environment conducive to identity development, and I believe that many parents are doing their best to seek this balance. Brandon's situation, in which one or both parents are not supportive of the developing person, is not unique. Aside from sexuality, there are many instances when parents exert undue influence on their children or withhold support if their children do not fit their desired model.

Lack of affirmation of a person for who they are makes it highly likely that the person will seek recognition from other sources. In the social media age, it has become more difficult to resist the values of the larger cultural forces of materialism, appearance standards, and objectification. Social media has created a nearly constant presence that reinforces the split between the authentic self that owns all of a person's experiences and the false self that is culturally scripted to gain approval from others.

IDENTITY ON SOCIAL MEDIA

Most of my clients were born between 1980 and 2005. These Millennial and Gen Z cohorts are the most prolific users of social media. Identity formation in the social media age is a difficult task. Much of the identity searching of these cohorts is done via social media and other online activities. Developing identity through social media is potentially detrimental for all individuals, but especially to those most susceptible to cultural messages of the thin ideal and to those who have not received the necessary affirmation. Adolescents need affirmation from their parents and other significant people to develop a foundation for authentic identity. Unfortunately, Brandon is more susceptible to the cultural messages about thinness because has not received adequate affirmation from his parents.

Although Brandon was in his early twenties and was highly articulate, he seemed much younger emotionally. Some have compared young people in the social media age to the lost generation. The lost generation was a term that was originally applied to the generation coming of age after the first World War. Writers such as Hemmingway and Fitzgerald decried the death of the American dream, pointing to social and cultural upheaval as the precursor to the disillusionment that led many to abandon expected life paths in favor of frivolous pastimes to divert their attention from the tasks of growing up—also a common criticism today. What were previously considered the developmental tasks of adolescence are now more realistically viewed as developmental tasks of young adults. Brandon had taken a leave of absence from college and was spending his time reading fantasy novels, scrolling on his social media accounts, and playing video games in his parents' basement. He habitually stayed up until the early morning hours and then slept until early afternoon. No longer dangerously underweight, Brandon continued to restrict at times and to binge and purge three to four times a week. He rarely went out and showed no interest in returning to school or obtaining a job. By the time Brandon came to see me, he met the diagnostic criteria for bulimia nervosa, major depressive disorder, and generalized anxiety disorder.

Brandon is a representative of Millennials, who are the first generation to spend their time watching large amounts of visual content online rather than watching television. Millennials continue these visual content habits through social media use and online gaming. Gen Z, the generation after the Millennials, are the first generation to have lived their entire lives with social media and ever-present mobile devices. They prefer making visual content online rather than merely watching it. This generation prefers to communicate through images, such as emojis, instead of words and expects instant responses from others. Like Millennials, they too are struggling with the challenges of technology. During the years of identity development, social interactions with peers play a vital role. Social media is a natural platform for both social interaction with peers and for self-presentation that is deliberately designed to portray a desired identity. Immediate feedback from a potentially large number of peers makes social media an alluring place for identity experimentation, but it has also enlarged the arena of social comparison, self-evaluation, and self-presentation.[30]

Social media expands the realm of social comparison groups, which are no longer only school mates and celebrities. A new category spans the gap between these two extremes and includes YouTube stars, Instagram influencers, and lifestyle bloggers. This new category represents average people who have become celebrities, or at least have a massive online following. Heightened appearance standards and unnatural body types abound in those who have become online celebrities or stars. This reinforces the idea that if adolescents or young adults create a desirable external identity, they can attain the same status. On social media, individuals tend to deem personal identity as a fluid creation, achieved rather than bestowed and alterable via the image put forth. Video games play into some of these same desires. Identity is expressed through the characters the players create and inhabit in virtual reality environments designed to trick the brain into believing the characters and situations are real. The characters often epitomize an ideal appearance.

Resources for identity development are broadened as the Internet and social media expand exposure to novel ideas and people. Seeming to be a certain way is valued above underlying character or personality traits. In short, personal identity is attained and displayed through external characteristics. Creation of the self becomes fixated on the exterior and the belief that this exterior can be reshaped to express culturally sanctioned ideals. If identity can be acquired, much like a commodity, a person can try on various identities. What begins as an experiment with an anorexic identity, for example, can become a perilous pursuit that is not easily reversed. Giving up behaviors of control, temptation-resisting, and perfectionism run counter to the cultural messages of the thin ideal. For Brandon, social media was a place to gather aspirational information for how he wants to be. He is also heavily involved in online gaming, where he can experiment with identity and escape from reality into role-playing games.

To understand how these messages become dangerously detrimental for some, we must gain access to information the person may not be consciously aware of. Unconscious influences are models for how the world operates based on lived experiences—expectations, emotional patterns, models of relationships, and general outlook can be beneficial or harmful. At times, those with eating disorders exhibit an element of avoidance of the adult world. While eating disorder behaviors are undoubtedly not frivolous, there certainly are elements of avoiding expected responsibilities. Brandon's father saw the time Brandon spent on eating disorder behaviors and online activities as the embodiment of a refusal to grow up and be a man, which had become a source of conflict between Brandon and his father. Brandon's difficulties in social interactions extended to his refusal to leave the house and his extreme fear of talking to others, especially adults.

Popular media is rife with headlines bemoaning the effects of the social media age on the skills required for succeeding in the adult world. The consistent theme is that young people are not engaging in the type of social experiences that prepare them for life. Screen time is taking the place of face-to-face interactions that require them to carry on conversations and resolve conflict with others. They have relied on apps to conduct the business of life. They order food, obtain information on health and fitness, and meet entertainment needs without interacting with others. In short, today's adolescents and young adults struggle to understand how they are perceived by others and how to build relationships because they have little experience with these behaviors. The multidirectional perspective discussed earlier in this chapter indicates that lack of relational experiences is impacting identity formation. Relationships are central to how the brain creates identity in the mind.

PROMOTING AUTHENTIC IDENTITY

The first task for the therapist is to engage the client in a relationship, since relationships are central to developing identity. Once a relationship has been established, the therapist's role in promoting authentic identity development begins with acknowledging the client's preoccupation with self. The constantly shifting sands of identity in adolescence and young adulthood are reflected in the larger culture, where tastes and opinions shift overnight. The average young person is trying to determine who they are and how they fit in. Sadness, dejection, fear, and anxiety are common responses to discrepancies between their actual selves and who they feel they should be.[31] This stage of development is rife with pain and insecurity, yet there is enormous potential for growth. Mary Pipher points to the gap between the surface structure and the deep structure issues in therapeutic work with young people.

> *Deep structure is the internal work—the struggle to find a self, the attempt to integrate the past and present and to find a place in the larger culture. Surface behaviors convey little of the struggle within and in fact are often designed to obscure that struggle.[32]*

The surface structure content and behavior are coded to mask deeper issues. To develop an authentic identity, we cannot be blind to the deep structure themes that are essential containers for the shifting sands of identity.

To get at the truth beneath the surface, we begin with the stories that people construct about themselves. Narratives serve to integrate the many aspects of the self into a coherent identity, one that is somewhat stable, yet also amenable, across time. "To make a claim to separate, individual status we need a plausible history of ourselves, which recounts our past in such a way as to confirm our identity."[33] Brandon began his time with me by relaying the narrative of his past. In recalling memories of his past, Brandon attempts to validate who he is. Incongruence between who he sees himself as and the messages he receives from others left him confused. There was little congruence between his exterior life and his interior life, between his past and who he wanted to be, between the surface structure and deep structure of Brandon.

For therapists interested in the role of social media, and I argue that all of us should now bring this knowledge into practice, the images a client has access to can provide insight into the deep structure issues and supply the medium through which the narrative work can take place. Images provide a way to delve beneath the surface to emotions and to evoke deeper structure issues, while ironically providing the necessary distance for safety. These images may include social media images or other images on the Internet, but they can also include those images deeply engrained in a person's past, family images. Pictures of family are visible reminders of the past, allowing clients to look back at their lives and experiences, potentially from a new vantage point. Memories are made, as much as they are recalled, from images. Memories are subject to how others believe we should remember ourselves and to changing recollections as we reassess the past, the present, and the future.

Like all memories, autobiographical memories can be modified over time, a natural artifact of reconsolidation that can be positively facilitated in therapy. Resolving these incongruities through narrative construction integrates the life story and enables the expression of thoughts and feelings. The insight and wisdom of retrospection links the past selves with present and future selves to consolidate identity.

Images in family albums have the unique ability to reveal information that the client may not be aware of or has chosen to avoid. Identity is constructed in relation to outside influences including family, history, surroundings, and the interconnected systems and messages that are transmitted across generations. Family images have the power to impact identity as long as they hold unquestioned authority about reality. Early sessions with Brandon illustrated this power and laid the foundation for further exploration of the impact of social media on his identity. The following chapter illustrates how these images can be integrated into narrative identity work.

REFERENCES

1. Baumeister, R. F. (2005). Self-concept, self-esteem, and identity. In V. J. Derlega, B. A. Winstead, & W. H. Jones (Eds.), *Personality: Contemporary theory and research* (pp. 246–280). Belmont, CA: Thomson Wadsworth.

2. Damasio, A. (2012). *Self comes to mind: Constructing the conscious brain.* New York, NY: Vintage. Books.

3. Burke, P. J., & Stets, J. E. (2009). *Identity theory.* New York, NY: Oxford University Press.

4. Oyserman, D., Elmore, K., & Smith, G. (2012). Self, self-concept, and identity. In M. R. Leary & J. Price Tangney (Eds.), *Handbook of self and identity* (pp. 69–104). New York, NY: Guilford Press.

5. Damasio, A. (2012). *Self comes to mind: Constructing the conscious brain.* New York, NY: Vintage. Books.

6. Damasio, A. (2012). *Self comes to mind: Constructing the conscious brain.* New York, NY: Vintage. Books.

7. Swann, W. B., Jr., & Bosson, J. K. (2010). Self and identity. In S. T. Fiske, D. T. Gilbert & G. Lindzey (Eds.), *Handbook of social psychology* (pp. 589–628). Hoboken, NJ: John Wiley & Sons.

8. Hood, B. (2012). *The self illusion: How the social brain creates identity.* New York, NY: Oxford Press.

9. Siegel, D. J. (2012). *The developing mind: How relationships and the brain interact to shape who we are* (2nd ed.). New York, NY: Guilford Press.

10. Panksepp, J., & Biven, L. (2012). *The archaeology of mind: Neuroevolutionary origins of human emotions.* New York, NY: W. W. Norton & Company.

11. Hood, B. (2012). *The self illusion: How the social brain creates identity.* New York, NY: Oxford Press.

12. Ma, Y., & Han, S. (2011). Neural representation of self-concept in sighted and congenitally blind adults. *Brain: A Journal of Neurology, 134*(1), 235–246.

13. Siegel, D. J. (2012). *The developing mind: How relationships and the brain interact to shape who we are* (2nd ed.). New York, NY: Guilford Press.

14. Swann, W. B., Jr., & Bosson, J. K. (2010). Self and identity. In S. T. Fiske, D. T. Gilbert & G. Lindzey (Eds.), *Handbook of social psychology* (pp. 589–628). Hoboken, NJ: John Wiley & Sons.

15. Hood, B. (2012). *The self illusion: How the social brain creates identity.* New York, NY: Oxford Press.

16. Oyserman, D., Elmore, K., & Smith, G. (2012). Self, self-concept, and identity. In M. R. Leary & J. Price Tangney (Eds.), *Handbook of self and identity* (pp. 69–104). New York, NY: Guilford Press.

17. Siegel, D. J. (2012). *The developing mind: How relationships and the brain interact to shape who we are* (2nd ed.). New York, NY: Guilford Press.

18. Panksepp, J., & Biven, L. (2012). *The archaeology of mind: Neuroevolutionary origins of human emotions.* New York, NY: W. W. Norton & Company.

19. Stone, G. P. (1962). Appearance and the self. In A. Rose (Ed.), *Human behavior and social processes* (pp. 86–118). Boston, MA: Houghton Mifflin.

20. Wilson, T. D. (2002). *Strangers to ourselves: Discovering the adaptive unconscious.* Cambridge, MA: Harvard University Press.

21. Mond, J. M., Mitchison, D., & Hay, P. (2013). Eating disordered behavior in men: Prevalence, impairment in quality of life, and implications for prevention and health promotion. In L. Cohn & R. Lemberg (Eds.), *Current findings on males with eating disorders* (pp. 195–215). Philadelphia, PA: Routledge.

22. Bruch, H. (1979). Island in the river: The anorexic adolescent in treatment. In S. . Feinstein & P. L. Giovacchini (Eds.), *Adolescent psychiatry* (Vol. 7, p. 27). Chicago, IL: University of Chicago Press.

23. Mond, J. M., Mitchison, D., & Hay, P. (2013). Eating disordered behavior in men: Prevalence, impairment in quality of life, and implications for prevention and health promotion. In L. Cohn & R. Lemberg (Eds.), *Current findings on males with eating disorders* (pp. 195–215). Philadelphia, PA: Routledge.

24. Amianto, F., Northoff, G., Abbate Daga, G., Fassino, S., & Tasca, G. A. (2016). Is anorexia nervosa a disorder of the self? A psychological approach. *Frontiers in Psychology, 7*(849). doi:10.3389/fpsyg.2016.00849

25. Winnicott, D. W. (1962). Ego integration in child development. In *Maturational processes and the facilitating environment: Studies in the theory of emotional development.* New York, NY: International Universities Press.

26. Miller, A. (1981). *The drama of the gifted child.* New York, NY: Basic Books.

27. Harter, S., Bresnick, S., Bouchy, H., & Whitesell, N. (1997). The development of multiple role-related selves during adolescence. *Development and Psychopathology, 9*(4), 835–853.

28. Winnicott, D. W. (1962). Ego integration in child development. In *Maturational processes and the facilitating environment: Studies in the theory of emotional development.* New York, NY: International Universities Press.

29. Winnicott, D. W. (1962). Ego integration in child development. In *Maturational processes and the facilitating environment: Studies in the theory of emotional development.* New York, NY: International Universities Press.

30. Dorster, L. (2013). Millennial teens design and redesign themselves in online social networks. *Journal of Consumer Behaviour, 12*(4), 267–279.

31. Swann, W. B., Jr., & Bosson, J. K. (2010). Self and identity. In S. T. Fiske, D. T. Gilbert & G. Lindzey (Eds.), *Handbook of social psychology* (pp. 589–628). Hoboken, NJ: John Wiley & Sons.

32. Pipher, M. (1994). *Reviving Ophelia: Saving the selves of adolescent girls* (pp. 53–54). New York, NY: Ballantine Books.

33. Abercrombie, N., Hill, S., & Turner, B. (1986). *The sovereign individual* (p. 33). London, UK: Allen and Unwin.

Chapter 4
IDENTITY IN FAMILY IMAGES

The curious paradox is that when I accept myself just as I am, then I can change.
—**Carl Rogers**

Identity dwells within stories of self; the two are inseparable. Oliver Sacks, the well-known neurologist and writer, infers that "to be ourselves, we must have ourselves—possess, if need be re-possess, our life-stories. We must 'recollect' ourselves, recollect the inner drama, the narrative of ourselves. A man needs such a narrative, a continuous inner narrative, to maintain his identity, his self."[1] The narrative is the story we construct of our life from our experiences and memories. Narratives are universal to human culture. We are told stories from childhood and continue to tell stories throughout life. Through stories we entertain, educate, and remember. We cannot live without telling stories for it is through these that we make sense of the world, of ourselves, and of our lives in relation to others. We configure our lives into a narrative by choosing the experiences and memories that become part of the story of how we came to be who we are.[2] How we make sense of our experiences and tell our story to others shapes our identity. Our narrative signals who we are.

Meaning surfaces in the process of organizing and interpreting what may appear to be random experiences into a cohesive story. Narratives always take meaning from and reside within the larger culture. Once a narrative becomes embedded into the culture, it can become a standard by which personal narratives are structured. What one's culture expects acts as a roadmap for life. Standard narratives, such as those that prescribe an expected path—education, gainful employment, fulfilling marriage, and having children who then repeat the same life path—provide structure for the life narrative. Life seems less complicated if you want what others tell you to want. These same narratives can also be problematic if they set up unrealistic expectations of a perfect life for those who follow the prescribed path or punishment for those who do not follow the prescribed path. Identity formation can be an arduous process if one's narrative veers from the expected path. Brandon, introduced in the previous chapter, lacked needed support and affirmation as he sought to develop his identity. In attempting to be who he wanted to be, he deviated from family expectations.

Brandon's case highlights the role that others play in shaping narrative and identity. Within the larger culture in which we live, relational experiences with parents sculpt the sense of self.[3] Early relationships build the brain and the mind, assembling the template for relating to self and others. Growth and integration of neural networks are optimized by parental attunement, support, and proficiency in expressing emotions. According to Cozolino, "Parent–child talk, in the context of emotional attunement, provides the ground for the co-construction of narratives ... that become the mass of our inner experience and the parameters of our personal and social identities."[4]

As I came to know Brandon in the early days of our work together, I was often drawn to Cozolino's words as I tried to make sense of Brandon's story. His narrative of failure and unacceptability, learned from his early interactions with others, impacted his sense of self and led to self-defeating behaviors. Brandon isolated himself from others out of fear of rejection, and when he did go out, he made poor choices that put him in danger due to his desire to please others. Frequently feeling overwhelmed by emotions, he had no skills to express or tolerate the intensity of his experiences. At these times, he saw no clear path out of his situation, and he was often suicidal. Brandon had no sense of self, so he was hiding from life in his parent's basement, spending his waking time avoiding emotions through food and online activities.

While the early childhood years are foundational for identity development, it is in adolescence and the years of early adulthood that narrative construction escalates. Exponential growth in the ability to describe how one event led to another and to identify recurrent themes among experiences intensifies the yearning to put together a coherent narrative. Narrative coherence imparts a unifying link between otherwise disconnected and separate memories. For this to occur, a person must be able to restructure a memory by reviewing it in the mind, without being emotionally overwhelmed, while taking the perspective of the current self. Often, a person like Brandon is not able to calm and distance themself from the emotions of the experience, even at a later point in time. They lack the ability to look back on an earlier experience and evaluate how it fits with the overall understanding of who they are.

False selves and incoherent narratives expose disconnects between experiences, feelings, attitudes, and behavior and usually echo unconscious memories hidden from conscious consideration. Unconscious memories are often expressed as themes in narratives. Once clients recognize underlying unconscious thought processes, they can begin to generate an understanding of why they make the choices they do. Understanding unconscious thought processes is the precursor to enacting behavior change. Clients must have the capacity to reflect on underlying motives to understand themselves. Reflecting on underlying motives generates brain reorganization through new neural integration of thoughts, emotions, and behaviors. Memories are recast to include newfound wisdom attained from melding the unconscious and conscious. When the conscious and unconscious merge, the client's narrative expands. After all, the life story is not written in permanent ink; it is always open to revision because memories undergo continual modification, making identity formation an ongoing process. Clients can choose how to rewrite the story.

Current research acknowledges the value of narrative in the organization and integration of neural networks.[5] Both left-right and top-down/bottom-up processes integrates information from various neural networks into a cohesive story of the self that blends sensations, thoughts, and emotions into conscious awareness. Autobiographical narratives combine the sensory information of the left hemisphere language network with the emotional networks in the right hemisphere. The power of visual images to elicit emotion occurs from stimulation in the amygdala in response to both bottom-up neurological processing of visual and sensory perception and the top-down cognitive process.[6] Vertical integration enables unification of body, emotion, and conscious awareness. Therapy is successful to the extent that it enhances this neural integration. In Brandon's case, as he began to unpack his story he effortlessly pulled up photos on his phone to supplement his descriptions. This action introduces current visual input and indicates the usefulness of images to evoke and enhance memories as well a willingness to explore narrative through images.

As Brandon introduced photos into the narrative process, the implementation of photo therapy techniques begins in the therapy process. Photo therapy is a collaborative therapist–client approach in which the therapist guides the client to reflect on the feelings, memories, and thoughts stimulated by photographic images that have meaning for the client. Images infused with meaning document the personal narrative.[7] Vision supplies a great deal of the information we use to make sense of what we encounter. When we view an image, our brain relies on memory to fill in information. Images have an incredible propensity to trigger existing memories, instilling them with the power to access embedded meanings. The ability to access embedded meaning gives the therapist a window into the world from the client's perspective. In working with images in a therapeutic setting, the task of the therapist is to unravel the personally, socially, and culturally constructed meanings that each image has for the client. What the client notices in an image is always based on their own memories or mental maps, created from personal experiences.

We think, feel, and recall memories not in verbal form but as visual images. Verbal language is employed when we attempt to make what is in our mind comprehensible to someone else. Some clients naturally flow through a narrative of their life, while others tell stories that are seemingly unrelated or provide little information about how they have come to be who they are in life. Therapies, like photo therapy, rely on nonverbal means of accessing and working with unconscious aspects of the self that are essentially nonverbal and predominately visual.[8] Photo therapy bypasses verbal translations that obscure protections such as defenses and rationalizations, thereby permitting connection with the thoughts, feelings, and memories that are embedded in images. Accessing these can promote self-disclosure about personal experiences and emotional expression. The family album preserves memory, history, and cultural identity,[9] and the images in the album open a window into this secret family history. Clues as to family and individual identity, as well as public and private identity, abound within these images. A rich source for the autobiographical narrative, the family album illustrates what it was like to belong to this family and how early experiences impacted the client.

"Photographs and family albums . . . provide the richest source of collected memories and traditions of the family."[10] Images for the family album are selected to ensure that certain memories are made permanent and that the ideal or desired family story is illustrated. Thus, images are chosen to display important milestones and celebrations in the family life cycle such as births, graduations, reunions, weddings, holidays, and vacations. On the surface these images may appear generic or clichéd, yet when viewed with an eye to the story these images tell, the album shows deeper dimensions of the family. Repeated patterns, positions, themes, nonverbal messages, and emotional expressions suggest underlying meaning, thereby giving direction to future areas for exploration.

The therapist's role is to help the client discover and make sense of what they already know unconsciously. Until the patterns of their lives are brought to light, the client cannot benefit from the insights, processing of emotions, and linking of memories that enable them to create a coherent narrative. From a multigenerational family systems perspective, family images are a rich source of information about family dynamics.[11] Here is a list of information that may be revealed in family images:

1. Visible content regarding family heritage or roots can signal enculturation, the importance to the family of retaining native culture, and the degree of pride in the family heritage. Open questions showing interest often produce a great deal of information on the family roots and how clients feel about their heritage.

2. Physical similarities may reveal similarities in other areas. Information on the favoring of certain family members by other members, alliances, and the effects of these similarities on the rest of the family can emerge from conversations on similarities. Asking what it means to the relationship when one member favors another can elicit information on family dynamics.

3. Emotional content captured in spontaneous photos can reveal how the family truly is, rather than how they would like to appear to others. Spontaneous images are the best clues to family relationships and interactions. Notice whether there are spontaneous images only with certain family members because this can offer clues to relationship dynamics such as connectedness and distance. There may be numerous spontaneous images that include certain family members, while excluding others. A family member may be absent from spontaneous images because they fill the role of family photographer. Few spontaneous images with certain family members may also indicate a lack of interaction or discomfort with a role, such as when there are few images of a parent and child together.

4. How the family poses in most of the formal portraits gives information into how they wish to be seen by others and the power structure in the family. Notice who is usually included and who is usually close or distant to whom. Notice if certain members are placed in ways that demonstrate power or lack of power. Is someone always in front or appears to be the leader in the image? Clients can offer additional information such as who usually planned family portraits and was responsible for arranging the family members. Some clients will remember details about a specific image or the event of having family portraits taken. Even formally posed photos can reveal significant patterns that are not intentionally transmitted.

5. Notice the contrast between formal and spontaneous images.

6. Family scripts and gender role expectations are often demonstrated through how children are dressed for photographs and the activities depicted in family images. Patterns can show parent's expectations for how the family members are expected to be.

7. Intergenerational interactions in photographs indicate continuity through generations. Are grandparents included in the family album? What other family members are present?

8. Images may vary depending on who is the photographer. A person who is designated as the family peacekeeper may stage photos that bring the family members together. Some family members may isolate by remaining in the role of photographer to distance themselves from the family.

9. Triangulation may be exhibited through the positioning of family members. A pattern of a child or pet repeatedly aligned with one parent may signify triangulation between the parents because parental alignment with a child takes the pressure off of the parents to interact with one another. Notice if certain family members routinely shield or block another member from others in the image or from the camera.

10. Family dynamics of alignment, alliances, and enmeshment are likewise exhibited in positioning of family members. Which family members usually appear together or never seem to be together unless forced to pose together? When the client was young who held them most often? Are there differences in how the parents attend to or interact with the client in the images? Where is the gaze in the images? Who touches or makes eye contact with whom? Who mirrors one another? Is any-

one avoiding doing these things? Are there nonverbal clues that indicate boundary violations or expectations for behavior such as a parent restricting a child or the child's movement? What do facial expressions reveal in terms of family emotions?

11. Lack of differentiation may be exhibited by images that indicate the family is a single entity rather than a collection of individuals. Can children be who they are, or do they appear as extensions of the parents?

12. First born children are usually photographed more than siblings as the novelty of milestone events decreases with subsequent children. An overabundance of images of a later born child may provide hints of favoritism. Viewing family images can also challenge client memories of favoritism that is not born out in the family images.

13. Family cut-offs and secrets may appear in the family album through who has been left out or pushed to the side. Therapists may inquire about family members who are present at one point in time and then disappear.

14. Gaps in the family album suggests periods of stress, crisis, or a significant transition for the family such as deaths, separation, divorce, and heightened conflict.

15. Status symbols such as homes and cars, as well as pets that are given primary importance in images may indicate preference for these above people or relationships.

As the client's album is viewed therapists must remember that one image may or may not be significant. The true meaning of the images for the client is formulated from the patterns that repeat across the pages. These patterns illuminate the client's personal historical context, connecting the private and family definition of their identity. Helping clients see how these identities have developed enables them to understand current family dynamics and their emotional responses to their environment. The therapist aids client exploration by drawing out the client's perspective on their family images and honoring their perceptions as true representations of how they experience their family. The collection of images becomes a map to better understand the family from which the client originates.

To begin this type of work, I tell clients that I would like to do some work based on images from family photo albums to explore how they have come to be who they are today. I explain how identity formation and the development of an eating disorder often go hand and hand. Photo therapy is an exploration of what the images mean to the client. Although I could speculate on the meaning of the images for Brandon, he is the person with the key to unlock the meaning of an image and the memories it reveals. Photographers and album keepers undeniably have intentions, but it is the client's interpretation of the image that holds the client's truth. The therapist's role is to draw out and explore the truths the client already knows, the truths that are locked in their unconscious.

Photo therapy with family images was used with Brandon to access information of a historical nature. Images "used in therapy are connected to client's mental images, beliefs and memories of self."[12] Recognizing and expressing emotions in response to this information promotes self-understanding. Brandon was experiencing trials in developing his identity as a separate yet connected individual within his family system. Viewing family images can activate old memories and identities that take a client back to childhood. There is interest in the story each picture tells, but it is the reoccurring patterns that guide the direction of the therapeutic work. I asked Brandon to bring a family album so we could explore topics related to his identity in the coming weeks.

Brandon's childhood was during the time when family photos were still printed and the images gathered in family albums, so he had access to a family album and agreed to bring it to the next appointment. What follows is a detailed overview of five family-image sessions with Brandon. This overview of the photo therapy sessions with Brandon does not account for all the therapeutic work that was done to address Brandon's eating disorder and other difficulties. The focus here is limited to our use of family images. Other photo therapy techniques are covered in subsequent chapters.

SESSION ONE: FAMILY RULES

Family album sessions begin with the therapist taking a few minutes to quietly look through the album to get an overall feeling for the content and tone. Family albums are put together by the family member who has an unconscious agenda for how the family will be portrayed. As a result, conflicts and power struggles are not always apparent in the images chosen for the album.[13] As in most families, Brandon's mother is the family album keeper.

While Brandon and I surveyed the images in his album I asked, *What photo shows the rules for how someone must be to be included in your family?* Brandon immediately searched for what seemed be an ordinary family photo taken on a camping vacation when Brandon was about nine. It was a candid image of the family at the campsite. Spontaneously taken photos often give the clearest views into family relationships and dynamics. Brandon's mother, the photographer, caught an image of Brandon's father and brother engaged in some type of rough play that resembles wrestling, typical of what Brandon remembers of their relationship at the time. In the image, his older sister is sitting on a nearby stool watching the action. Brandon, on the other hand, is visible in the far left of the image, making direct eye contact with either the camera or his mother. As we explored this image, two discrete yet interrelated memories rose to the surface.

The first memory that came to Brandon was a general memory of what it felt like to be him during childhood. Brandon's brother was drawn to sports and seemed to bond easily with their father, who shared this interest. Brandon recalled lectures from his father on the benefits of exercise and being involved in team sports. Brandon did not excel at athletic activities. Brandon's father would point out the more masculine traits of other boys to Brandon in his efforts to toughen him up. Brandon's voice faded to a hoarse whisper, "I felt so rejected, like he would rather have any other boy as his son. I'm just not the person he wants me to be. I'm good at art and literature, but these don't fit with my father's view of how I should be." Nor did it provide the exercise Brandon's father felt he needed. Viewing this image took Brandon back to a painful experience that communicated to him that he did not measure up to his father's expectations.

The second memory from the vacation depicted in the image suddenly came to Brandon. He was not sure if it occurred before or after the photo was taken. Brandon spent the better part of the vacation sketching pictures of imaginary creatures, enjoying the afternoons when his father and brother were off fishing. One evening his father became angry at him for showing no interest in helping clean the day's catch and threw his drawings in the campfire. Devastated by this act, Brandon began to cry, which further enraged his father. Tears welled in Brandon's eyes as he relayed this story, frustrated and embarrassed that the event still upset him even after so much time had passed. I asked him what the photo he selected says about this memory, and he immediately focused on the way his eyes are locked on his mother, the photographer. "Mom gets me. I think I was looking to her for what I wasn't getting with my dad and brother. She included me, maybe even protected me. I'm still afraid of letting emotions out around my dad, but with her I can be more myself."

Brandon went on to explain that his parents had different expectations for his sister than they did for him and his brother. He showed me other images in his album, some posed and some more spontaneously taken. The combination of photos provided insight into how the family wanted to be viewed. The photos also clearly showed the emotional intimacy and emotional distance between the family members. In the posed images, there appeared to be an alliance between father and oldest son, with Brandon often appearing to be shielded or protected by his mother. Perhaps this was due to his position as the baby of the family, but he insisted that he is no longer a child and is tired of feeling intimidated and dismissed by his father.

This first foray into photo therapy illustrated a deeper sense of Brandon's childhood experiences than could have been obtained by verbal means alone. When using photo therapy, a therapist takes in a vast amount of visual information about the family from the album that lingers in their mind long after the session ends. The therapist can identify patterns and use them to inform the direction of future exploration, but the client benefits most from the insights, processing of emotions, and linking of memories. As our session ended, Brandon stated that he was curious to see what other images could teach him about himself and his family.

SESSION TWO: TRUE CHILDHOOD

The question *Is this family album a true picture of your childhood?* started the second photo therapy session. Brandon thought for a few seconds. "Yes and no. I mean, when I really look at some of the pictures, like we did last week, I see the real story—like how I felt left out of the manly stuff my dad and brother did. But I didn't really care. I didn't like those things, and that's what bothered my dad. I think he wanted me to feel left out, so I'd try harder to be like my brother." Momentarily sidetracked by this thought, Brandon returned to answering my question as he flipped through the album. "There's some pictures in here that don't tell the true story, like these Christmas ones." When I asked, *What do these images say?* he said that they show them as the perfect family, but that they posed for these, sometimes weeks before the actual holiday, so the pictures could be made into Christmas cards.

In these images the family appears perfect even if things were not so good. Brandon shuffled through the pages looking for evidence of a point he wanted to make. When he found what he was looking for, he showed me a holiday image of his smiling family, dressed in coordinated clothing. He remembered the day the photo was taken as an especially stressful one because he had at first refused to get dressed for the photo session, feeling unable to shake the self-loathing and shame he had been feeling for weeks. Earlier that same year, Brandon had been diagnosed with depression, but the medication prescribed by the family physician was not helping. He shared with me that he had given up by the time this photo was taken, feeling like he would never fit in with his family or with the other kids at school. Brandon had not thought of this time in his life in a long time; but in this session, he talked of this dark time in his early teen years when he wanted friends so badly that he had no boundaries. He wanted to please others, but he couldn't seem to do so, no matter what he did. He continued to earn good grades, but only to make his family proud because academic achievement was important to them.

Brandon decided to make some changes in his life by changing his body. At first, he cut out junk food and ate only the healthy meals that were the norm in his home. As he began to drop weight and get positive comments on the changes in his appearance, he became more restrictive with his eating, often skipping family meals as he got involved in more school activities. He even made some new friends at school and felt that, at last, he was accepted. In some ways this period in Brandon's life fits with the type of stories we all love: The story starts off bad and ends on a positive note. Redemption narratives like this are linked with more positive mental health, particularly if a person feels they are in control of their life and they have good relationships.[14] At this point, Brandon's story exemplifies both. He felt optimistic as he looked ahead to a promising future, but his story also has a contamination component. Contamination narratives start good and end poorly, resulting in poorer mental health. This one family image had given me an abundance of information about the development of Brandon's eating disorder and depression.

I wanted to end this session on a positive note to give Brandon the power to reimagine his story. I asked him *What would you change to make the images more accurate?* so that Brandon could begin to rewrite his narrative to focus on the skills he used to survive rather than the problem narrative. This is a difficult question for the client because it requires them to leave the hurt place represented by the images and to move toward the unknown. A creative person like Brandon is more likely to already have the ability to build this alternative storyline. Brandon responded: "I'm taking things into my own hands, even if they don't like it." With this attitude, he can reimagine himself as someone more at peace with who he is, a necessary step in becoming who he is.

SESSION THREE: BODY IDENTITY

Food, weight, and body issues often have roots in family attitudes toward appearance. My initial observations told me that Brandon was not comfortable in his body, so exploring where this came from would be helpful in countering the family and cultural messages he received while growing up. As a child who was perceived to be overweight, Brandon received critical messages about his body from family. I asked him to review photos of himself across time to get a truer picture of his weight trajectory. Brandon initially told me that he became overweight in early elementary school, but the pictures we saw did not support this memory. In Brandon's class photos, where children are lined up on risers, he is in the back row, well above many of his classmates in height. In these pictures, he does not seem to be an overweight child, but rather a robust one. Why he was labeled overweight was a mystery to me, but it is not uncommon for someone with an eating disorder to recall that they were overweight in childhood, only to be baffled by photographic evidence that refutes this recollection. It is also common for a person to be falsely labeled as overweight by a family member. My next prompt was *Tell me what these images say about your body.* "I am just so big, bigger than the other kids, but also not like a big kid should be. I feel younger than my classmates even though I'm not. I was definitely not strong like a big kid should be." His response held much more than the acknowledgement that he was not overweight during this period. His response revealed feelings of not measuring up in other ways.

Middle school, when he did begin to put on weight, was a painful time for Brandon. I asked him what he saw in the family images that reflect his family's messages about weight and appearance during this time. He remarked that no one in his immediate family was overweight, other than him. The family message was that you must be in control of your eating or you will shame the family by being fat. His father openly disparaged him. "It wasn't okay that I was fat, and he let me know it. I felt bad when I ate junk food, but at the same time it felt good to not be doing what he wanted me to do." Peers also taunted him about his weight, so he started restricting food. Photos of him taken during the last two years of high school show an emaciated young man with hollow cheeks. In most of these photos, he is shirtless or has on tight fitting clothes, as if he is trying to accentuate his overly lean body. Brandon commented that he felt good about his weight at this time. He identified as gay at this point, at least internally if not to others, and felt that he had finally acquired the expected body type to go along with his desired identity: that of a somewhat small and lean gay male. He still felt too tall and that his frame was too large, but at least he was no longer overweight.

There are few images of Brandon from his first years of college in the family album. This can be attributed to several factors: He was no longer living with his family, and by that time most images were taken and kept on phones instead of being carefully placed in family albums. Sometimes the number of images of a family member declines if that member falls out of grace with the family.[15] Brandon came out to his family after his first year in college, and while they continued to support him financially, he felt a shift in his relationship with them. The few images of Brandon from this time period depicted him as closer to a healthy body weight, although he remembered feeling too heavy at the time. At this session, he was continuing to restrict food to hold his weight below the norm, only to give in to binging and purging. He talked openly about how these behaviors had taken over his life in recent months, a huge shift from his avoidance of the topic in our first session.

Next, I prompted *Tell me about your favorite image of yourself.* Not surprisingly, he chose an image taken in his senior year of high school. When I asked what he likes about the image, he declared that he looks more confident than he really was. He received attention for his appearance, and he loved hearing how good he looked, especially after feeling overweight and unacceptable for most of his childhood. But then Brandon's demeanor changed quickly, as a wave of sadness came across his entire face. "This didn't last too long though. About the time I started thinking things were going pretty good, everything got more complicated with the move to college." I agreed that this can be a big transition in a young person's life. Brandon went on, "I didn't know how to handle all the new freedom I had at college. Guys paid me attention. I didn't always choose the nicest or the most emotionally available guys. I'm so desperate for attention that I'll try to be whoever-I'm-with-for-a-minute wants me to be."

I asked Brandon if there was someone like that in his life at this time, and he silently nodded his head. For the first time, Brandon was putting some of his unconscious knowledge into words. He realized that he tends to lose his identity in relationships, attempting to get the affirmation he believes will make him feel whole. He didn't yet recognize the probable link between his choices of emotionally unavailable men and his thwarted attempts to get recognition from his emotionally distant father. Because photo therapy work is based on the client's perceptions rather than the therapist's, I didn't share this thought. Brandon's awareness of this dynamic came later in our work.

SESSION FOUR: FAMILY RELATIONSHIPS— INTERGENERATIONAL TRANSMISSION

Many of my clients grow up in families that offer conditional acceptance, granted only if they live up to nonverbalized expectations for how they should be. Often the expectations are so vague that the client is unable to access this information, so they blame themselves for a perceived failure to be loveable and acceptable. In photo therapy work, images reveal the family's desired public presentation of the client and the family. Identity work requires finding ways for the client to reclaim and rewrite the narrative that was created by others. This is especially important for clients who have been devalued by one or both parents. Therapy, in these cases, must delve into the complex nature of the parent–child relationship.

Family albums convey the complicated family connections and interdependencies from which a young person emerges as they seek their own identity. As family relationships and communication patterns are explored, this focus on the family is ultimately also how clients learn about themselves. I began this session by asking Brandon to again leaf through his album and note who is in the photos. He discovered images mostly of his nuclear family, as expected, with a few scattered images of grandparents, aunts, uncles, and cousins. His family does not embrace many from outside the nuclear family into their immediate circle. To guide discovery of alignments and power structures in the images, I prompted Brandon: *Observe who is standing next to or touching whom in the candid photos.* Spontaneous snapshots automatically contain physical representations that signal unconscious dynamics.

Brandon's gaze stopped on a snapshot of his family taken at what appeared to be a larger family gathering. He looked to be three or four years old and was sitting in his mother's lap, her arms wrapped loosely around his torso as he leaned back comfortably against her. In this photo, his sister sits nearby, at the edge of the image, and is also leaning on their mother. Brandon's father is on the other edge of the image looking rather rigid and bored. At his father's feet, Brandon's brother mimics their father's attitude. His mother is looking at his father, as if trying to read his thoughts. I asked Brandon *What's important for me to know about your family as I look at this image?* Brandon obviously felt drawn to this image out of all the others he flipped by in this session. He began his response with noticing how comfortable he looks in his mother's lap, and then noted that his sister appeared to feel the same. Linking this with the present, he commented on the closeness between the three of them. His eyes then went to his father, "This is an accurate picture of him, not very interested in family get-togethers. He's very narrow-minded and critical of everyone, so he doesn't get along with many people." Someone had captured this image without preparing the family, yet it spoke volumes from Brandon's perspective. Together, we looked at other images in his album that showed similar expressions of the family dynamics.

These family images prompted additional thoughts on the family dynamics. Brandon spoke of feeling attacked by and detached from his father. He shared that when his father was angry at him or disproved of his actions, he complained to Brandon's mother, who tried to intervene and fix the issue. It seemed to Brandon that he didn't want to deal with Brandon's emotions, which Brandon acknowledged can be intense. Labeling this behavior—his father bringing in someone else to do the relationship work that should occur between him and Brandon— as *triangulating* generated relief, based on this being a common enough issue to have a name. Brandon realized that his alignment with his mother enabled him to interact well with females. After his mother, Brandon was closest to his sister and a few female friends. Brandon's relationships with males tended to be with dating partners and characterized by seriality, superficiality, and attempts for approval. Not only was he fearful of interacting with his father, Brandon had difficulty with all male authority figures. He was intimidated by male professors and adult men in general, which caused problems in school and with seeking employment. He confided that he had been avoiding looking for a job since leaving school because he cannot summon the courage to interview.

I wanted Brandon to know more about his father so that he could have a fuller perspective of his father as a person. There were a few images of his father in the album from the early days of his parent's marriage, when he was not much older than Brandon was in our sessions, as well as some pictures of Brandon's paternal grandparents, taken around the same time. One photo of Brandon's father and paternal grandfather standing together shows their similar physical stature and serious demeanor. Brandon observed that he does not take after them in either aspect. He noted that he is tall and broad like the men on his mother's side, and he is obviously more expressive. He wondered what it is like for his father to have this son who is physically so much larger than himself but who does not fit his picture of masculinity. I asked Brandon to do a brief exercise, pretending for a moment to be his father in that image and talking in the first person as if he was his father. What follows is a brief overview of what happened in this exercise.

Brandon timidly stood up and began to talk to his grandfather about the difficulties of life and taking care of his young family. He pulled out of character as his father and told me that he has heard stories of how harsh his grandfather was with his father, so his grandfather probably would have told him to "buck it up and be a man." I urged Brandon to imagine this conversation and then to imagine how this made his father feel. After he completed this, he stated that no one taught his father how to deal with feelings, and now he doesn't know how to help his own kids deal with them. To close this out I asked, *What would you like to tell the men in this photo?* He responded that he would say he will be okay, even though he is just now learning things he wishes he had learned from them. Brandon remarked that this was a powerful realization for him; these thoughts came to him without much effort, yet they felt true. When he stepped into his father's shoes, he was able to draw on knowledge that he had from what he'd heard about past family history, from his own memories, and from the feelings these images brought forth to broaden his perspective.

This type of exercise is adapted from the well-known empty chair technique, a key method in Gestalt therapy for addressing relationship difficulties by helping the client gain insight into another's emotions and attitudes. The German word *gestalt* means "whole," which alludes to this technique's emphasis on bringing all aspects of the self into awareness: the interconnections with environment, relationships, and conscious and unconscious thoughts, emotions, behaviors, and sensations.[16] Likewise, photo therapy techniques that are based on this principal can directly tap emotions and communicate meaning not accessible by other channels.

SESSION FIVE: BRANDON'S TRUE SELF

Finding the true self depends on individuation, which provides a sense of being separate and distinct from others and differentiating oneself from family of origin. "The goal in differentiating is not just how to discover how family members are different, but also to find out (and accept) some of the areas of sameness, without those similarities meaning fusion or lack of individuation."[17] Photo therapy can illuminate the parts of the self that are unique from the family as well as those that may be enmeshed with outdated family identities. Finding balance between deciding to retain the parts of the family identity that fit with the true self, deciding to discard those that do not, and identifying one's unique contribution to identity allows one the freedom to construct the true self.

To encourage Brandon to a more future orientation of self, I asked him to make copies of his favorite photos of himself from the family album that he can then use to make a timeline of himself throughout his life and into the future he imagines. Once he does this, the images can be manipulated in any way he wishes while preserving the integrity of the originals. The images he selected could have other people in them, but he needed to be a central feature in them all. I wanted him to see himself as an individual in his own right, but also connected to the important people in his life. Neural networks involved in remembering the past are also used in creatively imagining future events and perspectives.[18] Past, present, and future orientations contribute to identity. Brandon returned the following week with his timeline. What follows is an overview of some timeline events relevant to Brandon's difficulties at the time of our sessions.

Together we traveled through his early years as he pointed out what he likes about each photo he chose for his timeline and explained his reasons for including each. When we reached his early teen years, his tone changed. When I pointed out this change in his affect, Brandon stated that creating this timeline led him to realize that he has few memories of his childhood and very few positive ones. I was not surprised by this news because many people who do not receive positive nurturing early in life relegate their painful memories to their unconscious as a survival mechanism, thus they find it difficult to recall these early memories. Early, prolonged stress triggers the release of cortisol, which can damage explicit memory, upon which autobiographical memories rely. Further, implicit memories residing at an unconscious level lead to dysfunctional patterns of thought, emotion, and behavior.[19] Brandon's recall and interpretation of his experiences, as well as his current perceptions, are negatively biased by difficult childhood experiences. This illustrates the influence of early relationships on present and future interpretations of events and who one is.

It is not surprising that Brandon was drawn to online activities once his social relationships became nonexistent partially due to withdrawal from school. In our sessions, he was in a vicious cycle of anxiety, binge eating, purging, and depression. The Internet is always available to meet needs that are not met elsewhere. It is still too early to know with certainty how mental health and social media use are linked. Among the vast numbers of studies conducted since the ascension of the Internet, technology use has been linked with poor mental health, but the pathways and strength of this association are likely based on numerous factors, including frequency and levels of use, as well as the actual online behaviors and reasons for use. Concerns about the addictive potential of technology is rising.

Adam Alter, a professor of marketing at New York University, explains how the widespread use of technology has led to Internet-based addiction for almost half the American population. In his 2017 book, *Irresistible*,[20] he discusses the intent of technology developers to capitalize on behavioral addiction to their products to fuel profits. Media addiction is fueled by attempts to meet needs for social engagement, mental stimulation, and sense of effectiveness. Social media uses the irresistible and unpredictable qualities of social engagement to keep people coming back to their sites to see who has liked a photo. Likewise, online gaming employs mental challenges and a strong social component to bond users with other gamers. Depressed or lonely people like Brandon are likely to turn to social media or gaming to lessen their pain. Addiction occurs when people learn that the experience lessens, at least temporarily, their psychological pain. Seeking body perfection, a core aspect of identity for those with eating disorders, is likewise driven by attempts to feel a sense of effectiveness.

Through our conversations, Brandon began to acknowledge that he engaged in these behaviors to numb his overpowering emotions and escape to a fantasy world where he could be who he wants to be. I asked him what he has learned about himself from playing video games, and he described the characters he creates as strong and assertive, unlike how he feels in other parts of his life. This topic moved him forward on his timeline, as a result of his relating these feelings to his current state of confusion about what he wants for his life. Anxious about making the right choices and unsure about his ability to withstand the pressure and criticism of a career in the arts, he avoided making any plans for his future. He knew what he wanted in a relationship, but he didn't know how to get it. He did not want to be in what he calls a "hook-up scene." Rather, he desired more depth than what he was experiencing in his current relationship.

Brandon had much work to do in the coming months. After session five, we began to work on one of the most crucial pieces: that of exploring the historical context in which Brandon's identity deficits emerged, using his autobiographical narrative. The images Brandon brought into sessions opened a window into the emotional turmoil he was unable to express with words alone, and they provided structure for building his narrative. Activation and integration of left hemispheric thought processes with the emotional right hemispheric brain processes help the brain make sense of experiences and promote a more coherent narrative. A safe therapeutic relationship guides the client back and forth between thoughts and feelings to integrate cognitive and affective networks and consciously consider feelings.[21] The power of the therapeutic relationships to repair early damage to sense of self relies on emotional attunement, memory talk, and co-construction of the narrative.[22] The therapist is present to support affect tolerance and regulation, to which we now turn.

Brandon was using multiple harmful behaviors to avoid feeling the strong emotions he has not learned to handle. Neuroscientist Daniel Siegel states that emotion regulation is at the core of the self because self-organization depends on the ability to regulate appraisal of and response to experiences.[23] A primary goal of the neural integration process referred to above is to prevent "amygdala highjack,"[24] which occurs when high levels of stress hormones, such as cortisol, prompt the amygdala to shut down higher level cognitive function. When this occurs, intense emotions can flood the mind, leaving the individual unable to use rational thought or reflection or to recover a calm state.

Explaining this process to Brandon helped him make sense of his previous patterns of shutting down in difficult situations and gave him hope that he can increase his emotional tolerance. I taught him a simple calming technique, which I use with many of my traumatized clients, to evoke a soothing image of an attachment figure while engaging in bilateral stimulation (BLS). The favorite image of Brandon and his mother from his timeline is the image he uses in this method. The technique is based on resource tapping,[25] a method associated with the practice of Eye Movement Desensitization and Reprocessing (EMDR), which will be discussed in more detail in Chapter 12. When Brandon notices an increase in anxiety, he holds a mental image of his mother, as she represents safety and support to him, while engaging in BLS by tapping his hands alternately on his thighs until he feels more relaxed. With practice, this gives him access to calm, positive feelings and, over time, decreases the frequency and intensity of anxiety. Competency in the ability to calm down from overwhelming emotions gives Brandon hope that he will be able to be present with himself without seeking distractions.

The self needs room to emerge and develop, space to know the self, and the practice of self-compassion, a rare commodity for many today. It's not that the space is unavailable, but sensory overload and distraction are the norm in the social media age, leaving young people with a limited capacity to tolerate unfilled minutes. When the self-reflective processes that arise in these situations are pelted by intrusive thoughts and feelings, an abundance of sensory input from social media can distract one from unmanageable feelings, but distraction does little to facilitate growth. In contrast, it is in quiet moments that a person finds the self through inward thought, listening to oneself, and imagining a future. Here is where *what is* and *what can be* are integrated into identity. Solitude is essential for the mind to organize the self and create meaning and for one to filter input from others and heal the self.[26] It is in finding balance between social engagement and solitude that authentic identity can form. This topic will be explored in more detail in Chapter 10.

For identity to be stable, problematic self-evaluations, narratives, and ways of interacting socially must be altered.[27] The family image sessions with Brandon brought new information into his awareness. While he continues to have a difficult relationship with his father, he moves from feeling that he is to blame for not being who his father wants him to be toward a greater recognition of his father's difficult upbringing and difficulties in relationships. Much work lies ahead for Brandon and his family. Photo therapy work opens Brandon to the self-compassion that will be necessary for his recovery. Self-compassion is a difficult task for many, but it is the basis of managing difficult circumstances and building a healthy sense of self.[28] When the harmful narrative is made conscious and associated beliefs about the self are challenged, one shifts toward acceptance of an updated identity, and greater self-compassion begins.

REFERENCES

1. Sacks, O. (1985). *The man who mistook his wife for a hat and other clinical tales* (pp. 105–106). New York, NY: Summit Books.

2. Lawler, S. (2014). *Identity: Sociological perspectives* (2nd ed.). Cambridge, UK: Polity Press.

3. Damasio, A. (2012). *Self comes to mind: Constructing the conscious brain.* New York, NY: Vintage. Books.

4. Cozolino, L. (2017). *The neuroscience of psychotherapy: Healing the social brain* (3rd ed., pp. 230–231). New York, NY: W. W. Norton & Company.

5. Damasio, A. (2012). *Self comes to mind: Constructing the conscious brain.* New York, NY: Vintage. Books.

   Cozolino, L. (2017). *The neuroscience of psychotherapy: Healing the social brain.* (3rd ed.) New York, NY: W. W. Norton & Company.

6. Carr, S. M. D. (2014). Revisioning self-identity: The role of portraits, neuroscience and the art therapist's 'third hand'. *International Journal of Art Therapy: Inscape, 19*(2), 54–70.

7. Weiser, J. (1999). *PhotoTherapy techniques: Exploring the secrets of personal snapshots and family albums.* Vancouver, BC: Judy Weiser and PhotoTherapy Centre Publishers.

8. Weiser, J. (1999). *PhotoTherapy techniques: Exploring the secrets of personal snapshots and family albums.* Vancouver, BC: Judy Weiser and PhotoTherapy Centre Publishers.

9. de Bernart, R. (2013). The photographic genogram and family therapy. In D. Loewenthal (Ed.), *Phototherapy and therapeutic photography in a digital age* (pp. 120–127). New York, NY: Routledge.

10. Entin, A.D. (1982). Family icons: Photographs in family therapy. In L.E. Abt & I.R. Stuart (Eds.), *The newer therapies: A sourcebook* (pp. 207-227). New York, NY: Van Nostrand.

11. Entin, A.D. (1982). Family icons: Photographs in family therapy. In L.E. Abt & I.R. Stuart (Eds.), *The newer therapies: A sourcebook* (pp. 207-227). New York, NY: Van Nostrand.

    Kaslow, F.W., & Friedman, J. (1977). Utilization of family photos and movies in family therapy. *Journal of Marriage & Family Counseling, 3*(1),18.

    Star, K.L., & Cox, J.A. (2008). The use of phototherapy in couples and family counseling. *Journal of Creativity in Mental Health, 3*(4), 373-382.

    Weiser, J (1999) *PhotoTherapy techniques: Exploring the secrets of personal snapshots and family albums* (2nd Ed.). Vancouver, BC: PhotoTherapy Centre.

    Weiser 2001. PhotoTherapy techniques: Using clients' personal snapshots and family photos as counseling and therapy tools. *Afterimage: The Journal of Media Arts and Cultural Criticism*, 29(3), 10-15.

    Wheeler, M. (January 2019). A review of the literature published by family therapists on the use of photographs in their practice. doi: 10.13140/RG.2.2.26499.96803

12. Halkola, U. (2013). A photograph as a therapeutic experience (p. 21). In D. Loewenthal (Ed.), *Phototherapy and therapeutic photography in a digital age* (pp. 21–30). New York, NY: Routledge.

13. Martin, R. (2009). Inhabiting the image: Photography, therapy, and re-enactment phototherapy. *European Journal of Psychotherapy and Counseling, 11*(1), 35–49.

14. Adler, J. M., Turner, A. F., Brookshier, K. M., Monahan, C., Walder-Biesanz, I., Harmeling, L. H., . . . Oltmanns, T. F. (2015). Variation in narrative identity is associated with trajectories of mental health over several years. *Journal of Personality and Social Psychology, 108*(3), 476–496.

15. Kaslow, F. W. (1979). What personal photos reveal about marital sex conflicts. *Journal of Marital and Sex Therapy, 5*(2), 134–141.

16. Cozolino, L. (2017). *The neuroscience of psychotherapy: Healing the social brain.* (3rd ed.) New York, NY: W. W. Norton & Company.

17. Weiser, J. (1999). *PhotoTherapy techniques: Exploring the secrets of personal snapshots and family albums* (p. 295). Vancouver, BC: Judy Weiser and PhotoTherapy Centre Publishers.

18. Schacter, D. L., Addis, D. R., & Buckner, R. L. (2007). Remembering the past to imagine the future: The prospective brain. *Nature Reviews Neuroscience, 8(9),* 657–661.

19. Cozolino, L. (2017). *The neuroscience of psychotherapy: Healing the social brain.* (3rd ed.) New York, NY: W. W. Norton & Company.

20. Alter, A. (2017). *Irresistible: The rise of addictive technology and the business of keeping us hooked.* New York: NY Penguin Press.

21. Cozolino, L. (2017). *The neuroscience of psychotherapy: Healing the social brain.* (3rd ed.) New York, NY: W. W. Norton & Company.

22. Cozolino, L. (2017). *The neuroscience of psychotherapy: Healing the social brain.* (3rd ed.) New York, NY: W. W. Norton & Company.

    Siegel, D. J. (2012). *The developing mind: How relationships and the brain interact to shape who we are* (2nd ed.). New York, NY: Guilford Press.

23. Siegel, D. J. (2012). *The developing mind: How relationships and the brain interact to shape who we are* (2nd ed.). New York, NY: Guilford Press.

24. Goleman, D. (2006). *Emotional intelligence* (10th ed.). New York, NY: Bantam Books.

25. Parnell, L. (2008). *Tapping in: A step-by-step guide to activating your healing resources through bilateral stimulation.* Boulder, CO: Sounds True, Inc.

26. Siegel, D. J. (2012). *The developing mind: How relationships and the brain interact to shape who we are* (2nd ed.). New York, NY: Guilford Press.

27. Swann, W. B., Jr., & Bosson, J. K. (2010). Self and Identity. In S. T. Fiske, D. T. Gilbert & G. Lindzey (Eds.), *Handbook of social psychology* (pp. 589–628), Hoboken, NJ: John Wiley & Sons.

28. Leary, M., Tate, E., Adams, C., Allen, A., & Hancock, J. (2007). Self-compassion and reactions to unpleasant self-relevant events: The implications of treating oneself kindly. *Journal of Personality, 92*(5), 887–994.

Chapter 5

PHOTOGRAPHIC IMAGES: THE LANGUAGE OF SOCIAL MEDIA

We do not err because truth is difficult to see. It is visible at a glance. We err because this is more comfortable.

—Alexander Solzhenitsyn

Perhaps truth is difficult to see because we avoid looking at aspects of ourselves that we would rather not acknowledge. Self-reflection can bring discomfort if feelings of vulnerability arise in response to discovering thoughts, desires, or even actions that have previously remained hidden from our awareness. Yet we also have an innate curiosity or desire to know ourselves. We want to understand what is going on beneath the surface: who we are and why we do certain things. Since the dawn of time people have drawn or painted pictures and told stories to make sense of their lives. Once the medium of photography became widely adopted, the camera became another way for people to tell their stories and find meaning. This chapter looks at the unique applications of this new medium for understanding ourselves and the world around us.

In the 1990s psychologist and author Mary Pipher referred to adolescent girls as "saplings in the storm" when she wrote that girls of this age were struggling with a host of issues due to the girl-poisoning culture in which they attempt to mature. She sounded the warning that a crisis was underway. As girls enter adolescence, they are encouraged to develop a false self to gain the approval of the larger culture. Girls who are able to hold on to their uncensored selves from their earlier childhood days are often punished in early- and mid-adolescence when they do not conform to cultural expectations.[1] They often clash with a culture that holds a narrow view of female appearance and behavior. Today, twenty-five years after Pipher's warning, the cultural conditions that negatively impact young people have heightened. One of the largest cultural shifts of our time—the proliferation of visual images—has placed greater pressure on young people. Pipher focused exclusively on adolescent females, but my work has taught me that males, as well as females in their adult years, also have trouble navigating the hurricanes of visual images that blow through their worlds each day.

If identity is comprised of personality, character, feelings, thought processes, motivations, emotional reactions, and behavior, why does the physical realm dominate a person's sense of self at this stage? The answer lies in understanding the concurrent developmental processes in the search for identity and how technological advances have altered the search for personal identity. Adolescence is a time of rapid change in the self, particularly the physical, emotional, thinking, and social aspects. With physical changes throughout adolescence and a cultural obsession with appearance, many in this age group place more emphasis on how things appear on the outside than they do on being true to themselves. Hence, we witness a preoccupation with the tangible self as adolescents attempt to develop a coherent sense of who they are at the same time as their abilities to process thoughts and ideas beyond their concrete world are expanding. It is as if their rapidly developing brains are overwhelmed by too much information, and to cope with this deluge, adolescents attempt to simplify identity down to observable characteristics by placing others and themselves in easily identifiable categories.

Most adults have lived through similar experiences, in which belonging to a desired group, such as the athletes, cheerleaders, band members, brains, or any other number of less than flattering categories, was used to simplify and define one another. The search for identity and belonging continues as young people transition into their twenties. Whereas in previous generations young adults in their twenties married and started families and careers, young adults are now addressing these tasks in their thirties. Many young adults now postpone these activities due to educational pursuits, a changed economy, and a general shift toward the twenties being a time of finding oneself before committing and settling down. Many twentysomethings I see in my practice continue to struggle with the issues of identity that first emerged in adolescence. These young people have spent most of their lives "connected" to their larger peer group through social media, and they are much more likely to feel the effects of existing in a public sphere than previous generations.

THE SMARTPHONE AND BEYOND

To set the stage for appreciating the cultural context in which visual images are made more powerful than personal attributes, we should first establish how images have come to exert such a powerful force on us. From the earliest times until recent history, people had minimal exposure to visual representations of objects. Most people viewed only what was present in their immediate environment. While the development of the printing press in the mid-15th century cannot be underestimated for its impact on the transmission of knowledge, visual representations of people in that era still relied heavily on drawings and commissioned portraits. This began to change in the early 19th century, following inventions in photographic technology and the advent of professional photography.

The production of photographic images is a three-step process: image creation, image processing, and image distribution or sharing. These steps shape the very meaning of photography at any given time because developments in each of the stages are interrelated yet occur at different rates.[2] Photography combines technological developments from multiple fields (cameras, image processing, smartphones and their related apps, and the Internet, as well as others). Photography is also a practice imbued with social meanings. The cultural influence of photography is best examined through the alliance of technology and meaning. What follows is a brief overview of technological developments that led to the fusion of the three steps into one device: the smartphone.

In its infancy, the photographic process relied on a detailed knowledge base and the use of toxic chemicals, thereby ensuring that the practice of photography was left to those with expertise in both mechanical and chemical technology. Creativity was constrained by the limitations of large equipment and limited settings in which the exposure could be completed. Exposure times were long and required the subject to remain perfectly still while the photo was taken, so photographs of people had an air of formal portraiture. This period, termed the first moment in photography, initiated a cultural shift in the use and, ultimately, the meaning of visual images despite these limitations. At the outset, only people of means were commemorated by photographic images.

Distribution of photographs initially relied on traveling photographers selling tintype portraits. Toward the end of this era, small black and white images became available to the masses, as photography studios appeared in towns and cities alike. This period initiated changes in the importance of visual images to identity development as the photograph became a reference point for perceiving oneself and communicating to others.

The professional photography monopoly didn't last long. The presence of visual images in daily living soon exponentially exploded, introducing the second moment of photography. In 1888, the Eastman Company initiated the era of snapshot photography with its release of the Kodak camera.[3] By the turn of the century, the first of the Brownie cameras, available for as little as $1, brought photography to the masses. It is at this point that we can say photography became vernacular, a language common to all. The photographically unskilled public who purchased these cameras had only to point the camera and press the shutter release; no technical skill was required to create accurate and mostly clear images. The Eastman Company slogan "You press the button, we do the rest" represented a revolution in photography. Creation and processing were distinctly separate. Once the 100-exposure roll was exposed, the entire camera was mailed to the Eastman factory, where the film was processed and printed. The camera was then reloaded with film and returned to the customer. Photography was now an affordable pastime for many, and the focus changed from documentation, through the monumental formal portrait, to portrayal of everyday domestic living and travel. Newspapers and magazines also capitalized on these developments by distributing photographs to sell products and sway opinions.

The third moment of photography came a mere thirty years later, as advances in photographic technology began to drive the frenzy of excessively documenting life that we see today. Amateur photographers—like my maternal grandmother, raising her brood of ten children on a cotton farm in Texas in the 1930s and early 1940s, and in later years in the wooded areas of Oregon—documented their families through a series of black and white images. My family members say that my grandmother always had a camera around and made sure to gather the family for informal family portraits. Of course, these photos were all taken outside because adequate lighting was still a limitation. Periodically, she would send her camera off for processing, despite the economic difficulties of a rural lifestyle and of raising a large family in that era. Along with the stories she wrote of her life on the farm, these photographs are readily shared among her descendants; they document a lifestyle that no longer exists. They are part of the life story she left.

Kodachrome film made color images available to amateur photographers in 1935. My grandmother, though, did not have the means for this luxury until much later. Her family photos in the 1950s were still shot in black and white. By the 1960s, Instamatic cameras, which allowed the user to take a single photo and eject it instantly, were so commonplace that an estimated 50 million users were suddenly able to immediately view their photographic images. Most households had at least one camera ready for commemorating significant family rituals, vacations, and mundane events alike. While these photographs may be best understood as "sophisticated constructs of reality,"[4] there is no doubt that the families who took them wanted them to reflect happy times and familial bonds. Viewing and sharing of images in this era was done by mail, thumbing through the shoeboxes and albums of photos, or during face-to-face interactions.

Personal photography seemed to have reached unthinkable levels of saturation at this point as a result of relatively inexpensive film and processing fees. The coming developments would show just how much further this technology could soar. The mid-1970s saw the emergence of digital photography, although it would take several years for this new technology to become widely adopted. By the start of the fourth moment in photography, which began in the 1990s, everyone with a digital camera was a photographer and image processing was immediate. The photographer can shoot with abandon and simply delete undesirable images. Digital cameras are ubiquitous—no longer is the camera an object that is pulled out of the closet only for family events. Images are now downloaded to a personal computer and distributed on the rapidly expanding Internet, home to the newly emergent social networking websites that are further shifting the landscape of photography. Digital photography allows users to control all aspects of photography: creation, processing, and distribution of images.

The most recent shift in photography occurred with advent of the camera phone and smartphone. Approximately four billion people have a digital camera with them at all times. It is estimated that over a trillion photos were taken in 2018, and 90% of people who take pictures today have done so only with a camera phone.[5] The quality, ease, and ability to manipulate images on these camera phones surpasses professional equipment of generations past. We even have a new niche for professional photographers, those whose work is done exclusively on a camera phone This is the fifth moment of photography, the key distinction from earlier moments being the pervasive presence of the smartphone, which enables almost instantaneous connection to the Internet and social media from anywhere. Images are shared in real time, a change that has shifted the focus from monumental events to common, daily phenomena. Flat rate Internet access and the ease of uploading images from phones to websites make smartphones the progenitors of prolific photo sharing. Apps designed for smartphones make it possible to control all three photographic processes of creation, processing, and distribution in one device. Visual culture in the digital age is a new frontier that we must acknowledge as a force in massive cultural shifts.

INVENTING REALITY

The proliferation of photography can be attributed to technological advances and the ease of capturing and sharing images, though focusing only on these changes ignores the deeper meaning of how photographs have become embedded in our lives. Since the advent of photographic images, people have desired to own images of themselves and others. Has the purpose of photography changed now that many of us take and store hundreds, if not thousands, of images on our phones? Are these photographs an attempt to catalog our world, capture our experiences, or prove our existence? Do we inadvertently believe in a photograph's ability to capture the soul? Building on the technology of photography allows us to explore the essence of photography today, how the meanings and uses interact with the technological advances. This can help us to better understand how images impact clients with eating disorders and how to address social media usage with clients in recovery.

In her collection of essays *On Photography*, published in 1977, Susan Sontag explains that photography is "mainly a social rite, a defense against anxiety, and a tool of power."[6] Despite the cultural changes since Sontag's thoughts were published, these tenets are still evident. Family life is chronicled to commemorate the connectedness, thus taking photos becomes a rite of family life and a means to commemorate family rituals. The photos themselves are "proof" that an experience is real and may mitigate feelings of anxiety that occur during periods of rapid change. Photographs are imperfect attempts to deal with the complex world and our own inner workings. This might explain why many adolescents and young adults today are obsessed with taking photos of themselves. Do the clichéd images simplify their increasingly complex inner and outside experiences during this developmental time frame? Perhaps photographs enabled us to own pieces of the world, to verify experiences and prove that we were there, long before the advent of the smartphone fueled a desire to chronicle even the smallest life events. To photograph something is to give it importance, at least in the photographer's eyes. Now that the photographer is often the subject as well, we can convey our own view of what is important with the push of a button. Cameras have always been instruments for identity expression. Digital cameras expand the use of photography as a tool for identity formation. Editing apps allow us to modify images to represent who we want to be and how we want to remember experiences, endowing the user with power to shape autobiographical memories, and thus identity.[7]

When I view a painting in a gallery or museum I want to get as close as possible. I want to see the brush strokes, to marvel at the skill through which thousands of tiny brushstrokes transform colors into a recognizable image. I might note the ability to realistically illustrate a dancer's movement, be transfixed by beauty or the likeness to a famous historical figure, or indulge a fascination for a particular artistic technique. Yet I have no sense that this representation is anything other than a likeness. A painting is a resemblance; we know and say it is a painting of . . . With a photograph, that line is blurred. We show others photographs and state, "This is . . ." Our filters for reality have been bypassed.

The tendency to believe photographs accurately depict the lives and appearances of their subjects is not unique to the digital or social media era. In *Camera Lucida*, Roland Barthes studied the superior ability of photographs, when compared to other images, to provide concrete evidence of what has existed.[8] Because photographs have inherent properties of reality, we have difficulty questioning the veracity of an image. The photograph is not viewed as a photograph; it is not separate from what it represents. We collect photos in family albums, and now more often in vast digital archives, to preserve a moment that no longer exists. Author and photographer Teju Cole classifies photography as a memorial art, a reminder of something that is lost.[9] The photographed moment in time is frozen, never to be experienced again, but the photograph attempts to duplicate what has passed, thus lessening anxiety over the disappearance of the fleeting moments.

For Sontag, photographs are "not so much an instrument of memory as an invention of it or a replacement."[10] Given our constant exposure to visual images, most of what we have experienced visually has occurred indirectly. That is, we are, today, more likely to view our world photographically than directly. Hence, a "memory" may be taken at face value with little reflection. We experience a reality trap when viewing a photograph. We view the photograph as if we are viewing the subject, without any cognitive filters that tell us it is only a depiction or image. This reality trap, a term borrowed from the photo therapy literature, allows us to believe that the photograph represents physical reality.[11] When an image is viewed or uploaded online, viewers enter a world of fantasy, to believe that the photographer's image represents a truth of what would have been witnessed had the viewer been present.

The photograph's weakness lies in its inability to convey the truth reliably, but a photograph is merely a representation. It is the human brain that has capitalized on this weakness, thereby giving photographs unparalleled power to convince us that what we see is the truth. Additionally, if viewers make comments or *like* an image, the reality trap may be reinforced for the original image maker. We think it must represent reality if others affirm its veracity Ansel Adams summarized this succinctly, "There are always two people in every picture, the photographer and the viewer."[12] Hence, a social media photo can be thought of as an attempt to package and present an idealized life to anyone who will view the image, including the photographer.

CLIENT IMAGES

The first sessions with a client give us an initial peek into their world. The first-time client has no idea what to expect of therapy. Tia is an example of such a client: a willing, yet skeptical, adolescent. She slid into my office as if she did not want to be seen and melted into the large, soft sofa. The floor held her attention as if there were some problem within the rug that needed resolution. She quietly responded to my attempts to draw her story out. Her mother had contacted me the week before with concerns that her 16-year-old daughter was wasting away into a shadow of the passionate, artistic girl she had been before she became obsessed with her weight. Slim and blonde with intelligent, sea glass eyes, Tia had lost over 25 pounds in the last six months. This is not an excessive amount of weight loss for a larger person, but for a small framed adolescent such as Tia, this is a considerable loss. Individuals with anorexia who are between the ages of 15 and 24 have a five- to ten-times higher likelihood of dying than their peers,[13] making early intervention imperative.

Adolescents often warm up very slowly when they are brought to therapy by their parents, and Tia was no exception. While she wasn't outwardly resistant, she offered little information. What I gathered in the first session was that she had few close friends and was only marginally engaged in her high school culture. She seemed more mature than many of her peers, yet also childlike in a fragile, sad way. I was not surprised to learn that some of her closest friendships had withered in recent months. Individuals who restrict their food intake and engage in other eating disordered thoughts and behaviors tend to isolate from others physically and emotionally as the disease dominates their time and energy.

We didn't discuss the eating disorder much that day. I view these behaviors as symptoms of deeper hungers and voids in sense of self, so I initially prioritized attempts to connect with her as an adolescent and to build trust. Tia did affirm that she felt detached and alone. She expressed profound sadness as she talked about feeling that she does not fit in with others her age. While this is not a unique perspective, it does partially explain her self-imposed exile from her high school culture. My first glimpse of her level of insight occurred from a comment she made as the session ended, "I guess I'm trying to find my identity."

Identity is not a term that I often hear directly from the mouths of my adolescent clients. More often, they tell me that they don't know who they are, or they simply state that they have low self-esteem. By defining her problem as a search for identity, Tia is expressing her need to determine the unique characteristics, both physical and mental, that distinguish her from others. Perhaps adolescents are reaching the core of these concepts in a rudimentary way when they simply state, I don't who I am.

Tia was not as active on social media as some of my other clients, due to her self-imposed isolation, yet her sense of self was nonetheless being influenced by the visual images that she accesses in both print and online media. When Tia returned to my office the following week, we delved into the topic of identity. She described herself as quiet and introverted, perfectionistic, and controlled. She spoke of her discomfort with her appearance and anxiously divulged that she fears not being exceptional. To her, normal was equivalent to bland or even bad and she desperately wanted to stand out. She revealed a confusing dilemma: She did not want to have to look or be a certain way to be accepted, yet she constantly compared herself with others to see how she measures up, a self-defeating practice termed *lookism*.

In my conversations with Tia over the next few weeks, I learned that she spent most of her out of school time with her family or engaging in her love of photography. When I was sixteen, the same age as Tia, I obtained my first point-and-shoot camera, on which I shot roll after roll of images. Be young adulthood, I was developing the images I captured in my dual-purpose laundry room/dark room. Like many amateur photographers, Tia is intrigued with film and manual processing, despite her expertise in the newer, digital technology. Through the years, I transitioned from film to digital images, so Tia and I speak a common language. There are distinct differences in our focus though. Tia has an intense interest in fashion photography and loves to look through online fashion and photography sites on her iPhone for inspiration. She carries her iPhone wherever she goes and uses this activity to avoid interacting with peers when she feels anxious or awkward in social situations.

Thoughts about identity and sense of self surfaced as I worked with Tia. As with many of my clients, she reminded me of what being at that stage of development was like: searching for who you are, yet focusing mostly on external characteristics. Although these outer aspects reveal little about a person's true nature, most adolescents are challenged to recognize this incongruity. Tia slowly acknowledged that she is deeply impacted by the images she is drawn to. Her photoshoots and viewings of her beloved fashion images trigger feelings of inadequacy and a need for control.

Tia had difficulty separating the images she exposed herself to daily from external reality. She tended to believe that these photos accurately depict the appearance and lives of the subjects, and she took this a step further in believing that she must look like the images she views in fashion magazines. On a logical, cognitive level she was aware that photo editing software is used to create fantasy in images. Still, on an emotional level she was unable to discern the truth. She experienced nearly constant thoughts that she does not measure up to her idealized version of the female form. These thoughts led to episodes of allowing herself to eat only a few small bites a day, in hopes that she would transform herself into a likeness of her idealized images. She reluctantly conceded that the thoughts and the restricting occurred more often when she engaged in her photography pursuits. Why do these images have the power to render incapable of discernment an otherwise intelligent, logical human? The answer may lie in photography's ability to trigger the limbic system.

Located deep within the limbic system, the amygdala is involved in the processing of emotions. The amygdala's neural connectivity ensures its role in the integration of all senses, especially visual input. Visual and emotional systems in the brain are extensively interconnected. Emotions are triggered by images of people, objects, or events that are occurring in the moment or that have happened in the past.[14] MRI scans are verifying today what has been theorized for over a century: the emotional power of photographs to make the viewer identify with them is unparalleled. A photograph stimulates brain areas relevant to what would occur if the subject of the image were present. When emotions are also triggered, this process is likely to be amplified. Whereas ideas were transmitted and interpreted through speech or written language for most of history, the visual nature of a photograph and our life experiences with photography imbue this medium with extraordinary power to cue the limbic system to react in nearly the exact ways it would to the actual presence of the person portrayed in a photograph. Citizens of modern culture have become indoctrinated into a world in which visual images define reality. Thus, these images have the capacity to bypass psychological defenses because both conscious and unconscious processes are activated by the visual stimuli.[15]

Barthes gave us language to understand the unique emotional impact of some photographs. He contrasts the themes of studium and punctum, dual elements which exist in certain photographs. The studium reflects a range of meanings in a photograph that may be clear to everyone and discerned without much effort. Studium represents interest in a photograph that leads an individual to desire to explore the meaning of the photograph. The punctum, in contrast, is the element that incites such a strong emotional reaction or connection to the image that the viewer attaches an unexpected, intensely private meaning to the photograph. The punctum ensures that the photograph is remembered, although often beyond the capacity of language to describe. A photograph's punctum blurs the line between the object depicted and the viewer who strongly identifies with the image. When strong emotion is elicited by a photograph the brain is tricked into taking the image at face value, as truth. A photograph has the potential to be experienced emotionally, as a participant, rather than from the detached perspective that allows rational evaluation.[16] The actual brain processes that allow this reality gap are only now beginning to be understood.

Photographs impact us in ways that were previously unimaginable because we now interact with the medium on a universal, intimate level. In the early days of photography only people and events of significance were photographed. The focus of the camera has shifted away from recording what is significant to attempting to make ordinary events significant. The average person simply views so many images that they are unlikely to react unless there is something about the image that triggers an immediate, personal reaction—punctum. The weight of this reality is reflected in Tia's fear of being normal or bland. She views photographs that trigger an emotional longing in her to achieve perfection, and so she creates photographs with the intent of evoking strong emotions in her viewers. Initially, she did not grasp that perfection is a fantasy and she was hesitant to acknowledge that she was heavily impacted by her visual habits. The first step toward self-awareness involves self-reflection, becoming conscious of thoughts, beliefs, and feelings in response to her created environment. Tia came to see herself photographically and to equate beauty to looking like a photograph, and often a retouched one at that. Not only did she desire to create an idealized version of herself, she had difficulty sustaining the awareness that the images she sees do not reflect reality in the first place. Their punctum overrode her discernment.

In Sontag's musings on photography, she noted that photographs have changed our understanding of what is real. With insight into the age of avid social media use she proclaimed, "Needing to have reality confirmed and experience enhanced by photographs is an aesthetic consumerism to which everyone is now addicted."[17] Confirmation of reality is clearly evidenced in a photograph—images provide proof of existence. The photograph is now the standard for the way things (and people) appear and this has ultimately heightened the value of appearance. Appearance is a mere surface level abstraction that does not require the viewer to question whether what is depicted is real. We view a photograph and believe that the fantasy created by the image is the truth, rarely considering what the image or the act of sharing the image may be saying. What our culture needs is the ability to look away from photographs long enough to question our own enculturation and physiological responses to images, to override the power of our limbic systems to convince us that this two-dimensional image is more than just that.

DIGITAL HOSTAGES

The veracity of a photograph is even less easily discerned when viewed on a smartphone screen than when viewed as a printed photograph. Because most images are now viewed on a phone screen or, less often, on a computer screen, the instantaneous conversion of a four-dimensional scene, existing in time and space, into a two-dimensional image, on a tiny screen that is ever-present in everyday life, leads to even greater difficulty separating the visual input from the emotional reaction. Recall that the visual system, due to massive interconnections with the limbic system, elicits a much more immediate impact than the written word does. Interpreting the written word requires conscious processes, whereas photographs influence us on an unconscious level and are now a language unto themselves. When images no longer seem to be representations, they are taken as truth. Exposure to digital images with punctum makes ascertaining the truth a highly unlikely prospect. The proliferation of images magically reconstructs our reality and inhibits our ability to decode their symbolic meaning.

Smartphone photography and online sharing, especially on social networking sites, introduce a new line of inquiry into the psychological dimensions of image taking, processing, presentation, and viewing. Capturing digital images for online posting is influenced by conscious and unconscious considerations of how the image will be seen by viewers on their screens. The very nature of the deep enmeshment between an individual and their phone leads to entanglement of a false sense of truth with actual reality.[18] This is especially true for those in the throes of identity development. The developing sense of self is impacted by the virtual, or cyber, reality that has become the new norm. Some individuals have a limited to capacity to decode the images they are continually subjected to, and this is made especially challenging by the pervasive nature of smartphone use.

Therapists who strive to alleviate the suffering of clients impacted by the proliferation of social media must implement strategies to counteract the effects of being socialized in a world increasingly reflected in digital images. With skill and effort, the conscious processing of images can quiet intense emotions stirred by the limbic system. Chapter 6 focuses on self-reflection, a necessary process if a person is to find their way through the overwhelming world of visual images. Self-reflection requires safety, low defensiveness, and an openness to exploring one's innermost being. Therapeutic relationships are helpful to the degree that these requisite characteristics are present.

Self-reflecting to expand their awareness of their true self is critical to the client's recovery, but this can be a painful process. Clients may not want to explore feelings and emotions that have been relegated to the unconscious realm. On the other hand, basing your identity on the degree to which you feel you measure up to altered digital images in fashion layouts is painful itself. The following chapter illustrates how to utilize client-created visual images to self-reflect on underlying desires and meaning.

REFERENCES

1. Pipher, M. (1994). *Reviving Ophelia*. New York, NY: Ballantine.
2. Gómez Cruz, E., & Meyer, E. T. (2012). Creation and control in the photographic process: iPhones and the emerging fifth moment of photography, *Photographies, 5*(2), 203–221. doi: 10.1080/17540763.2012.702123
3. Thompson, C., (2014). The invention of the "snapshot" changed the way we viewed the world. *Smithsonian Magazine.* Retrieved from https://www.smithsonianmag.com/innovation/invention-snapshot-changed-way-we-viewed-world-180952435/
4. Gómez Cruz, E., & Meyer, E. T. (2012). Creation and control in the photographic process: iPhones and the emerging fifth moment of photography, *Photographies, 5*(2), 203–221. doi: 10.1080/17540763.2012.702123
5. Harrington, R. (2013). 90% of people have only taken a photo with a camera phone in their lifetime? Retrieved from https://communities-dominate.blogs.com/brands/2013/03/the-annual-mobile-industry-numbers-and-stats-blog-yep-this-year-we-will-hit-the-mobile-moment.html
6. Sontag, S. (1977). *On photography*. New York, NY: Picador.
7. van Dijck, J. (2008). Digital photography: Communication, identity, memory. *Visual Communication, 7*(1), 57–76.
8. Barthes, R. (1980). *Camera lucida*. New York, NY: Hill and Wang.
9. Cole, T. (2016). *Known and strange things: Essays*. New York, NY: Random House.
10. Sontag, S. (1977). *On photography*. New York, NY: Picador.
11. Wheeler, M. (2013). Fotos, fones, and fantasies. In D. Loewenthal (Ed.), *Phototherapy and therapeutic photography in a digital age* (pp. 40–52). New York, NY: Routledge.
12. Attributed to Adams. A. Retrieved from https://photographyicon.com/quotes/
13. Hoang, U., Goldacre, M., & James, A. (2014). Mortality following hospital discharge with a diagnosis of eating disorder: National Record Linkage Study, England, 2001–2009. *International Journal of Eating Disorders, 47*(5), 507–515.
    Fichter, M. M., & Quadflieg, N. (2016). Mortality in eating disorders: Results of a large prospective clinical longitudinal study. *International Journal of Eating Disorders, 49*(4), 391–401.

14. Damasio, A. (2010). *Self comes to mind: Constructing the conscious brain.* New York, NY: Vintage. Cozolino, L. (2017). *The neuroscience of psychotherapy: Healing the social brain* (3rd ed.) New York, NY: W. W. Norton & Company.

15. Flusser, V. (2000). *Towards a philosophy of photography.* London, UK: Reaktion Books.

16. Barthes, R. (1980). *Camera lucida.* New York, NY: Hill and Wang.

17. Sontag, S. (1977). *On photography.* New York, NY: Picador.

18. Kopytin, A. (2013). Photography and art therapy. In D. Loewenthal (Ed.), *Phototherapy and Therapeutic Photography in a Digital Age* (pp. 143–155). New York, NY: Routledge.

Chapter 6

DECODING CREATED IMAGES

Seeing is no longer believing. The very notion of truth has been put into crisis. In a world bloated with images, we are finally learning that photographs do indeed lie.

—Barbara Kruger

Visual images have unparalleled power to alter the very notion of what is real. A digital image can be modified until the photograph has little semblance to the original subject. Even for an image creator like Tia, there are neurological barriers to separating what is known regarding the image from how she responds to the image. Each time an image is edited, the reality trap is reinforced for both the creator and the viewer. When we are saturated with altered images, the value of perfection increases, and reality is redefined by unlimited possibilities. Images, created and maintained by technologies that our brains have not developed the skills to handle, are now an replacement of reality.

Images that reflect a person's innermost desires have the potential to convince the limbic system that what is photographed is real and exists in the present. There is no training to address the psychological effects of nearly constant exposure to altered images. Images are transmitting cultural imperatives to a society that lacks the cognizance required to question the veracity of the images' messages, thus people are led astray through the emotional high they get from viewing images that portray fantasy as if it is real. Sontag stated that the camera "makes everyone a tourist in other people's reality, and eventually in one's own."[1] As we gaze upon these cultural artifacts, we must learn to question their authenticity. Do they represent reality or are they merely staged performances for the entertainment of the uninformed tourist?

IDENTITY DILEMMAS

Social and cultural experiences certainly have an impact on a person's sense of who they are and how they fit in the world. The unparalleled changes brought forth in the digital age are creating a milieu for identity formation that has yet to be explored, one in which identity is generated and exhibited in the public sphere. We have neglected to fathom the online world of today's youth in which the larger culture fosters and sustains identities based on external standards and toxic messages. A systemic view of identity formation as emanating from within a culture that barrages young people with unrealistic standards and unhealthy messages provides a greater understanding of how eating disorder symptoms are the expected manifestation of trying to live up to toxic cultural standards.

The appearance standards and the pursuit of sexual allure, traits idealized on social media, undermine healthy identity by focusing only on external appearances and gaining approval from others. For many, these traits are considered to be the only viable ways to gain status and recognition. The underlying message creates the real dilemma. The message is that teens will suffer the consequences if they resist striving to meet the impossible standards. Social media demands conformity to expectations, but elevating physical allure as the pinnacle of achievement narrows possibilities and trivializes life, leaving little room for other pursuits. Concern for body size, shape, and weight places one's focus on reshaping the physical body, heightening the risk of developing an eating disorder and diverting attention from the more important task of discovering who one is.

A 2018 study in the Journal of Eating Disorders clarified the association between identity disruption and susceptibility to eating disorders by pointing to early negative life experiences, such as childhood trauma and other adverse family environments, as risk factors for placing high value on societal appearance standards.[2] By disrupting normal identity development, these early adverse events predispose individuals to look to external sources to define sense of self. Adhering to cultural appearance standards is one way to define the self, but the internalization of these standards of attractiveness raises one's risk of developing an eating disorder. Engaging in appearance comparisons and feelings of body dissatisfaction increase the likelihood of disordered eating. A most intriguing finding of this study is that the paths of the model did not differ for males and females. Not surprisingly, females are more susceptible to internalizing the thin ideal and males to internalizing the muscular ideal, but both are susceptible to these cultural messages. Pressures from media, friends, and family to meet appearance standards heighten one's risk of developing eating disordered thoughts and behaviors.

As therapists, we are also aware that being seen or known plays a vital role in the development of self. Naturally, development of sense of self is optimized by a positive early environment, one that facilitates feelings of safety and positive affect regulation to create a calm internal setting in which the developing mind can integrate experiences. Early interpersonal relationships lay the foundation for the subsequent ability to reflect on the self, but we formulate interpretations about our existence across time.[3] To develop a positive sense of self, young people require safety, love from family and friends, emotional connection, respect, challenges that provide a sense of purpose, and an identity that is based on more than physical appearance. Knowing and adhering to one's values and convictions are at the core of authentic identity.

Our young clients are the proverbial canaries in the coal mine. They are the brave souls who tell us that all is not as it appears; something is happening that needs to be addressed. They reach out for help and, in doing so, give us the opportunity to learn about the struggles of a generation before they themselves can name the problem. What they can name are their reasons for coming to our offices in the first place—eating disorders, depression, anxiety, substance abuse, suicide attempts, bullying, and self-harm—reflections of a void in sense of self.

I see a good number of adolescent girls in my practice who are struggling with anorexia. While rates of anorexia have remained stable in other age groups over the last 50 years, this dangerous disease is on the rise in females between the ages of 15 and 24.[4] Many in this life stage have a narrow sense of who they are and limited exposure to their potential.

SELF-REFLECTION

There are, perhaps, many ways we could define the concept of self-reflection. Self-reflection, or introspection, allows us to achieve self-knowledge by directing our attention inward. Self-reflection creates an awareness of shifts in our perspectives, emotional states, and ways of using language. Two levels of language underlie self-reflection: social reflexive language, which represents how a person has been socialized to interact with others, and the internal dialogue of private thought, which develops from the critical or supportive voices in our early life experiences. Reflecting on both of these levels of language allows a third level of language—self-reflection—to emerge. Self-reflection affords a window into the unconscious aspects of the self.[5] Much of therapy focuses on exploring the first two levels of language, which inhabit the mind (social prescriptions and internal dialogue), as a way to develop the language of self-reflection.

Some useful ways of encouraging self-reflection include asking a client to be attentive, alert, or vigilant to their reflexive thoughts, feelings, and behaviors. In the safety of therapy, clients are guided to be more conscious or mindful of desires that drive social media use or the internal dialogue that emerges around the viewing of an image. Identifying emotional reactions to images can stimulate discernment of and introspection into the effects of social prescriptions and internal dialogue. Clients learn that they can choose whether to listen to the internal dialogue and how to react to the expectations of others. Though this process is challenging, clients are guided to access this internal information to elevate their competence in self-reflection while in the supportive context of the therapeutic relationship.

Use of photographic equipment or engaging in viewing of photographs does not result in enhanced self-awareness any more than self-documentation through photographs will without the subsequent reflection into the underlying thoughts and emotions. To gain insight into mental images, beliefs, and memories related to self, the client must reflect on the thoughts, sensations, and emotions that arise in the taking, sharing, and viewing of the images, as well as their expectations of others' reactions to the images. When client reactions are accessed, a language of self-reflection can develop, a language of careful consideration and potential change, which is the basis for re-authoring the narrative.

Tia's calm exterior belies a hidden internal struggle that was voiced only through food restriction. Soon after Tia and I began working together, I encouraged her to explore a deeper level of self-reflection. Tia was a natural for this type of work. Cerebral and insightful by nature, she has an inquisitive mind that seeks resolution. To begin this process, I initially asked Tia to monitor her contact with visual media in any form. For many, this can be simplified to asking them simply to monitor their use of their phones, but since Tia is an avid photographer, she was asked to record time she spent viewing fashion images as well, the sources of inspiration for her photo sessions. The actual time spent at photo shoots was also documented. Logging the time spent in these activities was recorded for only one week initially, because the goal was to increase her awareness of the behavior. Even though she does not spend as much time on social media as many of her peers, I wanted her to include this time in her logs because I suspected there was some overlap between this and her time on online fashion sites. When Tia returned the following week, we found her logs confirmed my suspicions. Unsurprisingly, she averages three to four hours each day in some type of interaction with social media or visual images. While some clients may resist this important step, it provides a benchmark for change and lays the groundwork for the work that follows.

Next, I suggested Tia again log her time in a similar manner for another week but this time to also provide a more detailed description of what she was viewing and to include her thoughts, emotions, and behavioral reactions to her visual image engagements. I provided her with a simple format for recording this, with five columns: the date and time, what she is viewing, her thoughts, her emotions, and her behaviors. This format provides a clear structure and the separation of each component. I instructed Tia to record data throughout each day and also to underline what she viewed on her recorded content that elicited the strongest response each day. The purpose of identifying the content that produces the strongest response is to identify those images, or exchanges with images, that incite punctum. Recall that punctum overrides the viewer's ability to take a detached perspective, thereby inhibiting rational evaluation of the image. Here is a sample of Tia's self-reflection logs:

SELF-REFLECTION LOG

DATE & LENGTH OF TIME	VISUAL MEDIA (how and what you are viewing)	THOUGHTS (how you have been socialized to interact and the critical or supportive internal dialogue)
Sept. 8 30 minutes	Looking at magazines	These girls are perfect. I have to look like them to be successful. If I would quit eating so much I would look better.
1 ½ hours	Phone - looking at photos online to get ideas for tomorrow.	
Sept. 9 45 minutes	Phone – Instagram, Flickr – looking at the people I follow and at some friends too	I should comment on my friends' posts. It's exciting to see what is posted, but seeing their pictures also reminds me that everyone looks better than I do.
3 hours	Camera – taking photos with friends	I need to make sure everything goes smooth. My friends seem to be having fun. I miss being with them, but then they all wanted to go eat and I shouldn't eat just because everyone else wants to.
2 hours	Computer - editing photos	I'm tired, but I need to do some work on these and then I will go work out since I ate so much.
Sept 10 3 hours	Computer - editing photos	I need to work harder if I want to be a successful photographer.
2 hours	Computer – looking at fashion online Phone – Instagram, Flickr	Looking for ideas that will set my work apart. This always makes me feel like a loser
1 ¾ hours	Camera – taking photos	Being outside made me feel better.

SENSATIONS EMOTIONS	BEHAVIORS (actions taken in response to what is viewed, thoughts, and emotions)
I feel sick to my stomach. Sad	Didn't eat dinner tonight
Excited to see what people posted. Then started feeling bad about myself.	I'm late to meet my friends so I skipped breakfast.
I felt good that I didn't eat earlier, but after eating I felt too full! Guilty for eating a hamburger and fries.	Ate junk food
Feeling very tired and heavy	Tried to take my mind off what I ate by editing and then going to work out. Didn't eat anything else today.
Anxious	
Sick to my stomach Depressed	Got very irritable with my family Felt sorry for myself, ate a snack.
Peaceful	Decided to go take some photos

This sample of Tia's self-reflection log demonstrates how recording thoughts, sensations and behaviors in response to images can aid self-reflection. Tia realized that she is heavily impacted by exposure to images portraying idealized versions of appearance and was surprised that she had not noticed these reactions before. Mindfulness of her actions assisted her in connecting her reactions to the images she viewed with her desire to restrict. Tia was not yet proficient in identifying her emotions or internal dialogue. As all therapists know, this content cannot be blocked or numbed out without unintended consequences, but when clients push these responses from awareness, they are temporarily guarding against emotions they do not yet know how to handle.

In the coming weeks Tia grew in her ability to self-reflect. Reviewing logs in session often elicited memories underlying the negative view of self. She learned to identify negative mental images of herself as well as beliefs expressed in her critical internal dialogue that drives perfectionism and heightened appearance standards. Self-reflective language allowed Tia to observe and evaluate societal expectations and mandates that were previously accepted without questioning the source of this learning. The ability to self-reflect grows out of awareness of unconscious aspects of the self that are expressed in reflexive thoughts, feelings, and behaviors. Clients often need repetition to develop and maintain self-reflective behaviors, so logs may be used throughout treatment. A blank self-reflection log is included in Appendix B.

PHOTO THERAPY WITH CREATED IMAGES

Now that Tia had a rudimentary knowledge of how images were triggering her behaviors, we needed to go deeper into the meaning she was taking from and attempting to express in images. Most of us now create and collect vast numbers of images on camera phones. Prompting clients to share what it is about an image that makes it special, how it makes them feel, and what the image is saying are only a few of the possible avenues for work with created images. Construction and presentation of the client's visual story through created images is a powerful conduit to self-reflection and awareness. Self-reflection is a necessary skill for recovery from anorexia. Exploration of the messages being transmitted in her photography can give Tia the skills she needs to decode cultural messages and to gain a sense of who she is.

Photo therapy is a method for exploring the ways in which photographs depict underlying meanings, regardless of whether the photographer or viewer is aware of this process. All types of photographs express the concrete, objective existence of what is being depicted. Symbolic, subjective meanings are also hidden within the images.[6] Created images describe the creator along with the content of the image. While the image creator may not be aware of the underlying messages, an image is a visible extension of the self, even when the person is not in the photo. Through an image, clients display their personal constructs of what is real, how they relate to the world, and how they view themselves.

Images can accelerate self-reflection by opening a portal into the inner workings of the mind. Images often show things that were not intended when the image was taken. The subject and the exact moment an image is taken are chosen for a distinct reason, often outside of awareness for the photographer. These moments, taken in sum by viewing a collection of a person's images, reveal personal patterns that have symbolic meaning. This is where photo therapy work has the potential to create new associations and explore emotional reactions. The following two photo therapy techniques involve the use of created images and are illustrated in my work with Tia.

Meaningful Images

In the first technique, the client is asked to bring 8 to 10 of their favorite images to the next session. The client chooses images with private meanings, images that they feel drawn to, often for unknown reasons. These images have exceptional punctum for the client and often express what is valued. In *A Photograph as a Therapeutic Experience*, psychotherapist Ulla Halkola states that "taking a photograph is always the photographer's expression of mind, his/her choice and thus a personal individual product. Photographs themselves do not tell truths; however, they offer symbolic material and open doors to a world of possibilities that can be discussed together."[7] Much like self-portraits, all created images hold information about the person who took the photo.

To get a sense of the overall mood or feelings present in a client's images, we initially want to view them as a group. Repetition of patterns, symbols, themes, or messages in the images may be seen by the client while viewing the selections this way. The images Tia chose were all taken in a studio setting with dramatic lighting. They appeared to be carefully staged images of a person, of a small group, or of objects. Right away, I detected an element of fantasy in the images she was drawn to, but it was Tia's interpretation that I was interested in.

What follows is an overview of the questions I used in working with Tia and these images.[8]

As we viewed Tia's images spread out on the table, I asked, *What do you notice about these images as you see them all together?* Tia's response was to look at them photographically, to evaluate their artistic merit. After gently redirecting her toward the emotional aspects by asking, *What were you hoping these images would capture emotionally?* She gave a one-word reply, "Alone," and then she expounded by saying that this is the first word that comes to mind when she views them all at once. Although it was not her intent to convey aloneness, she saw it even in the images of more than one person. They are posed together, yet they are separate, as if they are in their own worlds with nothing happening between them. She elaborated on her own feelings of loneliness. When she started trying to lose weight, she no longer wanted to spend time with her friends or go out because food was always involved, so it became easier to isolate herself. She expresses\d a desire to rebuild friendships but also sees herself as very different from others her age and wonders if being an only child has somehow left her without the ability to relate. She voiced a desire to feel like she fits in and belongs, but she doesn't want to fake who she is to be accepted.

Tia is artistic, soft-spoken, and somewhat introverted, traits that can make it difficult to fit in with the constantly connected world of adolescence. She is not interested in the dominant culture of her high school, which centers around athletics and partying, but she had a small group of friends prior to the start of her eating disorder. Isolation is common in those with eating disorders, as the desire to avoid food and to maintain secrecy around the behaviors creates barriers to connection. Viewing her created images allowed Tia to concede the costs of the eating disorder for herself rather than being told by someone whom she might perceive as having an interest in pushing her toward change.

Photographs are considered symbolic projections of the self,[9] so I next asked Tia to pick the one image that is most representative of her. She chose an image with a child, or small person, in partial shadow that is so dark that it is difficult to discern if the subject is indeed human. The hand reaching from the shadow convinces the eye that the subject is a person reaching for something. On the ground are an array of carved wooden objects. Other than these two focal points, the image is barren. Inanimate objects can represent the client or some aspect of them, yet the therapist wants to leave interpretation of the image to the client. So I asked Tia a series of open-ended questions to stir her telling of the image's story. I asked *How did you decide what would be in this image?* hoping this would clarify the nature of the figures. She explained that the subject is a friend who agreed to do a photo shoot with her some time back. She found some old wooden animals in a box in the garage and chose them for their graphic appeal and for sentimental reasons: she'd played with them in childhood.

How did you decide how much of your friend to include in the image? "I purposely chose to keep her hidden, with the lighting and by keeping most of her outside the frame of the image." I wondered if Tia saw that she was also keeping herself hidden, by isolating and starving herself into the smallest possible version of herself, but I didn't ask this directly because I wanted her to make her own sense of this image. Questions are phrased to guide the therapeutic process. Instead I asked Tia if this image had a message to give. After a long pause, she described the message in the image as the girl wanting to reclaim an earlier, simpler time in life when things were less complicated, so she is reaching from a place of darkness to the familiar.

Tia was expressing inner dissonance to the changes occurring in her life as she leaves childhood behind. Dissonance declines when conflicted feelings are brought to light and change can be viewed as manageable and even desirable. Once something is consciously accessible, it can be dealt with rather than avoided. Projective photo therapy techniques allow insight into unconscious values that dictate expectations for the self.[10] I asked Tia to inquire of the image, *What do you say about my own life?* This question prompted the thoughts: "I always felt like I needed to be a good little girl, and now to remain innocent and young." This type of thinking is common in those with anorexia.

Where does this message come from? Societal expectations, rules, and norms specify that young women like Tia should be remain vulnerable and dependent. One way this message is transmitted is through the thin body ideal, a code that tells women they are objects of male attention rather than worthy by their own right. The message is one of restraint and compliance, of shaping the body and self to others' approval. Restricting food takes the mind off thoughts about not measuring up to societal standards of perfection. She recalled that she had always had extra weight to lose, so she started counting calories to drop a few pounds. Although she ate a fairly healthy diet, she thought she had room to improve and found losing weight exciting. As the weight loss continued, she cut protein, dairy, and fats from her diet. Controlling how much she takes in felt good to her, and she liked her current size, but because she was consuming less than 1,000 calories a day, food thoughts were unremitting. She lived in constant fear of overeating.

Girls like Tia need to learn how to question the scripts and expectations that they must be perfect and please others. Questioning the scripts that have been written for them by others allows them to write their own stories. Work like this is most effective in the trusted context of relationships, like therapy, where the adopted conventions can be examined and challenged rather than in more traditional educational settings.[11] Tia was in an inner struggle with societal and personal expectations for how her life should be. Her battle with anorexia is the personification of this struggle. Tia and I went on to work with the material that was brought up in her newfound self-reflection as her emotions, thoughts, and behaviors were made comprehensible to her. We discussed her desire to self-present in a positive manner. Throughout, we mined her internal dialogue for clues to the origin of critical voices that lead to perfectionism. This first foray into photo therapy moved her self-reflection beyond what was attained in previous sessions.

Photo Narratives

Encouraged by Tia's progress in working with her images thus far, we moved to a more active photo therapy technique: assigning the client to take photographs in response to the question "Who am I?" Taking photographs can be healing in much the same way that creative art processes free the expression of emotional content. This two-part assignment is based on a photo narrative revision approach to personal control that uses client images to externalize thought processes and stimulate self-reflection.[12]

Therapists often attempt to raise clients' recognition of their inner dialogue or self-talk to illustrate the pervasive nature of critical or demeaning thoughts that permeate their daily life and negatively impact their sense of self. Clients find it difficult to recall occurrences of internal dialogue for several reasons. First, it is challenging to begin noticing what have become normative thought processes over time. Second, the societal scripts and rules are deeply engrained within self-talk, to the degree that they may be unrecognizable. Finally, the intimacy of self-talk is intruded upon by the presence of the therapist. In the photo narrative, images elicit inner dialogue by bringing implicit meaning into awareness.[13] The essence of this assignment is to broaden self-understanding through self-reflection without the presence of an audience, the therapist is a notetaker, recording the client's thoughts when the narrative is presented in session.

The following instructions, adapted from the photo narrative approach, were given to Tia:

1. *This assignment asks you to communicate with yourself about yourself.*
2. *Take 8 photographs to tell the story of you to yourself.*
3. *Your images can be of anything, as long as they tell the story of you over time, including your future if you wish.*
4. *Create an eight-page book of your images.*
5. *You are the creator and the audience for the story you will tell through this photo narrative. This is your story that you show in images and we will view in the images.*

On an agreed upon date, clients are invited to bring their images in to session and tell their story to themselves, with the therapists acting as recorder. In this session, internal conflicts are externalized through the images so the client can gain a more objective view as they narrate their story. The following paragraphs include my descriptions of Tia's photos and what I recorded of her photo narrative story.

Tia's first image was actually an image of some of her previous work scattered on a table. She said, "All of these photos mimic what I see in fashion layouts. I'm drawn to creating something that can completely shift what is real. These are dreams brought into reality, and I like to be able to make a perfect world. Maybe all of this shows how much I want to be perfect."

Image two depicted a shattered piece of delicate, flower-covered china. "This photo shows how I fear things changing, no matter how good the change is. I'm thinking of going away to school in a few years and that seems so scary. Actually, I'm afraid of everything—losing control of eating and becoming obese, not having my parents around to help me, not making them proud of me, not being liked, really everything! I feel anxious all the time and I'm tired of feeling like a scared little girl. This broken teacup symbolizes the end of tea parties and make-believe."

The third image showed rows and rows of cotton growing in a field on the outskirts of town. "It symbolizes my natural tendency toward logic, being able to think things through without being too dramatic about things. I think I've lost some of that. Now I let anxiety override everything else."

Tia said, image four "is more of that logical side of me. This is my favorite camera. You know, cameras are logical. If you know how to use them, you can predict how the photographs will turn out. That is why I like photography—it's a mechanical process but also has that artistic part. I was thinking how I logically know how ridiculous my eating disorder is, how my perfectionistic thoughts are not logical, but sometimes I just forget."

Image five depicted a plate holding five grapes, a small bundle of carrot sticks and half a sandwich. Tia described this image as "my lunch" and then continued her narration: "This is what I typically eat for lunch. I know exactly how many calories I'm eating so it feels safe to eat this every day, but now that I see it for what it really is. I have to admit that this is the reason I'm so hungry all the time. Sometimes I have better food days, but then I feel guilty for eating so much so I go back to what is safe. I'm constantly craving something."

The sixth image appeared to be a black and white abstract, like rows of columns. "This photo is of some of my art markers. A few are long and thin, but most are these bigger ones. It symbolizes the pressure I feel to be naturally slim. One of my friends is really skinny and eats all the time and that is what makes her stand out, that's what she's known for, this really skinny girl who eats all the time. I don't stand out for anything. I try to make good grades, but I'm not really that smart. I'm not one of the truly beautiful girls and I don't have any special talents. I want to be exceptional, like the thin markers, to stand out, but I'm not exceptional."

Image seven was of "my cat, Mabel. I've had her since I was 10 and she is my best friend. She's pretty independent and like really aloof to everyone else, but she likes to cuddle with me. I think she is pretty confident and doesn't care what anyone thinks or what she looks like. I want to be more like her in that way. I don't want to be sick to make myself feel better about the way I look. I do want to grow up and do exciting new things, but sometimes I also want to return to childhood, so I don't have to make all these changes."

Image eight depicted a mountain range that Tia told me her family visited on a recent trip to New Mexico. "What makes this photo special to me is the grandness of these mountains. I don't usually take many photos like this, but that morning I was so in awe of how the light plays on these mountains. The colors changed before my eyes and I realized that change is not always a bad thing, sometimes the change brings even more beautiful colors. I think this reminds me not to fear something just because it's not the same as before."

Tia and I revisited the themes she brought up in her photo narrative. She was surprised at the number of memories these photographs brought up for her as we processed her emotional reactions to the photographs she selected. Tia's photographs expressed a longing for perfection and control, both of which are common goals in disordered eating. She realized she was trying to impose order in this chaotic time of life by controlling her physical appearance. Seeing these longings expressed in her work was much more powerful than simply talking about these desires. Emotionally meaningful images facilitate emotional processing, one of most important and effective means for psychotherapeutic change.

In our time together, Tia gained self-reflective insight into the underlying thoughts and emotions triggered when she views images, and together, we developed strategies for dealing with the emotions. Once she made this connection, she decided to carefully monitor and change her habits. She can now reflect on her response patterns and is learning to detach from the images long enough to regain her logical self. Self-reflection prompts knowledge of self and lays the groundwork for change. Perhaps the most important initial outcome for Tia is her newfound awareness of how her actions, even commonplace ones such as viewing an image or a simple Internet search, impact her sense of self.

The second part of the photo narrative assignment occurs a few months later. In this assignment, clients are encouraged to re-author their narrative to reflect any changes in the story. Old, out of date perceptions are challenged to create a more accurate story of self and place in the world. Specifically, Tia was given the following instructions:

1. *Review the original photo narrative and ask yourself how you might retell the story.*
2. *Record your thinking by taking 8 more photographs that depict yourself as you now see yourself.*
3. *Include these photos in your revised book.*
4. *Like before, you are the creator and the audience for the story you will tell through this photo narrative. This is your story that you show in images and we will view in the images.*

Tia chose to rework her photo narrative by placing a new image on the back of each of her previous images. On the back of Tia's first image, she placed a photo of her previous works scattered now on the ground. She commented that she sees the value in making beautiful photos but knows that life is not going to perfect, like some staged photo. "Even those photos aren't perfect. Not everyone appreciates my work, and I have to grow thicker skin if I want to be a photographer." She paused and then continued, "and to be honest other people don't understand or always like what I'm trying to say, so I guess it's true that you can't please everyone."

On the back of her second photo, of the broken china teacup, she has placed another image comprised of images. This one was made up of photos of herself across her life. "This photo shows how I have changed over time and how I now know that change is certain. Even though I am no longer quite the same, not that innocent little girl, I am still the same, too."

The image on the back of her third image of the cotton field shows the field now stripped of the white bolls, like part of a time lapse series that started in the photo from set one. She pondered, out loud, the natural rhythm of crops that she witnesses each year, how this cycle brings positive things along with the change.

On the back of Tia's fourth photo of her camera was an image of Tia's parents. "When I started trying to lose weight, I thought I could become perfect, and now I've caused all this stress for my parents, which is opposite of being perfect. I know they are always there for me and they don't expect me to be perfect."

Image five of the plate of food was answered on the reverse side by an image of a plate of fruit that can only be described as destroyed. The fruit was hardly recognizable as such, but among the destruction were remnants of banana peel and half smashed melons. Tia narrated her thoughts about her fear of losing control. "This image is symbolic of the way I thought I needed to be to get approval. It felt good to smash the fruit because there was so much of it, but then I had another thought. I think the fruit represents being female, how we are not valued for our natural bodies. I'm not going to be crushed to make others like me. I want to learn to like myself and eat again without beating myself up."

On the back of Tia's sixth image, the abstract image of her markers, was an image of a flower in an unusual glass vase. Regarding this image, Tia announced that she wants to counter the statement that "the flower is exceptional because it is better than other flowers. It's beautiful on its own merit. I don't need to compare myself with others. What makes me feel alive is creating art through my photographs. When I look at this flower, it reminds me of how important that is."

The image on the back of Tia's seventh image of Mabel the cat was of a series of jet trails across a very blue sky. This image reminded Tia of the exciting things she wants to do in the future. She is no longer willing to allow the eating disorder to ground her plans.

The final image in Tia's book showed the flower from image six, now from a different angle. What is clearly visible from this angle is the missing petals on one side of the flower. She close her photo narrative by stating that she still thinks the flower is beautiful. "Just because it is not what's expected doesn't mean we should throw it out. I am working on accepting my imperfections."

Re-authoring through the photo narrative helps clients discover that they can intervene in their own lives to reconstruct the self, rather than allowing previously unexamined scripts to create their story. By facilitating self-reflection, the photo narrative exposes internalized conflict and offers a medium in which to rework the conflict with updated knowledge. In Tia's case, her first set of images presented desires she felt, such as the desire to be perfect and exceptional. Anorexia plays a part in her narrative, although she did not name it directly. Instead she verbalized her inner struggle between trying to be perfect and exceptional and dealing with hunger and comparing herself to others. Tia's fear of change as she transitions from childhood to adulthood are evident throughout. In the last two images, she began to resolve some of these conflicts, as she spoke of her desire to be more like her cat, independent, yet connected, and she appreciated the beauty of the mountain as it changed, a movement toward appreciating herself.

The second self-narrative expanded on Tia's growing appreciation for who she is. She reworked two of her images in response to increased self-awareness: the first in response to accepting the futility of making images of herself only to please others. The second reworking, of image five of the fruit, illustrated Tia's increasing awareness of gender expectations and the self-empowerment she is experiencing by taking action to strengthen her identity as a woman. As a narrative, Tia's images traced her acceptance of the changes she will make to mature into the adult world and a recognition that she will retain some of her valued qualities. This shift demonstrates her identification with a future in which she can write the story as she redefines her sense of who she is in relation to others and to her environment. This second self-narrative is not the finished product any more than Tia's life is laid out exactly as it will occur. Instead, it is a moment in the process of self-construction that is ongoing and subject to revision.

Tia's images allow her to transform her private thoughts into language. Finding meaning through visualizing and deciphering her experiences is central to verbal expression. Metaphors set "the imagination free to integrate memories, anticipations and wishes into images that are charged with symbolic associations".[14] Metaphors, laden with symbolism, expand Tia's perspective on her lived experience as well as her vision for the future. When Tia revised the image of her restricted lunch to the image of the smashed fruit, she was moving from recall of an event from memory toward an agenda of empowerment, again with the aid of an image. In the metaphor of the fruit, destroying it symbolizes fighting back against cultural imperatives and sanctions on the female body. The changes derived in the transformation of meaning reduced feelings of powerlessness by creating agency in her life.

Imaging and narrating lived experience imbue a person's story with meaning.[15] Reflection on images and dialogue go hand and hand in this exercise. In telling the narrative, Tia could reflect on life experiences, then gain necessary distance to see them from another perspective. Change ensues when the feelings, values, and anticipations inherent in the symbolic language of the images are made conscious so that new meaning or reformulation of lived experiences can be created.[16] As Tia and I continued to address her anorexia, she continuously reworked the content revealed in these initial exercises. Reaching a more normal weight again triggered fears that she is no longer exceptional. She continued to be challenged to accept her body as she matured over the period of her treatment. Many young women with anorexia have stored a mental image of themselves as they appeared in early adolescence, setting an unrealistic expectation as they transition into the later teen years.

Since Tia responded well to our initial photo therapy work, we continued to work with her metaphors for the self as she learns to question personal and societal scripts that limit her ability to negotiate the maze of identity formation. Her family history reveals numerous family members with eating disorders, anxiety, and depression, thus she has a genetic predisposition toward developing similar difficulties. In terms of her early environment, Tia is fortunate: she received stable, responsive care early in life and has a supportive family to aid in her recovery. Perhaps most importantly, she is motivated to fight for her mental health.

There is a tendency to consider the Internet or social media, or even the smart phone, to be the cause of the rise in problems in this generation that has lived their entire lives connected through these media. This would be understandable, given the rise in mental health difficulties in the last few decades, but we should not underestimate the role of the images themselves. Connectivity brings exposure to ideas, both positive and negative, that cannot help but impart new pressures, especially on the more vulnerable segments of society. Adolescents and young adults fit within this category and are the heaviest users of the new technology. As with all societal advances, there is little incentive to turn back the hands of time and forego the benefits these changes bring.

What is needed, therefore, is the willingness and awareness to examine the impact of photography itself, as Franz Kafka had the prescience to voice almost a century ago when this medium was still in its infancy:

> *In the spring of 1921, two automatic photographic machines recently invented abroad, were installed in Prague, which reproduced six or ten or more exposures of the same person on a single print.*
>
> *When I took such a series of photographs to Kafka I said light-heartedly: "For a couple of krone one can have oneself photographed from every angle. The apparatus is a mechanical Know-Thyself."*
>
> *"You mean to say the 'Mistake-Thyself,'" said Kafka, with a faint smile.*
>
> *I protested: "What do you mean? The camera cannot lie!"*
>
> *"Who told you that?" Kafka leaned his head toward his shoulder. "Photography concentrates one's eye on the superficial. For that reason, it obscures the hidden life which glimmers through the outlines of things like a play of light and shade. One can't catch that even with the sharpest lens. One has to grope for it by feeling.*
>
> From Gustav Janouch's *Conversations with Kafka*[17]

Like Kafka, Tia now understands that photos must be examined for the deeper meaning. She must be willing to feel what is going on underneath the images, a skill that will be examined more fully in subsequent chapters.

Exploring created images in the therapeutic setting can be an alternative way for a client to tell their story. It is in the telling of their story that greater awareness and understanding emerge. Tia's deep enmeshment with visual content, due to her desire for a career in photography, makes these techniques a vital component of her therapy. Although most of our clients are not aspiring professional photographers, we can argue that they are image creators, considering it is a rare individual who does not now take photos with their phone. This technology has made photographers of us all.

In the following chapter, we turn our attention to the newest expression of self in the digital age—the selfie—to explore how it is transforming the burgeoning online culture and the development of self. Tia is an observer of online images rather than a purveyor of selfies, yet she experiences the power of digital images to shape her sense of herself.

REFERENCES

1. Sontag, S. (1977). *On photography*. New York, NY: Picador.

2. Vartanian, L. R., Hayward, L. E., Smyth, J. M., Paxton, S. J., & Touyz, S. W. (2018). Risk and resiliency factors related to body dissatisfaction and disordered eating: The identity disruption model. *International Journal of Eating Disorders, 51*(4), 322–330.

3. Siegel, D. (1999). *The developing mind: How relationships and the brain interact to shape who we are*. New York, NY: Guilford.

4. Lucas, A. R., Crowson, C. S., O'Fallon, W. M., & Melton, L. J. (1999). The ups and downs of anorexia nervosa, *International Journal of Eating Disorders, 26*(4), 397–405.

5. Cozolino, L. (2017). *The neuroscience of psychotherapy: Healing the social brain* (3rd ed.) New York, NY: Norton & Company.

6. Saita, E., Parrella, C., Facchin, F., & Irtelli, F. (2014). The clinical use of photography: A single case, multi-method study of the therapeutic process. *Research in Psychotherapy: Psychopathology, Process and Outcome, 17*(1), 1–8.

7. Halkola, U. (2013). A photograph as a therapeutic experience. In D. Loewenthal (Ed.), *Phototherapy and therapeutic photography in a digital age* (pp. 21–30). New York, NY: Routledge.

8. Weiser, J. (1999). *PhotoTherapy techniques: Exploring the secrets of personal snapshots and family albums*. Vancouver, BC: Judy Weiser and PhotoTherapy Centre Publishers.

9. Weiser, J. (1999). *PhotoTherapy techniques: Exploring the secrets of personal snapshots and family albums*. Vancouver, BC: Judy Weiser and PhotoTherapy Centre Publishers.

10. Weiser, J. (1999). *PhotoTherapy techniques: Exploring the secrets of personal snapshots and family albums*. Vancouver, BC: Judy Weiser and PhotoTherapy Centre Publishers.

11. Hoskins, M. L. (2002). Girls' identity dilemmas: Spaces defined by definitions of worth. *Health Care for Women International, 23*(3), 231–247.

12. Ziller, R. C. (2000). Self-counseling though re-authored photo-self-narratives. *Counseling Psychology Quarterly, 13*(3), 265–278.

13. Ziller, R. C. (1990). *Photographing the self: Methods of observing personal orientation*. Newbury Park, CA: Sage.

14. Sitvast, J. E., & Abma, T. A. (2012). The photo-instrument as a health care intervention (p. 179). *Health Care Anal, 20*(2), 177–195.

15. Gaydos, H. L. (2005). Understanding personal narratives: An approach to practice. *Journal of Advanced Nursing, 49*(3), 254–259.

16. Sitvast, J. E., & Abma, T. A. (2012). The photo-instrument as a health care intervention. *Health Care Anal, 20*(2), 177–195.

17. Janouch, G. (2012). *Conversations with Kafka* (2nd ed.). New York, NY: New Directions Paperback.

Chapter 7

SELFIE IMAGES

If a man has lost a leg or an eye, he knows he has lost a leg or an eye; but if he has lost a self—himself—he cannot know it, because he is no longer there to know it.

—Oliver Sacks

Commemorating life has never been easier or more prevalent than in the age of social media. Pausing to take a photograph has become a habitual action, an interruption of the most mundane activities, to capture the moment and post it to social media. Entire business models based on camera phones and photo editing apps are devoted to this seemingly innocuous pastime, all with the goal of streamlining the photographic process of image creation, processing, and sharing.

Each year Oxford Dictionary selects a word or expression that garnered a great deal of attention during the past year, reflecting the preoccupations or mood of that year and the expectation that the word will have long-term cultural significance.[1] The 2013 Oxford word of the year was *selfie*, a term coined around 2002 to describe the new medium in which the camera is turned on the self.[2] The selfie, a self-portrait photograph taken with a camera phone or webcam, arose out of technological developments, most notably social media platforms such as Facebook and Instagram. Initially many of these images were taken in the mirror, but as front facing camera phones became pervasive with the release of the iPhone 4 in 2010, the most popular selfie methods consist of taking the photo at arm's length or supporting the camera phone on a selfie stick. A front facing camera phone allows the photographer to view the screen while composing the photo.

While the word selfie is now common parlance, the desire to make self-portraits existed long before the art of photography was born. Remnants of self-portraits are documented in ancient Greek, Egyptian, and Roman art, and numerous intact examples exist, dating back to the 15th century. Artists well-known for their repetitive self-portraiture work, such as Vincent van Gogh and Frida Kahlo, are assumed to have used self-portraiture to resolve emotional difficulties. Less is known about the motivations of those who experimented with the earliest photography self-portraits, probably due to lack of interest in the lives of those individuals. Photographers rarely achieve the cult status attained by some artists of other media. Portraits were the most common subject of early photographs, making up 95% of early photographs and illustrating our long-time interest in images of people. The first known self-portrait photograph, a daguerreotype taken by Robert Cornelius in 1839, was made possible due to the long exposures required by this early photographic method.[3] The long exposure allowed Cornelius to uncover the lens and move into view of the camera for what was likely the minute or more required for the exposure. Self-portrait photographs became easier as technology progressed. It seems that photographers, much like artists, have a natural desire to turn the focus to themselves.

The introduction of the Kodak Brownie camera in 1900 allowed the amateur photographer to take self-portraits in a manner similar to the early selfie, by either shooting their reflection in the mirror or using a nearby object or tripod to prop the camera. The photographer could frame the photo and easily maneuver into the scene before tripping the shutter. The daughter of Russian Tsar Nicholas II, Anastasia Nikolaevna described, in an October 1914 letter to her father, how she used a mirror to capture her image for a friend.[4] She was 13 years old when she sent the picture to her friend. In her letter to her father, she described the trembling of her hands as she took the photograph. One can only imagine the importance of such a rare experience for this young girl and wonder how teens today experience similar moments as they casually take a multitude of selfies.

The ease with which selfies can now be taken and shared with an unlimited audience has made the selfie a transnational phenomenon. Due to the merging of self-portraiture photography with easy access to technological innovations that allow instantaneous image sharing, the selfie has democratized and normalized self-portrait photography. The resulting selfie phenomenon, or selfie pandemic as some call it, has created new categories of self-portraiture and vernacular photography that have transformed culture as dramatically as that first Brownie camera. The selfie is the digital self-portrait of our age, a cultural artifact that represents what is deemed to be of value: the self. The act of taking a selfie often surpasses the initial intent. A selfie begins with the individual but becomes a part of digitized archives, outliving the person and the time it was captured. Although more popular with younger generations, the selfie transcends age, nationality, and socioeconomic levels. A wide audience is now available on the ever-evolving social media platforms that support the selfie. Anyone who has a camera phone with access to social media can easily share selfies today.

One thing is certain: selfies are not a short-term trend but rather a new way of communicating. In *The Life of the Mind*, Hannah Arendt wrote about how important being seen by others is to our sense of self:

> . . . the fact that I am aware of myself and therefore in a sense can appear to myself, would never suffice to guarantee reality. . . . The urge toward self-display . . . seems to be common to [humans] and animals. And just as the actor depends on . . . spectators, to make his entrance, every living thing depends . . . on spectators to acknowledge and recognize its existence.[5]

Selfies have altered the very nature of the private self and the public self. This impetus to blur the line between public and private is a social change that coincides with the beginnings of photography itself. The very nature of privacy has changed as new avenues for presenting oneself have appeared. Self-portraits allow the subject to manipulate the image they want others to see. Selfies allow continuous rewriting and instantaneous distribution of that image. Celebrities, political figures, business moguls, and the general population alike share a fascination with selfies. The news reports an increase in head lice and neck problems in adolescents, resulting from their leaning together to capture group selfies. As we delve into this new territory, typical questions arise: Who takes selfies? Why do we take selfies? Are there potential gains from taking selfies? What about the possible downsides of taking selfies?

SELFIE PANDEMIC

As with most social trends, the advent of the selfie prompted predictions and concern regarding how this new technology would impact individuals and the larger culture. Since selfies are transmitted on social media, it is only natural that much of the research on this trend is conducted through these platforms. Metadata, stored with each image, provides information on image characteristics as well as time of upload and location coordinates.

One of the earliest projects studying selfies, the Selfiecity project, utilized metadata as a starting point to collect over 120,000 photos that were geotagged on Instagram from five major cities around the world (Bangkok, Berlin, Moscow, New York, and Sao Paulo). The photos were then visually inspected to determine how many were selfies and to approximate the gender and age of each person depicted. The study indicated that young people take the most selfies (median age was 23.7) and that women take more selfies than men— differences between the cities revealed a range of 1.3 to 1.9 times as many.[6] Projects like these will likely continue to develop and enhance our understanding of this worldwide phenomenon. Selfiecity has now launched a similar project in London.[7] Despite some interesting differences among the cities, this project convincingly illustrates that selfies transcend nationality and are truly a force to be understood.

In 2016, Google reported that an estimated 24 billion selfies were uploaded in the first year of the new Google Photos.[8] Depending on user age, selfies are most often posted on Facebook, Instagram, Snapchat, or WhatsApp. As of December 2016, there were 282 million selfies posted to Instagram alone with the hashtag #me.[9] It is estimated that over one million selfies are taken each day. Around one-third of the population has taken a selfie; 95% of American young adults surveyed in 2015 have done so. In fact, it is estimated that Millennials will likely take over 25,000 pictures of themselves in their lifetimes and spend more than 54 hours a year taking selfies.[10] Millennials are not the only people posting selfies. Over 90% of 12- to 17-year-olds post photos of themselves online.[11] Not surprisingly, these younger teens are unlikely to decrease their use of social media or selfie-sharing as they move into their twenties. This generation has lived their entire lives connected through this technology. As they enter their young adult years, they will be at the forefront in adopting new technologies, some that will surely target the sharing of selfies. As this generation continues their search for identity throughout their teen and early adult years, selfies will likely play in role in how they see themselves.

WHAT DOES THE SELFIE TELL US?

In the early ages of photography, staging a portrait or self-portrait would involve careful selection of clothing and background with the intent to illustrate the status of the person. For Europeans, this might have meant that the portrait would include props to reflect their status or might be set in classical Roman or Greek ruins. This would likely reflect ties with ancient civilizations, perhaps even hinting at lineage. For Americans, the portrait or self-portrait was more likely to express a sense of independence. An iconic portrait of the well-known photographer, Ansel Adams, comes to mind. In the photo, he is standing atop a platform built on a Woody Wagon of his era, looking through a large format camera that is perched on a tripod. A scene from Yosemite Valley with Half Dome is in the background. It is as if he is conquering the land with his camera. The image projects the vastness of Adam's talent and the grandness of the wilderness in which he created his art. The selfies of today speak their own language, a language that gives voice to this generation's longings for status based on modern priorities.

Photography may have begun as an expression of social identity or civil status, but more is always revealed if we are willing to look below the surface. Reflect on your experience of being photographed, or perhaps even of taking a selfie. Consider the underlying desires that led to a certain pose or attempt to capture a specific expression. If you look below the surface of the photo, you might catch a glimpse of your unconscious desire, perhaps the hope that in the act of capturing this moment, the essence of your individuality, who you truly are, will be expressed. "To photograph is to appropriate the thing photographed,"[12] therefore, a selfie may be an attempt to seize or adopt the self.

Cristina Nuñez, a photographer who practices self-portraiture, uses self-portraiture therapy as a means of expanding self-awareness. She refers to Barthes work on the meaning of self-portraits as a medium that "neither represents nor reflects reality, rather it gives it meaning. We are not our self-portrait; we are much more: The self-portrait does not define us. It is simply what needs to come to light; it is the voice of our unconscious that tells us what we need to know today."[13] If the photograph allows sight of the true self, and we are open to exploration, we can learn the language of selfies, which may provide an access point into identity.

SELFIE IDENTITY

When Macy first came to see me she was in her first year of college, but still moved like the high school athlete she'd been just a year before. Changes in her body since high school were troubling to Macy. Muscles developed from long hours in the weight room had softened to a more natural state, leaving her extremely self-conscious of her diminished muscle tone. Macy spent 12 of her 19 years playing a sport she missed intensely. Now in her first year of college, Macy binged more days than not each week. She openly discussed her past struggles with anxiety and obsessive–compulsive behavior. As she shared more of her story with me, bits and pieces of her social media habits were revealed as well.

Macy usually arrived for her sessions in an oversized T-shirt, each one commemorating a special event of a Greek organization at the large university she attended. Depending on the weather, she wore leggings or barely visible shorts underneath. She was tanning-bed bronzed and had her hair in a pile atop her head. The disheveled look seemed to say, "I don't care how I look," or "I am naturally beautiful and don't have to try." Macy cared a great deal, and she felt anything but beautiful. She expressed how much effort it takes each day to simply leave her dorm room to attend class, sorority obligations, or her sessions with me. Each day she changed clothes several times before being satisfied with her outfit. I was frankly a bit shocked that this look required so much effort to pull off. Other clients who come to see me have similar stories, they are young men and women who are seemingly unconcerned with their appearance, but who are wracked with an insecurity that belies their ostensible lack of effort. This dichotomy intrigued me as Macy began to spontaneously reveal her world of selfies. As she talked of her experiences and reactions, she often shared images from her frequent date-night parties or formal events.

Macy's selfies opened a window into her world and provided a language and richness she was unable to express verbally. She used this medium to explore her sense of who she wanted to be. At first, her comments were focused on concerns about her physical appearance. As we delved deeper into the underlying meaning of her comments, she acquired an ability to look beneath some of these surface concerns. I witnessed her use of selfies to explore and facilitate identity development.

A selfie provides a much truer picture of how others see us than does a mirror image. As I worked with Macy, I thought about how a photographer, as an artist, explores her own identity through self-portraiture. An artist seeks to gain the same kind of access to her own physical features as she has to the subject of any other portrait she might create.[14] The self-portrait provides a canvas that can be viewed as others see us. Taking a selfie is a form of self-exploration through images, for sense of self includes awareness of the physical self. The experience of sharing the selfie on social media may be more important than the selfie itself, in terms of identity development, as evidenced by the repetitive nature of posting selfies and the desire for feedback on each one.

Adolescence is a time of intense identity searching. Erik Erikson's classic psychosocial theory, in which each developmental stage is marked by a crisis that could have positive or negative effects on development, defines adolescence as a time of identity versus role confusion. During this stage, adolescents engage in a search for sense of self or identity. They examine values and beliefs to gain a sense of who they are. Erikson posited that successful resolution in each stage lays positive groundwork for subsequent stages. After adolescence, an individual has a clear identity and is prepared to move into the next stage, intimacy versus isolation, in early adulthood. In Erikson's opinion, if the individual has not resolved the search for identity, intimacy with others will be hampered. While Erikson's theory is not comprehensive in explaining how this development occurs nor, perhaps, accurate on the age spans, given that very few 18-year-olds qualify as having a clear sense of who they are, it does seem to reflect the yearnings of this age.

For teens and young adults, identity and intimacy are of central concern, and Macy is no exception. As a high school athlete, she had a built-in identity, even though it was primarily based on her membership on the volleyball team. She maintained few friendships from high school and was now most concerned about her social standing in her new college environment. Much of her anxiety centered on whether she is truly liked by her new friends. Some of them took advantage of her, expecting her to give them answers on homework or even complete papers she has written for her own classes. Difficulty saying no to these requests led to academic probation. Her relationships with males were similarly troubled. Macy's former identity as an athlete was no longer relevant. She had no sense of who she is nor how she fit into this new environment.

When teaching human development classes to 18- to 22-year-old college students, I poll students with the question of whether they think they have attained a sense of identity. Rarely do these students affirm identity resolution.

Instead, they reflect on their struggles to figure out who they are and where they fit into society. They are searching for acceptance and intimacy, and most feel lost in a maze of confusing choices. These students are active on social media and cannot imagine life without these conveniences, yet they are uncertain how to interact with others in ways that move them toward their goals of identity or intimacy. Like Macy, they think nothing of posting selfies in the moment, but most have also had negative experiences as a result. Guiding therapists to help youths, like Macy, navigate this cultural phenomenon is the greatest impetus for writing this book.

FUNCTIONS OF THE SELFIE

There are few definitive answers as to why people post selfies or what the effects of this practice are. There have been a good number of research studies, yet still no consensus exists. Internet searches of articles, blogs, and social media posts are likewise divergent. Some common themes emerge. The many ways in which identity, or sense of self, are explored encompasses most of the theorizing on why selfies have gained popularity. Purposes for taking selfies include maintaining personal and group memories, creating/maintaining relationships, self-presentation, and self-expression. All are likely actions of self-exploration, yet each deserves individual attention, as all are vital to identity formation and, thus, to our client's mental health.

Self-Exploration

Humans have an intrinsic need to explore the physical self. When mirrors first became affordable, there was concern that people would become overly focused on themselves. Perhaps mirrors did result in more awareness of appearance, as anyone who has passed a mirror and noticed their hair astray or a piece of spinach in their teeth can attest, but it is doubtful that mirrors alone have led to self-obsession. If the traditional diary's function is to explore and express innermost thoughts, the selfie may be more like a visual diary, through which the individual can look back and see how they dressed or what they looked like at a given time, thereby exploring physical identity in digital form. The selfie provides an alternative way to explore (and share) who one is.

Selfies allow a more in-depth method of examining multiple versions of the self, each time allowing a fresh viewing. Mirrors provide one view, but they do not reflect how we look to others. After all, we cannot see how we look in the mirror without directing our eyes to the image in the mirror. According to James Kilner, a London neuroscientist, selfies are helping us see ourselves the way we want to be perceived. People have an image of themselves as more attractive than they actually are, he says. Since we spend a lifetime observing others, and relatively little time observing ourselves, we are very inept at recognizing what our own faces look like. In Kilner's research, people were asked to choose the photograph that looks most like them from a group of photos that were digitally altered. The images that were altered to make the subjects appear more attractive were most likely to be chosen. He believes that this mismatch may explain why selfies have become so popular; they allow us to retake a photo until we capture an image that is closer to the way we think we look.[15] Popular photo sharing apps with built in editing features can beautify an image with a few taps, enabling a person to mimic a preconceived vision. It may not be a realistic version, but instead more of an exploration into how a person would like to be seen. Self-exploration also transpires through reflecting on memories.

Memory

As snapshots of our history that are tied together to form our story, memories are an autobiography that is continuously under construction. Filmmaker Luis Buñuel, in his autobiography, *My Last Sigh*,[16] reflected on the role of memory. "You have to begin to lose your memory, if only in bits and pieces, to realize that memory is what makes our lives. Life without memory is no life at all. . . Our memory is our coherence, our reason, our feeling, even our action. Without it we are nothing." In a similar vein, the short film, *The Last Mariner*, closes with the question "What kind of self is left when you've lost your past and your place in time?"[17]

Traditional definitions of memory have focused on the act of retaining or reviving facts, events, impressions, etc., or of recalling previous experiences. Neuroscientists, such as Daniel Siegel, build on this understanding of memory by focusing on the process by which the brain experiences the world and uses this information to affect future ways of responding. This suggests that the structure and function of the brain are unique to the individual: a person's experiences impact their brain structure and subsequently determine future responses.[18]

Memories are strung together into a narrative that gives structure to our sense of who we are. Some events are forgotten immediately, having little impact on the individual, while others can be recalled throughout life. Most day-to-day experiences are trivial and have little bearing on our functioning, but we can recall events that have significance. Emotionally laden input translates into significant memories.

Photographs have an elevated ability to impact memory. Visual input may enter through the eyes, but it is "seen" with the brain. The hippocampus, part of the emotional limbic system, plays a role in autobiographical memories. The hippocampus combines sensory information and transforms short-term memories into long-term memories. Alongside the hippocampus is the amygdala, a site of extensive neural connectivity essential for memory processing and emotional responses. That our autobiographical memories are overwhelmingly visual is no surprise. In terms of memory formation, vision is the most potent sense.[19]

Recall that a photograph with punctum arouses an emotional response in the viewer based on their personal response to the image. Those images often haunt our thoughts long after the image is out of sight. Neuroscientists are illuminating just how important emotions are to the formation of memories. Emotions not only motivate us to interact with and connect with our environment, but they also guide how learning controls memory formation.[20] That they are intricately tied to our visual experiences only further explains the power of the selfie.

Memory storage is the result of neural network potentiation. What is stored is the probability that neurons will again fire together in a specific pattern. Thus, memories are based on the strengthening of complex neural connections. The representations of the remembered experience are likely stored in the regions of the brain that were activated by the experience. Brain imaging studies have shown that when a person is asked to visualize an object, the areas of the brain responsible for visual processing become active. Retrieval of a memory activates the neural network associated with the event, along with elements of the memory such as sights, sounds, smells and words, and the present state of mind.[21] Hence memories are not static because new information and experiences can prompt reconceptualization of a memory. There are shifts each time a memory comes to mind, a necessary change if the past is to connect with the present.

Consider the importance of integrating new information, feelings, or visual input into previous experiences as a necessary process in the ongoing creation of personal identity. I witnessed this process as Macy pulled out her phone and showed me several selfies from a formal event she attended the previous weekend. Instantaneous cueing of memories and a strong emotional reaction support the idea of punctum in these selfie images. Macy recalled feeling anxious and self-conscious most of the evening and labeled the event as disappointing and boring. After spending a great deal of time shopping for her dress and then doing her hair and makeup that evening, she was disappointed that she did not receive the attention she desired. These memories and the associated emotions seemed inseparable.

Memory instability allowed Macy to integrate new information and develop a more accurate perception of the evening as she viewed the selfies from a calmer emotional state and processed her expectations of the evening. Reconsolidation underlies the ability to update memories with new information and lies at the core of therapy. A strong, stable sense of identity depends on strengthening of memory or memory reconsolidation that supports positive identity. This illustrates the connection between selfies and memory. A selfie provides information about the past, the time it was taken, but memories arise from our past experiences to affect the present, including our present sense of self. Selfies have the capacity to activate memory recall. They serve as a visual diary or repository of the past, a form of memory storage. Our autobiographical memory serves a similar function. It holds the story of what, where, and when events occurred in our lives, along with the emotional components of the events. Therapeutic processing of selfies can enable updating of the associated memories by promoting amygdala and hippocampal connectivity. This skill enables clients to balance emotional responses with conscious, logical thought about a memory.

Whether memories reflect reality is another matter. It is imperative to note the malleability of memory, even though one's memories may be held onto as if they are an exact recreation of an event. Since memory is encoded within neural networks rather than stored in an intact file as an exact replica of an event, the subjectivity of memory must be acknowledged. Sontag believed that photographs are "not so much an instrument of memory as an invention"[22] of it. Like some family stories, selfies may have more to do with selective memory creation than with preservation of actual memories. Examining memories and related photographs for accuracy can be a liberating experience.

A client's selfie collection serves as a visual diary of life that includes important events as well as the banal day-to-day activities of life. Selfies may enhance long-term memory in much the same way as storytelling is used to pass down family history. Through repetition, the memory becomes stronger and less susceptible to forgetting, although always amenable to change before reconsolidation. Through selfies, we can travel across time and space to the stored remembrances, especially to those with strong emotional salience, the memories that have significance for us and are clung to regardless of their validity. Perhaps in the future we will have the means to erase selected painful, traumatic, or even troublesome memories. For now, psychological interventions are able to renovate difficult memories, framing them in a more positive light. Since memory is an ongoing, dynamic process, damaging memories can be brought into an active processing mode and the inclusion of new emotional contexts that were not available when the original memory was formed can be added.

Collecting vast numbers of photographs, including selfies, can also be viewed as outsourcing of memories. The album is a concrete receptacle of memories, often displayed prominently in our homes and available for review. Technology takes over the process of creating and maintaining of the family album, which was previously considered an act of devotion and love. It remains to be seen whether selfies will achieve the same status as the family album. Methods of creating and maintaining albums of cherished images are transitioning as technology offers new options. Many albums are stored on cloud storage systems, never to be viewed again, making them even more ephemeral, as they are now out of sight.

While selfie memories are now easily transported, they also can disappear in a flash. Lack of storage, device failure, or actions of cloud-based storage companies can wipe these from our lives permanently. Despite the risks, the act of taking selfies continues to flourish.

Creating/Maintaining Relationships

Selfies are clearly related to our desire to maintain memories of our relationships and the groups to which we belong. Those responding to surveys about why they take selfies often mention that selfies signify relationship connections. When the selfie includes others in the photo and is shared, group memories are solidified, and membership is affirmed. As humans, relationships are vital for survival, and social connectivity is a central pillar of identity. Macy's lost social role provided status and stability in high school, but because these relationships were not maintained and new relationships were proving to be more difficult than anticipated, her identity was hampered by her lack of belonging.

Across the lifespan, we need others who care for us, make us feel safe, desire our company, and share in the discovery of who we are. Mirror neurons, which fire both while observing others in action and when we make those same actions, may be responsible for our capacity for empathy when viewing others' facial expressions, posture, and other nonverbal expressions.[23] We now consider the brain to be a social organ that is continually being changed by our experiences and relationships. Our brains are deeply connected to others; they reside within a social milieu. Fundamental to our ability to build relationships and develop sense of self, visual information prompts mirror neurons. Optimally, this allows us to read others' internal states and empathically attune to them.

However, in the process of trying to capture selfies, we may prevent ourselves from experiencing the very events and relational experiences we are trying to capture. This has never been truer than it is today, with our ever-present camera phones. I recently spent several months teaching and traveling abroad with a group of university students, and I was intrigued by their focus on capturing selfies of themselves engaging in the act of tourism, as if they were only living the experience if it was captured on the screens of their phones. This excessive documentation can get in the way of experiencing life and being present enough with others to build relationships.

Perhaps taking and sharing selfies serves a social function. With a notable emphasis on vision, the amygdala plays an important role in assessing the environment, evaluating sensory input, and activating responses. Its extensive neural connectivity promotes sensory integration. The amygdala is also involved in bonding and attachment due to its high density of opioid receptors.[24] Neural processes in the amygdala may facilitate the connection that is felt when the eye gazes on a photo that elicits remembrance of caring relationships. Long before the field of neuroscience confirmed the power of visual input to bring about strong affect, G. K. Chesterton said, "There is a road from the eye to the heart that does not go through the intellect."[25]

As I worked with Macy, I was intrigued by the social regulation in her peer group that occurs on social media. Suffice it to say that there are oftentimes unspoken rules of etiquette in terms of how a person responds to another's selfie. These rules, based on the closeness of the relationship, dictate whether someone posts a written response or simply likes a selfie. Those who are not considered a part of a young person's close social group overstep boundaries if they post a written response to a selfie, especially if the comment seems too familiar. It is a grave offense to post a comment that indicates a closer relationship than exists between the two people. The importance of these rules was reflected in my conversations with Macy as she talked about her own social media usage. She closely monitors any selfie she posts or is tagged in to see how many likes it receives and from whom. Her mood is negatively impacted if a person she holds in high regard does not respond to a photo. She second guesses her own responses to others, fearing more than once that she has committed a social blunder. Additional research from such fields as neuroscience, social psychology, sociology, and communication is needed to fully understand how the visual nature of social media impacts the experience of relating to others.

Self-Presentation

Some believe that the function of personal photography has shifted from remembrance and commemoration to self-presentation and affirmation of personhood.[26] Younger people today appear to be more comfortable being photographed than ever before. Their almost constant interaction with camera phones and social media across their short lifespan has fostered a nonchalance to moving their private lives into the public sphere. Social researchers and parents alike worry that excessive sharing of selfies is a cry for attention from insecure or self-conscious individuals. Some have linked selfies with narcissism, saying that the selfie both increases narcissism and is a product of it. No doubt, excessive perusal of social media can be a sign of narcissism, an inordinate fascination with oneself and with others' perceptions, but humans have an innate need to be noticed or known by others.

Young people are notorious for their concerns about how they appear to others. This is visibly played out in adolescence, when self-consciousness increases. Elkind coined the term *imaginary audience* to describe the feeling that one is the focus of another's attention. A related term, the *personal fable*, relates to feelings that one is unique or exceptional.[27] Originally applied to the developmental stage of adolescence, these beliefs can occur at other ages as well and can lead to extreme self-consciousness. Typically, undergraduate students in human development classes are not highly motivated to learn about the developmental stages that lead up to adolescence, but their attention intensifies when this topic is introduced. They recall worrying about facial breakouts or bad hair days to the extent that they avoided activities. Changing clothes multiple times before being comfortable enough to leave the house is not unheard of even in college students. College students relate to concepts such as the imaginary audience and personal fable, possibly because, when anonymously polled, many admit they still experience these beliefs. As a result, a significant number continue to struggle, like Macy, with self-consciousness.

Since the advent of social media, feelings of self-consciousness have increased because it is easier than ever to eavesdrop on others' opinions and conversations. We no longer need to rely solely on word of mouth or face-to-face interactions to know what is being said about us. This preoccupation with presenting oneself to others has led to a plethora of new social media platforms on which to operate. It is easier than ever to build a social media presence, gather a following, and monitor others' responses.

Posing for selfies provides a medium for self-presentation. Barthes reflected on this concept long before the selfie when he recognized in himself the tendency to transform himself in advance to the image he had of how the photograph would portray him.[28] Selfie-takers like Macy know the pose is important: cheeks sucked in, pouty lips to convey sexiness, and bodies angled to slice away pounds—a pose commonly known as the "sorority girl." These poses are obviously staged to convey desired attributes. The selfie can be retaken until just the right expression is captured, unlike the days when film was expensive and photos had to be developed and printed. Macy's slightly mussed, just-out-of-bed hair and wide–eyed stare selfies reflect an "I don't care" attitude, a message that the selfie was quickly taken and shared with no concern for appearance. Of course, my conversations with her tell a very different story.

Selfies can seem like the answer to self-consciousness. The use of apps to digitally manipulate or alter images before posting enables selective self-presentation. A person can take a photo over and over until one that matches the ideal, or at least reflects an image they are willing to share with others, is captured. Most selfie-takers admit to altering selfies to improve their appearance. Applying flattering filters and blurring outlines before sharing are just two means of impression management. Selfies are also cropped to exclude parts that may be deemed less desirable. If the image still doesn't pass the test, the delete button is another option for instant editing. If we don't like it, it's gone, along with the unconsciously expressed uniqueness of an individual that often comes through in more natural moments. The ability of the user to manipulate the image makes the selfie a state-of-the-art tool for identity formation.

If the selfie-taker's goal is to get likes or comments affirming the share, does digital manipulation erase the sense of who we actually are as we attempt to create a more appealing version? If we consider that photographs can express the underlying essence of a person, does the manipulation erase the truth? Does it repress unconscious material that would shine through in more traditionally made images?

My mind wanders to the memory of a photograph of my grandparents and some of their 10 children. I am not sure of the exact year it was taken, perhaps in the mid-1940s. My grandmother's hair is flying wildly in the Texas wind. With one hand on her hip, the tilt of her head seems to confirm her comfort with who she is. This photograph is, to me, the essence or personality of this woman, whom I knew well into my own adult years, a woman who could laugh regardless of the circumstances with little concern for posing or appearing as someone other than who she truly is. In contrast to this attitude toward the camera and akin to Sontag's "aesthetic consumerism," Teju Cole, a writer and photographer who writes extensively on photography, coined the term *aesthetic control* to describe how the camera is used.[29] The vast number of photos taken across a lifetime seems to be an attempt to commemorate life as it occurs, but with the option to control the image that others see. Because we can choose the setting and clothes, to edit or delete, we now have consummate control over how we are seen, and the end goal of these efforts is now often social reward, likes. Nothing expresses the desire to garner positive social responses in the current age more than the term *aesthetic control*.

Another new concept, at least as applied to humans rather than an object, is self-branding, an act of self-packaging or self-promotion. Arising from the Internet-connected reality of needing to have an online presence, today's youth are faced with the pressure to create a self-brand, which is much like a corporate brand. This brand should set them apart from others in the vast world in which we now work and interact. Ultimately the goal is to gain the social rewards of interaction and recognition from a desired audience. Developing a personal brand is now a commonly discussed goal among Millennials. As a business student, Macy is well-aware of how her selfies "promote" the brand she hopes to convey. The dissonance of her private struggles and her public persona often lead her into a frenzy of confusion.

Others are less affected by the need to self-present in a positive manner. One trend that some find difficult to understand is when intentionally unflattering selfies are shared on apps such as Snapchat. These may be an attempt at humor or another way for the person to thumb their nose at expectations of how they "should" appear. Since the Snapchat selfie is believed to be available for only 10 seconds, users see little danger in posting selfies that they might not share on other formats. These users may also simply be less self-conscious about their appearance. It is evident that selfies are a new way of self-presentation, exemplifying a fresh means of expressing oneself through images.

Self-Expression

Many proclaim that selfies are a form of self-expression, used in today's culture as a means of imagining the self or even creating a self. The selfie allows a young person to project who they are, or at least who they want to be seen as. The concept of *imaginization*, an idea taken from the organizational management book by the same name,[30] seems to be especially relevant when applied to creation of the self. This model, as it was originally developed, relies on metaphors and visualization to illustrate innovative management practices. Much like the use of metaphors in narrative therapy, imaginization of self plays out in the creative and innovative science of the selfie. As a way to explore identity through metaphors or visual stories, selfies may be the new canvas on which self-definition occurs.

Some selfies exhibit a characteristic trait that is enacted to set a person apart from the crowd, often a borrowed trademark or signature persona of a celebrity that has become a cliché pose by the masses. The self that is displayed is created to gain social status. It is a false self that corresponds to social pressures rather than reflecting the person's true self. The selfie is a new way of expressing the self to others, of communicating through images in a culture that increasingly relies on visual images to transmit information. The sharing of this selfie in the public forum creates a digital footprint or public identity that may have little semblance to reality, but it may also indicate one's attempt to express who they feel they truly are at that moment. The popularity of selfie-sharing among those searching for identity is no accident.

As their search for identity becomes prominent, young people experience intense self-involvement and focus on physical appearance while they try out new roles. For a person in search of self, controlling what is shared can provide a sense of personal power as well as connection with others. For identity formation, a young person must differentiate from family and others. This process of differentiation can be observed in the digital diary many adolescents create by their collection of selfies. By creating this diary, our existence is confirmed; there is concrete proof that we are here, that we exist, and that we are distinct from others. Sontag recognized this desire before technology revolutionized where this process occurs: "While many in non-industrialized countries still feel apprehensive when being photographed, divining it to be some kind of trespass, an act of disrespect, a sublimated looting of the personality or the culture, people in industrialized countries seek to have their photographs taken—feel that they are images, and are made real by photographs."[31]

The practice of taking selfies is not likely to abate. While this behavior may seem strange to some, if we view it in the context of developing a sense of identity, selfies may be the modern method of using social feedback to create a sense of who we are, a process that has long been recognized as foundational to the sense of self. The common practice of seeking affirmation through the posting of selfies is a particularly risky activity for those with eating disorders because responses to selfies can affirm their eating disorder behaviors. The next chapter describes the use of selfie images in therapy with Macy, a component of her binge eating disorder treatment.

REFERENCES

1. Oxford Word of the Year. Retrieved from https://en.oxforddictionaries.com/word-of-the-year/word-of-the-year-faqs

2. Word of the year. (2013). Retrieved from https://en.oxforddictionaries.com/word-of-the-year/word-of-the-year-2013

3. Rawlings, K. (2013, November, 21). Selfies and the history of self-portrait photography. Retrieved from http://blog.oup.com/2013/11/selfies-history-self-portrait-photography/

4. Diaries and letters: Letters of Grand Duchess Anastasia – Excerpts from the letters of Anastasia to her father. Retrieved from http://www.alexanderpalace.org/palace/adiaries.html

5. Arendt, H. (1981). *The life of the mind*. (Kindle version). Retrieved from Amazon.com

6. Selfiecity: Investigating the style of self-portraits (selfies) in five cities across the world. Retrieved from http://selfiecity.net

7. Selfiecity: Investigating the style of self-portraits (selfies) in five cities across the world using a mix of theoretical, artistic and quantitative methods. Retrieved from http://selfiecity.net/london/

8. Zhang, M. (2016). Google photos turns one: Now hosts 24 billion selfies. Retrieved from https://petapixel.com/2016/05/30/google-photos-turns-one-now-hosts-24-billion-selfies/

9. Lister, M. (August 26, 2019). 33 mind-boggling Instagram stats and facts for 2018. Retrieved from https://www.wordstream.com/blog/ws/2017/04/20/instagram-statistics

10. Glum, J. (September 22, 2015). Millennials selfies: Young adults will take more than 25,000 pictures of themselves during their lifetimes: Report. Retrieved from http://www.ibtimes.com/millennials-selfies-young-adults-will-take-more-25000-pictures-themselves-during-2108417

11. Teens, social media, and privacy. (2013). Retrieved from http://www.pewinternet.org /2013/05/21/teens-social-media-and-privacy/

12. Sontag. S. (1977). On photography. New York, NY: Picador.

13. Nuñez, C. (2013). The self-portrait as self-therapy (p. 103). In D. Loewenthal (Ed.), *Phototherapy and therapeutic photography in a digital age* (pp. 95–106). New York, NY: Routledge.

14. Wilson, D. (2013). Facing the camera: Self-portraits of photographers as artists. *The Journal of Aesthetics and Art Criticism, 70*(1), 56–66.

15. Kilner, J. (2014, January,17). The science behind why we take selfies. Retrieved from http:// www.bbc.com/news/blogs-magazine-monitor-25763704

16. Buñuel, L. (2003). *My last sigh.* (Kindle version). Retrieved from Amazon.com

17. Martin, T. (2014). *The lost mariner.* Animated film retrieved from http://www.tessmartinart .com/the-lost-mariner/

18. Siegel, D. J. (2012). *The developing mind: How relationships and the brain interact to shape who we are.* (2nd ed.) New York, NY: Guilford Press.

19. Sarinana, J. (2013). Memories, photographs, and the human brain. Retrieved from http:// petapixel.com/2013/07/20/memories-photographs-and-the-human-brain/

20. Panksepp, J., & Biven, L. (2012). *The archaeology of mind: Neuroevolutionary origins of human emotions.* New York, NY: W. W. Norton & Company.

21. Cozolino, L. (2017). *The neuroscience of psychotherapy: Healing the social brain* (3rd ed.). New York, NY: W. W. Norton & Company.

22. Sontag, S. (1977). *On photography.* New York, NY: Picador.

23. Cozolino, L. (2017). *The neuroscience of psychotherapy: Healing the social brain* (3rd ed.). New York, NY: W. W. Norton & Company.

24. Cozolino, L. (2017). *The neuroscience of psychotherapy: Healing the social brain* (3rd ed.). New York, NY: W. W. Norton & Company.

25. Chesterton, G. K. (1901). *The defendant.* Retrieved from https://www.gutenberg.org/ files/12245/12245-h/12245-h.htm Release Date: May 3, 2004 [EBook #12245]

26. Harrison, B. (2002). Photographic visions and narrative inquiry. *Narrative Inquiry, 12*(1), 87–111.

27. Elkind, D. (1967). Egocentrism in adolescence. *Child Development, 38,* 1025–1034.

28. Barthes, R. (1980). *Camera lucida.* New York, NY: Hill and Wang.

29. Cole, T. (2016). *Known and strange things: Essays.* New York, NY: Random House.

30. Morgan, G. (1997). *Imaginization: New mindsets for seeing, organizing, and managing.* Thousand Oaks, CA: Sage.

31. Sontag, S. (1977). *On photography* (p. 161). New York, NY: Picador.

Chapter 8

THERAPEUTIC USE OF SELFIE IMAGES

Until you make the unconscious conscious, it will direct your life, and you will call it fate.

—Carl Jung

Nascent technologies have long been viewed as purveyors of social ills, and the various developments that have sown the selfie pandemic are no exception. Perhaps the loudest critique of the selfie comes from those sounding the alarm about a rising trend of narcissism in younger generations. Millennial and Gen Z cohorts receive a great deal of consternation for their involvement on social media and passion for selfies. Some psychological assessments indicate rising rates of narcissism in these cohorts compared to older adults.[1] Inclinations toward community involvement and connection with others have been declining since the 1970s, indicating that this variation could merely be an indication of overall social change. It may be that correlations between narcissism and selfies are mere artifacts of a general cultural shift to a more self-absorbed norm.

WEIGHING IN ON SELFIES

Although selfies have been blamed for the uptick in narcissism levels, there is relatively little academic support for this assertion. One study indicated a positive link between narcissism and editing and posting of selfies for 18- to 40-year-old males.[2] Women post more selfies than men, and most studies that include both genders have found that various subcomponents of narcissism must be taken into account to evaluate how narcissism and selfie-sharing are related. Type of social media on which selfies are posted, culture, and the age of the sharer reflect different aspects of narcissism.[3] Rather than decrying selfie use in general, a greater benefit may come from studying where and why selfies are posted.

In one study that asked college students to report on their selfie behavior 55% of subjects conveyed that sharing their selfies on social media encouraged narcissism and selfish behaviors. These students admitted that they share their selfies to impress others with their social experiences and to garner as many likes as possible.[4] It seems that these individuals have an incessant need for affirmation from others. So, does narcissism lead people to use selfies in narcissistic ways, or do selfies encourage narcissism? While delving into this topic in greater detail may someday offer a clear analysis, the current state of this line of inquiry provides few definitive answers. It is clear that the inquiry into selfie-sharing and narcissism is far from complete. Narcissism is a term that is liberally thrown at a wide range of behaviors that may actually stem from cultural shifts rather than diagnosable mental illnesses. While beyond the purview of this discussion, these studies prove interesting for those desiring a more detailed perspective on selfies and narcissism.[5]

Another criticism leveled at selfie-sharing is that the practice encourages superficiality. If one shared image is more liked than another, should a person adopt the version that others affirm? Over 90% of college students in the above study said that they post selfies for the sole reason of receiving likes or positive comments from others. They believe that online profiles can elevate social status, and they estimate another's popularity on how many likes that person's profile picture receives. It seems that some base the attainment of a desired social identity, albeit a very superficial one, on how others respond to a shared photo.

The American writer John Paul Titlow pronounced selfie-sharing as "a high school popularity contest on digital steroids."[6] The hashtag #me is one of the most popular tags on Instagram, and with the pseudo-fame obtained by some young people solely from sharing selfies of themselves on social media, it is no wonder that this generation places a high value on being attractive. Social media stars may have thousands of followers based simply on their visual appeal, not any identified talent or achievement. The audience from which one may gain popularity is now virtually unlimited. In a world typified by perfected and stereotyped images, it is difficult to see beyond a flawless image to the individual underneath who is crying out for recognition of their uniqueness.

Getting noticed and standing out from the crowd is harder than ever in the digital age. Constant documentation on an ever-expanding array of social media sites provides infinite opportunities to create a public image. One way to garner attention is by posting selfies that document dangerous feats, and in today's image saturated world, an image is necessary to prove that a daredevil event actually occurred. The news is rife with stories of selfie-related fatalities: "Student Dies after Falling from Cliffs of Moher while Taking Selfie" and "Man Crushed to Death while Attempting Selfie before Moving Train" are two examples. Of 259 verifiable selfie-related deaths between 2011 and 2017, only a little more than one-quarter were taken while the user was in a nonrisky location or engaging in a nonrisky behavior.[7] Males and those between the ages of 10 and 29 are most likely to succumb to a selfie-related death, but all selfie-takers are at risk when their attention is fixated on taking the perfect selfie rather than on safety.

Are there positives to selfies? Some believe that selfies boost self-image, but whether selfies actually raise self-esteem is unclear. Selfies do allow the user an incomparable level of control over appearance. The selective self-presentation that selfies allow may give at least a temporary boost to self-esteem. While they may not raise self-esteem for long, if at all, selfies permit us to see ourselves in a more favorable light. They also offer an unprecedented view of what we look like or how our body language comes across to others.

Selfies allow exploration of the implicit self-knowledge that often lies outside our awareness. Implicit feelings about the self are thought to guide many of life's most important decisions.[8] In optimal situations, selfies can be used to express our moods and share important experiences. If an individual holds implicit, unfavorable views of themself, however, there is a tendency to present the self in an overly zealous manner.[9] This is easier than ever on social media. Selfies can also hinder relationship quality. Sharing selfies on Facebook correlates with shallow relationships, lower social support from friends, and negative romantic relationship outcomes.[10] So while there is a potential to use selfies as a means of self-exploration or self-expression, some users are at risk of suffering negative effects of selfie-sharing.

Researchers at the University of California, Irvine, found that positive affect can be enhanced with the use of smartphone photography.[11] By randomly assigning students to one of three groups who were either instructed to take a smiling selfie each day, a photo of something that made them happy, or a photo of something they believed would bring happiness to someone else, researchers discovered that students in all three groups experienced enhanced positive moods. Of course, each of these groups was interacting with photography in a positive manner. Interestingly, selfie-takers reported feeling greater confidence and comfort with the smiling photos over time, as well as enhanced recollection of the moment that the smile occurred. The group of students who took photos with the intent to bring happiness to another also sent this photo to that person. Mood measurements of these students revealed the behavior had a calming effect, likely due to the social connection this activity engendered. Selfies that connect the sender and the receiver may have the potential to build social connections.

If photography is an art, a controversial idea in the art world, then selfies may be the art of the masses, for the masses. Like self-portraits, selfies might be an art that can aid exploration of a person's unique appearance. In some ways, it may be a more authentic representation of beauty than other media images. Despite the common use of filters and other means of altering the image, unaltered selfies have the potential to counteract the standardized notion of beauty. In this sense, it can feel empowering to create and share a less-than-perfect selfie. More generally, selfies may help a young person accept how they appear to others, especially if explored in a therapeutic manner.

In the 2015 article in *Elle Magazine*, "Why Selfies are Good for Girls,"[12] Glynnis MacNicol touts the empowerment that she feels in taking a selfie. She prefers to be in control of her own image, and she stated that she knows how she wants to look and can portray that look better than others can. She goes on to say that the person being photographed by another makes the subject the object of the photographer's gaze. This thought originates in a historical context in which the absence of the female voice coincides with objectification. MacNicol sees taking a selfie as a feminist act and she quotes Sontag's words "to photograph people is to violate them, by seeing them as they never see themselves, by having knowledge of them that they can never have; it turns people into objects that can be symbolically possessed."[13]

To appreciate the difficulty of weighing in on selfies, we must be able to step back from the polarizing rhetoric that serves the sole purpose of attracting attention to calmly examine what this new form of communication offers. Therapists must become familiar with the effects of selfies so as to provide guidance for healthy use. Technological advancements will continue to introduce new forms of visual communication, and older forms will become obsolete. We can guide those who share selfies to express their authentic self and to explore how they fit into the world through this medium. We can raise people's awareness of safety issues and inform them of ways to harness the power of this new technology. Selfies are here to stay. Making peace with this practice may allow us to gain new insights into our client's lives.

SELFIES AND SELF-AWARENESS

Selfies bestow control of all aspects of the image making process on the individual. People are simultaneously creators, subjects, and viewers of the selfie. Thus, selfie images are endowed with meaning from multiple perspectives—rich material for the identity work that is central to eating disorder treatment. As we contemplate the selfie phenomenon, it is obvious that photography imparts a greater influence on society today than ever before. Never have so many people engaged in the creation of images. Camera use is at an all-time high, with smart phones producing more selfies than anyone could have predicted. What we consider to be a simple touch of a button on a phone often holds implicit meanings that are rarely explored. Selfies, often unknowingly, are a means to express what cannot be spoken.

When strong emotions are present, verbal centers in the brain are less proficient. We've all experienced this when at a complete loss for words in an intensely emotional moment. People use images to capitalize on the ability of visual stimuli to express intense emotions or confusing thoughts when other means of expression are inadequate or unavailable. These images range from internal images in the mind to external images that hold symbolic meaning. Both created and found images can be meaningful when they express what is not possible to express with words. The expressive power of images, including selfies, lies in examining what is underneath the surface.

Neuroscience research shows that there are two distinct forms of self-awareness: the autobiographical-self that keeps track of the self across time, through language, to form the story of self and the present-self that reflects moment-to-moment awareness based on physical sensations. These two kinds of self-awareness emanate from different brain regions and processes—language versus visceral body sensations. Whereas, words cannot make sense of experiences until the body-based self is engaged,[14] pairing the story with what registers in the body as the story is told creates a path to self-awareness.

The therapist's role is to guide the client to self-awareness, a paradoxical goal at best. In peering inside to understand our own nature, there is only the self to interpret what is seen. Complete self-awareness is an impossible task; to fully know oneself is unattainable. Still, self-knowing lies at the heart of the overarching identity process, and to know oneself requires self-awareness. Individuation and differentiation grow from self-awareness, as does the likelihood that clients will act in line with their personal values.[15] It is only through self-awareness that values can be identified.

Self-awareness grows from self-reflecting on social guidelines that are learned so a person can fit in socially and on the internal dialogue of private thoughts. Without self-reflection, critical voices from the past can intrude on the present. Self-reflection allows a person to uncover the unconscious programming of reflexive social language and internal dialogue, so clients can build an awareness of their own mind. The expanded self-awareness that develops over the course of therapy enables clients to observe their social reflexes and their internal voices and then decide whether to follow the mandates of others or to create their own story. Clients learn to think about their emotions and to have feelings about their thoughts as they process new knowledge about themselves.[16] Stressful situations are less taxing when clients have insight into who they are and how they react to the world around them. In quieting the mind, there is room to reflect and author new narratives of self. Self-awareness is epitomized by an openness to knowing and honoring the authentic self. We are all storytellers. Selfies are just one medium through which we can tell our stories.

PHOTO THERAPY WITH SELFIE IMAGES

Macy had little sense of herself or her place in the large university environment where she had just completed her first semester. In high school, she gained instant recognition for her talents on the volleyball court. Her days were filled with practice, and she had a large network of friends who had all grown up together in their small hometown. Without her high school identity as an athlete, she had little sense of self. Her energy was centered on adjusting to the demands of college, building a new circle of friends, and her physical appearance.

Macy's disordered eating began in high school when she developed a habit of binging late at night after socializing with friends, but this trend has intensified in college. An injury in her senior year of high school benched her for the second half of the season, and she gained around 20 pounds. The summer before college, she started restricting her caloric intake in an attempt to lose the added pounds. As the restriction accelerated, Macy became fixated on food and soon began to binge most evenings as her body attempted to make up for the calorie deficit. Binge eating disorder (BED) is common in those seeking weight loss through restrictive means and is more than three times as common as anorexia and bulimia combined.[17] Macy initially had difficulty identifying the emotions surrounding the binging behavior, but she did know that eating more than she planned triggers a binge. If she went over her self-imposed calorie limit, she would then continue to eat until she was miserable.

I initially worked with Macy as I did with Tia: on self-reflection. Macy has more difficulty with this concept; she is less reflective by nature and she desires immediate benefits from her efforts to notice her behaviors, thoughts, and feelings. Frequently, she simply wanted advice on how to handle her most recent social crisis or she wanted reassurance that she is likeable. An opening into her social media life occurred at Macy's third session when she revealed that she posts selfies on Instagram each day. I wanted to determine her awareness about her reasons for this behavior, so I asked her to tell me about her experiences on Instagram. She said she posts to see if others like her selfies, often taking them down when she becomes anxious or doesn't get the desired responses. As we discussed this further, it became clear that Macy was aware that her use of social media exaggerates her insecurity about her looks. She was often overwhelmed with anxiety over how others perceive her and her thoughts were dominated by her comparisons of herself with others She spent her weekdays binging and worrying about the upcoming weekend events, and her weekends were spent going to parties that often lead to behaviors she later regretted. Macy's self-destructive behaviors represent her deeper struggles with identity as she tried to fit into her new environment. Transition periods are risky times for the development or intensifying of eating disorders because the young person is working mightily to adjust to new demands without sufficient insight and skill to handle the challenges. If Macy could develop a sense of who she is, she would be less dependent on others for self-definition and approval.

The therapeutic use of selfies can enhance self-knowing by facilitating insight into the self. Through selfie images, clients can see themselves from an external perspective and can interact with the images at their own pace and open an inquiry into what they are attempting to communicate. Perhaps most importantly, selfies can allow a person to document their identity without the influence of others. In selfies, clients are simultaneously the photographer, the subject, and the viewer of the image and thus can speak from all three perspectives. Selfies free people to speak about themselves indirectly, to speak of their feelings about the selfie or even feelings of the person in the image rather than about themselves directly. Selfies can empower a person to take ownership of who they are as they move from this more distanced third person perspective to the more personal first person perspective as they become ready.[18] Macy's photo therapy sessions with selfies consisted of two parts: self-initiated selfies and, later, a selfie assignment.

Self-Initiated Selfie Images

Macy has literally thousands of images on her phone, many of them selfies she has taken while alone or with others. When asked to choose one that speaks to who she is, she picked an image she recently took while alone in her apartment. It is similar to many of the other selfies Macy has on her phone: a headshot of her smiling while looking directly into the camera. But this image is different from many others that represent her trite, disheveled look. It is not the selfie itself nor even the specific questions asked by the therapist that are important, but rather the meaning of the image in the client's mind that stirs the thoughts and feelings.

Selfie images have the capacity to reveal uncomfortable thoughts and emotions that confront the usual self-presentation, so begin this work from a safer perspective by discussing the creation of the image with questions such as: *What was it like to plan this selfie? What did you caption it with? How did you choose which version to post? Did it come out like you wanted? What do you like about this selfie?* Macy took the selfie that she thought best represented who she was one day after completing a class presentation. She felt good about how the presentation went, so she took it to post, along with comments about doing well on the presentation and being glad it was over, on Instagram. She was uncertain why she chose this selfie. She commented that she didn't look fat in this one, like she thought she did in some of the others, but still, she had a hard time deciding which one she liked best. She finally picked one at random because she was not happy with any of them.

Tell me a story about this person. "Well this girl is a mess. She hates the way she looks most of the time and feels pretty awkward. She is very competitive, even with her friends, mostly about wanting to be smaller than everyone and getting attention from guys. If she is bigger than her friend, she thinks she needs to lose weight. Winning would be losing weight, but then that would make others feel bad if she is smaller. She is always thinking about losing weight or what she will eat. She's too big and not pretty enough."

What's this selfie saying? "This is kinda me. I tried to look really good for my presentation, but I still didn't feel that great about how I looked. So why bother?"

What does she want? "For everyone to like her. I want to know a lot of people, so I go out every chance I get. And I've made some friends this semester, but if there's drama in my friend group, I think I have to fix it. If someone gets mad at me, I feel like I'm the one who needs to apologize quickly because I want to end it. Even if they're in the wrong, I don't like the tension, so I say it's my fault just to end it."

Where does that register in your body? "Right in here (pointing to her stomach). It feels awful. I know I'm right, but I give in. It's like letting someone else win, and they keep expecting that you'll always give in to them."

Notice how Macy automatically shifted from speaking in third person to first person as the conversation evolves, enabling her to own her thoughts and feelings. I gleaned a truer picture into Macy's unconscious thoughts and desires than she had been able to express up to this point. She continued to discuss how she suppresses her feelings to gain approval from others. Macy was acting as a people pleaser, passive and unassertive with others but angry at herself and others afterwards. Much of her binge eating occurred when she felt angry. She shared more about her negative body image and the importance she places on physical looks. She wanted to enjoy her college years, but she thought she could only feel good if she were thinner. She also placed high importance on having a boyfriend, believing that males will find her attractive only if she is very fit. Her acceptance of herself was based on her evaluation of her body. It is noteworthy that Macy's chosen selfie cut off all of her body, from the very top of her shoulders down. This pattern repeats in many of her later selfies, indicating a disconnect from her body.

As therapy progressed in subsequent sessions, Macy's selfies provided prompts to explore an inner world she has been blocking out with binging. We explored her desire for approval from others, personified by poor decisions that continue to put her at risk. During her first semester of college, Macy began drinking and using marijuana. It was a rare weekend, beginning on Thursday afternoon, that she did not abuse these substances. Up to 50% of those with eating disorders abuse alcohol or illicit drugs, and they are five times more likely to do so than the general population.[19] Macy admitted that she drinks or smokes to calm herself before going into social situations and usually blacks out at least one night each weekend. For the next few days she is extremely anxious as she tries to recount the events of that evening. Thoughts that she might have said or did something that will come back to haunt her produces a state of heightened anxiety.

Macy had little desire to change her use of substances due to her fear that she will no longer fit in with her friend group because using substances is at the core of their activities. On a few occasions, she declined to go out with them and ended up binging to try to calm her feelings of isolation. Macy was caught between two extremes—partying with her friends and isolating herself and risking binging. Macy continued to bring selfies into sessions, and we used these to explore her inner world. Her selfie images elicit feelings in sessions as she responds to questions such as: *How is this selfie feeling? What does this selfie want to be feeling?* and *What does this selfie bring up for you?* Macy's reflections built her awareness of emotions and helped her express her internal state, allowing her to integrate the emotions into her narrative and to develop calming skills to manage her turbulent emotions. Macy also responded well to visualization exercises and reaching out to a few trusted friends when she feels the urge to binge.

At the two-month mark of treatment Macy continued to occasionally binge in response to disturbing social situations, whether they occurred on social media or in person. In one instance a friend ignored her on social media, and she noticed that she felt competitive with this friend and binged later that evening. Another time, as she sat with some friends at a coffee shop reminiscing about a recent night out, they began to look at group selfies posted on Instagram. Macy fell back into the habit of comparing her appearance with her friends, which stirred up feelings of anxiety and a subsequent binge when she returned to her apartment. Both of these instances align with a 2018 research study by Saunders and Eaton [20] that found in-person and social media comparisons to be a hinderance to recovery from eating disorders. The majority of participant comparisons in this study consisted of comparisons to the eating disordered self, peers, and social media images. Participant photography and interviews were used by the researchers to learn about social and cultural influences on eating disorder recovery. The Saunders and Eaton study highlights the utility of bringing social media material into the session to address social comparison as clients are engaging in this online behavior anyway. Most clients continue to use social media during the recovery process despite the risks, and by openly talking about the images, we can guide social media use to promote recovery.

Whenever Macy pulled up a selfie, I asked her questions to help her analyze her images for unconscious motives for taking the image. We developed a title for this activity: *Today's Selfie Says. . . .* Some of the most effective questions included: *When you took this selfie, whom did you unconsciously take it for? How did you want them to react to it? What's the message in this selfie? What would you want to ask this person in the selfie? What do you like about this image? Where in your body do you register the feelings you get in viewing this selfie? Is this the real you in this selfie? If yes, how so?* or *If not, how is it not?* These questions help the therapist and the client gain access to the client's inner world, allowing them to learn a great deal from these sessions. More importantly, the client's self-awareness expands as they connect their story about the selfie to their internal reactions.

As Macy gained awareness of her motivation for positive self-presentation, she began to question her enmeshment with selfie images. She changed her social media presence as a result of her new awareness, and these changes have led her to initiate other changes in her relationships with self and with others. As she becomes less dependent on others for validation, she gains confidence in herself and she begins to accept herself in ways she had previously thought impossible.

One day Macy arrived with a story about a friend's suggestion that they post a swimsuit image to see how many people would respond to their selfie. Macy's newfound awareness of the negative consequences of posting to see if others affirm her posts led her to decline to do this with her friend. She told her friend about her struggle with posting for likes and how this type of behavior triggers negative self-evaluations of her appearance. Macy also now recognizes that her desire for popularity and to know a lot of people allows others take advantage of her. Some of the people she worked so hard to impress were more interested in what she could provide them with than in the friendship itself. Setting boundaries has become easier for her, and now she deepens her relationships with trusted friends. This growth in boundary setting and communication skills produce feelings of empowerment.

However, Macy still struggled with social media use, so she agreed to experiment with ceasing to post images on Instagram for one week. Not thinking about taking selfies reduced her anxiety and she felt better about herself in the absence of the constant check-ins to see how others had responded to her posts. Tempted to post at a party one evening, Macy was able to recall her desire not to go back to old habits. She recognizes how these behaviors impact her mood and trigger unhealthy thoughts and desire for affirmation.

Selfie Homework Assignment

For this selfie assignment, Macy was asked to take a selfie that reflects *the me I am today*. At the time of the assignment, she was almost four months into her treatment, and she reported that she had just completed her first week with no binging since the beginning of her treatment. We used the selfie Macy took to help her see how her presentation of self is changing. Prior to therapy, Macy was more concerned about being what others needed her to be rather than being her authentic self. Taking selfies and then exploring them in session has prompted Macy to reflect on her inner self. She was learning to identify hidden messages or scripts that have led her to place expectations on herself for how she "should" act or "ought" to look. She was questioning the messages that tell her to strive for self-perfection, yet there was still an element of perfectionistic thinking in her self-presentation in this selfie.

The selfie Macy created for the assignment was different in several ways from any she had previously brought to our sessions. Most noticeably, this selfie showed most of her body, not just the floating head that was typical of her prior images. My comment on this brought a smile to her face and she explained that she was trying to be more comfortable with her body instead of trying to control it because controlling it has not worked so well for her.

What would this selfie say if it could talk? "I'm tired of spending so much time focusing on my weight and believing I have to be thinner to enjoy myself. I want to be more independent, so I don't give in just to have people around." *What would this selfie say to the very first one you showed me?* Macy laughed and said, "Girl, you're a hot mess." *What does this selfie not show?* "That it took me a long time to take this one. I wanted to show myself that I could be okay with showing my whole body, but I had to take it a bunch of times. Guess I'm not completely there yet, but I'm more okay with myself than I was."

Social media use can be damaging to those susceptible to cultural messages that place an overvaluation on weight and shape. Manipulating images and investing in appearance comparisons and conversations are associated with greater body and weight concerns.[23] Just as there is a trend on social media sites away from posting flawless selfies in idealized settings toward more naturally posed selfies of mundane activities, perhaps there will also be a trend away from photo manipulation. For now, Macy sees the value in changing her habits, but she has resumed posting on Instagram. Like many in her age group, she feels that being absent from this online space is the equivalent of going into the witness protection program: You no longer exist.

While Macy's and other cases described in this book illustrate pieces of the dialogue that occur around photo therapy techniques, photographic images can also inspire a "deep nonverbal dialogue" that allows the unconscious to speak the truth.[22] Turning the camera on oneself allows one to contact the self in powerful ways that further self-exploration. And a person must explore the self to recover from an eating disorder. Incorporating other therapeutic strategies, such as journaling, are helpful with assisting clients in the exploration of unconscious material. Printing selfies and using them with journal entries can facilitate further processing of expression of self. When self-image and identity are strengthened, lasting recovery from an eating disorder is possible.[23]

Macy continues to grow in her sense of herself as she gains self-awareness of the unconscious motives that drive her behaviors. Congruence between conscious and unconscious aspects of self is key to emotional well-being.[24] The day she stopped using alcohol and marijuana to lower social anxiety and to mitigate her obsessive thoughts was a turning point in her healing process. As she developed healthy coping strategies and honed her social skills without the crutch of substances, Macy blossomed. When we ended treatment she had ceased bingeing, but she continued to use social media with her new awareness of her unconscious motivations.

Therapists use transitional objects with clients to represent the therapeutic connection and help them stay in touch with the positive changes they are working to maintain. Objects such as rocks, quotes, or other symbolic items that hold meaning for the client are frequently employed as transitional objects. In our final session, Macy told me that she sometimes looks back over the selfies that we talked about in session and is reminded of the goals we set and her commitment to live a binge-free life. Selfies or other client images are potent reminders of growth and newly acquired self-awareness. Selfies are infused with immense emotional power to benefit the client's emotional well-being. By extending the positive relationship with the self into the physical form, selfies provide proof of the progress made in therapy.

The power of selfies to harm sense of self lies partly in the ready audience, waiting to confirm or deny acceptance with the touch of a finger. The next chapter will examine how this audience impacts identity formation now that social networks have expanded into the social-media arena. Group membership in the social media age brings surprising changes along with inherent challenges.

REFERENCES

1. Twenge, J. M., Konrath, S., Foster, J. D., Campbell, W. K., & Bushman, B. J. (2008). Further evidence of an increase in narcissism among college students. *Journal of Personality, 76*(4), 919–927.

    Twenge, J. M., & Foster, J. D. (2010). Birth cohort increases in narcissistic personality traits among American college students, 1982–2009. *Social Psychological and Personality Science, 1*(1), 99–106.

2. Fox, J., & Rooney, M. C. (2015). The dark triad and trait self-objectification as predictors of men's use and self-presentation behaviors on social networking sites. *Personality & Individual Differences, 76*, 161–165.

3. Panek, E. T., Nardis, Y., & Konrath, S. (2013). Mirror or megaphone?: How relationships between narcissism and social networking site use differ on Facebook and Twitter. *Computers in Human Behavior, 29*(5), 2004–2012.

4. Wickel, T. M. (2015). Narcissism and social networking sites: The act of taking selfies. *The Elon Journal of Undergraduate Research in Communications*. Retrieved from https://www.elon.edu/docs/e-web/academics/communications/research/vol6no1/01WickelEJSpring15.pdf

5. Barry, C. T., Doucette, H., Loflin, D. C., Rivera-Hudson, N., & Herrington, L. L. (2015). Let me take a selfie: Associations between self-photography, narcissism, and self-esteem. *Psychology of Popular Media Culture*. Retrieved from doi:10.1037/ppm0000089

    Sorokowski, P., Sorokowska, A., Oleszkiewicz, A., Frackowiak, T., Huk, A., & Pisanski, K. (2015). Selfie posting behaviors are associated with narcissism among men. *Personality and Individual Differences, 85*, 123–127.

    Weiser, E. B. (2015). #Me: Narcissism and its facets as predictors of selfie-posting frequency. *Personality and Individual Differences, 86*, 477–481.

6. Titlow, J. P. (2013). #Me: Instagram narcissism and the scourge of the selfie. Retrieved from http://readwrite.com/2013/01/31/instagram-selfies-narcissism/

7. Bansal, A., Garg, C., Pakhare, A., & Gupta, S. (2018). Selfies: A boon or bane? *Journal of Family Medicine and Primary Care, 7*(4), 828–831.

8. Pelham, B. W., Carvallo, M., & Jones, J. T. (2005). Implicit egotism. *Current Directions in Psychological Science, 14*(2), 106–110.

9. Bosson, J. K., Brown, R. P., Zeigler-Hill, V., & Swann, W. B., Jr. (2003). Self-enhancement tendencies among people with high explicit self-esteem: The moderating role of implicit self-esteem. *Self and Identity, 2*(3), 169–187.

10. Ridgeway, J., & Clayton, R. B. (2016). Instagram unfiltered: Exploring associations of body image satisfaction, Instagram #selfie posting, and negative romantic relationship outcomes. *Cyberpsychology, Behavior, and Social Networking, 9*(1), 2–7.

11. Chen, Y., Mark, G., & Ali, S. (2016). Promoting positive affect through smartphone photography. *Psychology of Well-Being, 6*(8). doi:10.1186/s13612-016-0044-4

12. MacNicol, G. (2015). Why selfies are good for girls. *Elle.* Retrieved from http://www.elle.com/life-love/a29197/why-selfies-are-good-for-girls/

13. Sontag, S. (1977). *On photography.* New York, NY: Picador.

14. Cozolino, L. (2017). *The neuroscience of psychotherapy: Healing the social brain* (3rd ed.). New York, NY: Norton & Company.

15. Swann, W. B., Jr., & Bosson, J. K. (2010). Self and identity. In S. T. Fiske, D. T. Gilbert & G. Lindzey (Eds.), *Handbook of social psychology* (pp. 589–628), Hoboken, NJ: John Wiley & Sons.

16. Cozolino, L. (2017). *The neuroscience of psychotherapy: Healing the social brain* (3rd ed.). New York, NY: Norton & Company.

17. Hudson J. I., Hiripi E., Pope H. G., Jr., and Kessler R. C. (2007). The prevalence and correlates of eating disorders in the National Comorbidity Survey Replication. *Biological Psychiatry, 61*(3), 348–58.

18. Weiser, J. (1999). *PhotoTherapy techniques: Exploring the secrets of personal snapshots and family albums.* Vancouver, BC: Judy Weiser and PhotoTherapy Centre Publishers.

19. The National Center on Addiction and Substance Abuse (CASA) at Columbia University. (2003). *Food for thought: Substance abuse and eating disorders.* Retrieved from https://www.centeronaddiction.org/addiction-research/reports/food-thought-substance-abuse-and-eating-disorders

20. Saunders, J., & Eaton, A. A. (2018). Social comparisons in eating disorder recovery: Using PhotoVoice to capture the sociocultural influences on women's recovery. *International Journal of Eating Disorders*, 51(12), 1361-1366.

21. McLean, S. A., Paxton, S. J., Wertheim, E. H., & Masters, J. (2015). Photoshopping the selfie: Self photo editing and photo investment are associated with body dissatisfaction in adolescent girls. *International Journal of Eating Disorders, 48*(8), 1132–1140.

22. Nuñez, C. (2013). The self-portrait as self-therapy (p. 97). In D. Loewenthal (Ed.), *Phototherapy and therapeutic photography in a digital age* (pp. 95–106). New York, NY: Routledge.

23. The National Center on Addiction and Substance Abuse (CASA) at Columbia University. (2003). *Food for thought: Substance abuse and eating disorders.* Retrieved from https://www.centeronaddiction.org/addiction-research/reports/food-thought-substance-abuse-and-eating-disorders

24. Wilson, T. D. (2002). *Strangers to ourselves: Discovering the adaptive unconscious.* Cambridge, MA: Harvard University Press.

Chapter 9

SOCIAL MEDIA AND
GROUP MEMBERSHIP

I don't even remember the season. I just remember walking between them and feeling for the first time that I belonged somewhere.

—Stephen Chbosky, from *The Perks of Being a Wallflower*

The need to be loved and to belong is embedded the neural architecture of us all, so much so that each of us develops socially and emotionally only through interactions with others. Without social connections, we wither in all domains: physical, emotional, and cognitive. Connections with others shape the mind and the sense of self. It is within relationships that we learn indispensable skills such as attunement, reciprocation, and empathy. Relationships can be an invaluable tool in our pursuit of self-knowledge. Our sense of self originates from interactions and acceptance from others.[1] The need to fit in with others is so great that the fear of psychological or social death, no longer being known or accepted by others, holds primacy for all. Belonging confers a sense of identity as a person identifies with others, and associations with valued groups boost one's feelings of self-worth.[2]

Group membership can be based on anything from team affiliation, religious beliefs, and cultural identity to physical appearance and interests; people prefer to surround themselves with others who have similar views or traits.[3] Groups form when people assemble to share common interests, but proximity, once heavily influential, no longer limits group membership. Technology is changing the very landscape of social interaction as groups now affiliate with little need to be in the same locale. With 24-hour access to group communication, social media expands options for group affiliation and creates a forum for disseminating information about the self. Most notably, social media sites capitalize on the social nature of humans by providing a virtual space to hang out, interact with others, and even attain a sense of belonging.

The growing number of users on social media platforms attests to their popularity. In 2005, only 5% of Americans used social media.[4] By 2018, 88% of 18- to 29-year-olds were using social media, and most users visit social media sites every day.[5] Sharing images and connecting with friends through social media is the norm, especially for those who spent their formative years socializing on this medium. Social media use is almost universal among teens, with 95% of 13- to 17-year-olds having access to a phone.[6] As communication patterns and locations morph, many experts worry that young people are being negatively impacted by dependence on social media and that they are not being exposed to the types of social experiences that build the skills required to interact with others in real life.

SOCIAL DEVELOPMENT ON SOCIAL MEDIA

Indirect communication through social media erects a barrier to the type of communication that humans are hardwired to thrive on. In the absence of direct interactions, it is no longer possible to rely on subtle facial expressions, body language, or the fine sense of attunement to read others. Throughout life, our brains rely on social experiences to develop neural complexity that promotes these social competencies. Many young people who have spent more time with screens than in face-to-face social interactions have not learned to interpret the subtle visual cues that promote social competency. Miscommunication through text or social media is common even for those who have developed social competencies because without the cues that would be present in direct spoken language, meaning is confounded. Autocorrect and punctuation errors often bring humor to online interactions, but the detrimental effects of learning relationship skills online are more profound. Learning to make and maintain relationships requires practice; it is emotionally risky to say what you think and manage disagreements.

According to Catherine Steiner-Adair, a psychologist and author of *The Big Disconnect*,[7] the distance provided by social media does not provide the same type of learning experience as does face-to-face communication. Without the give-and-take of live communication, it is difficult to gauge how others are reacting to our words. The asynchronous nature of social media also allows more time to ponder a response, so many young people are not versed in how to carry on a conversation in real time. They do not have the ability to hold a conversation. Steiner-Adair states that many young people today find talking to someone on the phone too intense because they get little practice in talking directly to others.

Although teens still sometimes meet face-to-face at parks, malls, and coffee shops, social media is now the preferred hangout location. Media expert, danah boyd, observed and interviewed teens around the country to better understand their networked lives. She learned that social media functions much like the hangouts of previous generations by enlarging their social world beyond the home and providing a public space to socialize informally with peers out of eyesight of parents and others.[8] Today's teens and college students are the first generation to have moved the majority of their peer group interactions online, and they are navigating new pathways for how to move between the various groups to which they belong.

For those in their twenties who have moved on from age-segregated schooling for the first time, social media can be a lifeline for keeping in touch with friends who no longer live close by. Forming new relationships can be uniquely challenging for these young adults. Many people in this generation freelance or work from home, so they do not have regular contacts that might develop into friendships. Up to this life stage, many belonging to this generation always had access to same age peers and institutions that placed them contact with similar individuals. Once this is no longer the case, they may struggle to develop new relationships. Identities formed in high school may be based on activities they no longer engage in, as we saw with Macy in the last two chapters, and, like Macy, they may be ill equipped to build new relationships. Young and old alike are increasingly turning to social media to fulfill needs for connection, making it mandatory that we better understand the interface between this new medium and the attainment of belonging and connection.

Social interactions are both streamlined by and complicated by the mass adoption of social media. Young people today have larger social networks than any previous generation. Yet they are also presented with challenges that arise from near constant contact, intense pressure to present idealized versions of themselves, and fear of missing out on nonstop group interactions. They often equate social media likes with acceptance and lack of likes with rejection. Prior to the invention of social media, many of these same issues existed, albeit in different ways. Social media is also distinct from previous ways of communicating in that each person can potentially communicate with anyone in the world and with any group as a whole. Receiving comments or feedback from others is unlimited. There is simply so great an exchange of information with others that many feel paralyzed by the deluge.

Because group membership has moved into the online arena, young people today are constantly privy to 24-hour status updates on social media, and they feel pressure to respond to group posts immediately. This 24/7 activity leads some to fear turning off their phone to sleep, afraid they will be left out. Clients tell me that they are afraid they will be forgotten or pushed out of a group if they are not constantly present on social media. They seem to recognize that this way of interacting reflects a short attention span, and they do not want to fall off the radar of their peers. Social interaction has become an increasingly exhausting chore.

As therapists, we are seeing the effects of social media on those who enter our offices with their vast array of complaints. Common themes emerge as we attempt to unravel the layers of their experiences. Young people today have real time knowledge of what their peers are doing at any given moment, and they're receiving images and messages of activities they are not included in, all the while anxiously monitoring their own posts and photos to see how others react. Most of their online interactions are via visual images, thus bombarding them with others' images.

I learn a great deal about social media from my clients, who are often simultaneously uneasy about their social media experiences while also drawn to its powers. Sara, a 14-year-old first-generation teen whose parents emigrated from Mexico to the United States before her birth, is typical of these young clients. Although she was considered one of the more popular girls at her middle school and was active on Instagram and Snapchat, she felt disconnected and lonely. Heavily involved in the extracurricular activities of cheerleading and sports, she was overscheduled during the school term, but at the same time worried that she would have nothing to do over the upcoming summer. Most of her friends lived too far away to walk to one another's houses, not that their parents would allow it, and their parents were busy with work, so these middle-schoolers were stuck at home alone during the summer. Sara's story is illustrative of the relationship between social media and the desire to feel a sense of belonging to a peer group or crowd during middle school, a time when peer relationships intensify and the desire to belong peaks.

GROUP MEMBERSHIP AND IDENTITY

The power of the group to shape individual identity cannot be underestimated, for it is the group that provides the basis upon which social status is gauged. During adolescence, dependence on peers intensifies, as teens' emotional dependence on their parents lessens. Demands for autonomy increase during this stage; while teens are concurrently dealing with rapid changes in the brain as well as the body, leaving them unmoored from the known world of childhood and not yet ready to enter the world of adulthood. Affiliation with others who are going through similar trials can explain adolescents' preoccupation with peers at this life stage.[9] These relationships broaden the context for entertainment, support, and connection beyond the family. Friendships come to play a key role, and central to these friendships are the larger groups or crowds in which they reside.

More so than in any other stage of life, the group to which a teen belongs confers identity. The search for identity occurs in the social domain of peers and is based on validation from others for conformity or nonconformity to norms set forth by the group. Membership in these larger crowds signals social status and identity,[10] much as it has in past generations. Belonging to a group enhances a member's belief that membership makes them distinct from those who do not belong. When comparing their own group to other groups, there is a tendency to view their group more positively than other groups, a sense of us versus them.

Group membership also reduces uncertainty as the thoughts, feelings, and behaviors of self and others are categorized based on stereotypes of the group.[11] Although she cannot substantiate the source of her anxiety, Sara feared her membership in the popular crowd was tenuous. Making the cheer squad and sports teams tends to ensure popularity in her school, but Sara felt that other girls get more attention than she does and are included in outside activities more often than she is.

Unquestionably, group images on social media exhibit who holds membership. Social media provides the stage for identity construction because this is now where the social group confers membership and approval. Connecting and sharing of experiences are the social demonstrations of group meaning and membership. While this is alienating to nonmembers as well as to group members who were not present at a particular time, it serves as a bonding experience for those depicted in the images. With social media, who a person is or what they do is of no consequence unless it is made apparent to others.[12] During my time teaching and traveling abroad with university students, I was intrigued by their focus on capturing and posting images of each group activity. As the semester progressed and smaller crowds formed within the larger group of students, it was evident that their social media images served to bond them to one another and to cement their group identity. Some of these students spoke of the challenges of taking images to post on social media and of how to caption their images. They want to adhere to the group standards while also expressing their individuality in ways that will result in positive responses from others.

End of term projects for a course titled *Social, Group, and Personal Identity Across Cultures* this same semester reflected the visual nature of this generation in that all students included selfies and group images in their identity projects; all of the students were heavily influenced by the format of social media, Instagram and Facebook in particular. As these students reflected on identity development, they communicated in the most tangible medium for their generation: "communal photographic exchanges that mark their identity as interactive producers and consumers of culture."[13] Social media has birthed a visual language in which the images themselves speak much louder than the minimal text that accompanies them.

As social media becomes the dominant means of communicating, there is a reciprocal process in which we divulge more and more of ourselves through this medium and are influenced by what is returned via the same medium. Although most social media sites have privacy settings that enable the user to choose who can view their content, the default settings offered on some sites may cause some users to inadvertently expose personal information if they are careless or don't understand the importance of protecting personal contact details. Some parents are aware of the risks and allow their teens to have public profiles anyway, while other parents are unaware that their teens even have public accounts. Sites like Instagram and Twitter offer users the option to convert their private account into a public account, which gives the user access to an important digital popularity score: how many followers they have. Having a public account and a large following is a status symbol in the teen world. The social arena in which identity is constructed has expanded beyond the people these teens know personally.

Identity is ever evolving as young people fashion and re-fashion their online identities. One researcher aptly described the staging of the teen self on social media as an "identity project, . . . dynamically changing and constantly on display."[14] For many, this project is agonizing because they seek to control a social institution they do not fully understand. When young people post on social media, they are traversing both public environments and more intimate contexts. What they post to appear cool to their peers can be offensive to family or other adults. Demonstrating interest in a particular activity or topic can backfire if others in their crowd do not approve, and posts are easily taken out of context. Social media requires that individuals be constantly aware of diverse and incompatible audiences, a skill most young people are not equipped to handle.

CONNECTION ON SOCIAL MEDIA

An insatiable drive to be in contact with peers is a hallmark of adolescence that has changed little across time. However, the mass adoption of social media has altered how, when, where, and how often adolescents communicate. As more communication transpires online, there is less participation in face-to-face relationships. Jean Twenge, a psychologist whose research focuses on teens who have grown up with social media, cites downward trends in the amount of time that today's teens spend simply hanging out with friends. High school seniors in 2015 went out less than 8th graders did in 2009, and the number of teens who spend time hanging out with friends everyday declined by over 40% from 2000 to 2015.[15] Most young people today say they would rather use social media than talk face-to-face. Sara, like most of her friends, is frequently exchanging messages and images with a specific boy from school. The use of the term *talking* is a curious choice for a generation that prefers texting to actual conversation. Social media expands the ability to *talk* to peers anytime and anywhere, even if they are rarely meeting in person.

Many adults believe that true social connection is not possible on social media, yet young people are drawn to these sites to socialize with friends, to meet new friends, and to get to know people better. They connect by joking with one another, flirting, gossiping, and sharing videos and memes, the same things teens of past generations did when they gathered in public spaces. Of teens who use social media, an overwhelming majority cite connection to friends' feelings and knowing what is going on in their friend's lives as benefits of social media. Nearly seven out of ten teens receive support on social media from friends when they are going through tough times.[16]

When Sara lost social media privileges due to sneaking her phone late at night, she found it difficult to know what to talk to her friends about at school the next day because she was not privy to the YouTube videos that circulated the previous evening. She was shocked at her difficulty connecting with people because she considers herself to be someone who can hold a conversation with her friends. Being in the know, being one of the first to know about things, leads to feelings of importance, so being on the outside of the group's jokes put Sara at a disadvantage. Teens want to be noticed by peers, and what better place to do so than a very public post? Belonging to a group is expressed through participation in group comments, so Sara again felt left out when she missed some drama in her social group.

A podcast from 2017 provides a window into the social lives of three adolescent girls as they explain the intricate social dance of their status updates.[17] These three friends, who recently transitioned into high school, describe the process they go through to post selfies of themselves and the rules of their crowd for responding to others' selfies. Most times, selfies are circulated through a friend group, to determine whether close friends respond positively to the image, before being posted on social media. Of course, the responses in these smaller groups are affirming because to respond otherwise would mean you're not being a good friend. These responses are similar to the ones the image will garner when posted to social media, short comments such as "you're so gorgeous," "perfect," or "you're the cutest," often in all caps and with lots of emojis. There are subtle differences in the language of responses that indicate the closeness of the relationship, although to an outsider the differences are indistinguishable.

These girls also know that response time is important; ten minutes is the limit for responding to a close friend's post. The number of likes and comments are closely watched to see the reaction of others, for the group rules stipulate that close friends must comment on every selfie. A particular degree of social support is expected from friends, so being on social media at all times is important to live up to these social obligations. These girls admit to mindlessly scrolling through social media feeds and liking every image to fulfill this duty. They are image junkies whose tolerance is so high they no longer register what they are viewing. Yet, they also feel positive about responses to their own selfies, even with the knowledge that others are also liking all posts out of obligation. They understand that they must "promote" themselves and they use the term "relevant" to describe the goal of having people care about you and about what you are posting. They monitor what others post as well, to see what is termed the *whole social map*: the hierarchy of their social world and where everyone stands in relation to everyone else. In fact, they acknowledge that most of their social media time is spent analyzing and jockeying for social relevance.

Likes are the popularity contests of this generation in which people attempt to affiliate, compete with one another through comparison, and establish identity. Young people want to be accepted by their peers, but at the same time, forming a unique identity requires that a young person stand out or be set apart from peers. Posting is announcing their existence to the world, and the number of likes or comments demonstrates to others that they matter. Too few responses are sources of embarrassment. Social media epitomizes an approval dependent culture where identity verification is outsourced in a very public sphere and opportunities are manipulated to obtain feedback that reinforces the self-view.

Displaying symbols of identity through appearance and choosing who to interact with online are common strategies for obtaining verification. The number of social media views is so important that people will go to great lengths to surround themselves with those who will provide feedback that verifies what they consider important.[18] Another strategy involves using interpersonal prompts that lead others to respond in a manner consistent with one's self-views.[19] Because the means and methods of socializing now include tremendous visual content, posting certain types of selfies can be viewed as interpersonal prompts that nudge group members into providing verification. Those who receive verification of social identity as a group member feel a sense of belonging and self-worth,[20] but there is also a darker side to this pursuit.

Comparison is a natural part of identity formation as young people seek to define themselves based on how they measure up to others. It is through comparison that a young person judges their traits and abilities and sets expectations for how they desire to be. When used as motivation for positive change, comparison can have positive effect, but when social media assigns an explicit numerical valuation to people by tallying likes and comments, harmful beliefs about status can become solidified. A 2017 survey of university students found that believing that peers have more friends, even if this is not true, is harmful to mental health.[21] It seems relatively easy to misconstrue friendship when operating in the superficial social media realm. Beyond likes, social media makes it easy to compare one's own life unfavorably to friends' lives. Because social media posts are carefully curated highlights of life, viewing other people's posts undermines our self-satisfaction and happiness. Teens and young adults spend inordinate amounts of time planning how to present themselves on social media because they feel they must only post what makes them look good to receive positive comments. Social media seems to extend what is normally an adolescent obsession with making comparisons into subsequent life stages as well.

In independent cultures, such as the United States, people strive to outdo others and stand out from the crowd, thereby increasing the likelihood of comparison, but recently there has been a backlash against likes-counters on social media after ongoing concern that this feature contributes to technology addiction. In the spring of 2019, Instagram announced that they would be testing a version of the platform that focuses more on content by allowing likes to be seen only by the person who makes the posts. While it is still too early to see if social media platforms will adopt these types of changes, the move demonstrates a recognition of the vicious cycle of comparison entrenched in this practice. It also remains to be seen whether these sites can survive this type of change, considering getting approval from others in the form of likes and comments is a motivating factor for social media use in the first place.

SOCIAL MEDIA ADDICTION

Young people really don't have a choice of whether to be on social media because this is where friendships and connection now operate, but online interactions are different from real-life interactions, and to understand the psychology behind social media addiction, we must turn again to the like button. In a November 2017 interview, founding president of Facebook Sean Parker commented on the impetus behind the revolutionary experiment in social validation afforded by this button:

> *The thought process that went into building these applications, Facebook being the first of them, . . . was all about: "How do we consume as much of*

your time and conscious attention as possible?"... And that means that we need to sort of give you a little dopamine hit every once in a while, because someone liked or commented on a photo or a post or whatever. And that's going to get you to contribute more content, and that's going to get you... more likes and comments.... It's a social-validation feedback loop... exactly the kind of thing that a hacker like myself would come up with, because you're exploiting a vulnerability in human psychology.[22]

Social media likes exploit a social validation feedback loop by providing unpredictable feedback on posts. We are more motivated by feedback that isn't guaranteed, and every post has the potential to attract likes, comments, and shares. It is the social feedback mechanism that makes social media so addictive. Social rewards initiate the release of dopamine in the brain in response to attention or positive feedback from others. Even the anticipation of rewards can result in a flood of dopamine. A 2016 study published in *Psychological Science* found that the nucleus accumbens, a part of the brain's reward circuit, is activated when adolescents see large numbers of likes on their photos and that adolescents are more likely to click on an image that already has a high number of likes.[23] Validation from peers triggers the same dopamine release as chocolate, sex, and some drugs. Dopamine peaks also come from similarity to and comparison with admired others. Social media has the ability to produce unremitting dopamine highs, making addiction to it a real possibility.[24]

We know that anticipation of reward is so satisfying because expectancy triggers a release of anticipatory dopamine. Never sure of their own worth, users tend to go back to the social media platform to see if there are more likes or if someone has made a flattering comment. The intermittent reinforcement is what strengthens the behavior: one photo gets 50 likes and 15 positive comments whereas the next receives fewer than half those numbers. A person feels compelled to continue checking responses or to post another image. This behavior is especially addictive when it is used to relieve psychological pain.

Adam Alter, author of *Irresistible: The Rise of Addictive Technology and the Business of Keeping Us Hooked,*[25] believes that the potential for addiction is highest in young adulthood because young people are ill-equipped to handle the array of responsibilities this stage of life requires. When a young person feels overwhelmed by the tasks of becoming an adult, social media can seem like a solution to the psychological distress of uncertainty. Adolescents are also known to have high addiction rates because social media taps into a basic need for social bonding in a setting that also includes validation. It is not that people always prefer to spend their time on social media, but as more and more of our lives occur there and we are compelled by the need for connection, the risk of addiction to technology becomes more likely. Unfortunately, many social media users experience the opposite of connection when online communication is substituted for more traditional means of connection with others.

LONELINESS AND ANONYMITY IN AN ERA OF CONNECTIVITY

We are currently in what has been termed a loneliness epidemic, with those between the ages of 16 and 24 most likely to report feeling lonely.[26] Not only do these young people feel lonely, they also feel more intensely lonely than any other age group. Opportunities for interacting with others through social media are unprecedented, yet while this can promote connection, there is also acknowledgement that these relationships are distinct from those played out in more traditional contexts. Young people undeniably interact more frequently and with a greater number of peers today than in past generations, reflecting a shift from the smaller social networks of yesterday to mass connection. The days of talking to one peer at a time on the family phone or hanging out with a small friendship group have passed. Young people today are involved in multiple conversations simultaneously, scattered among various social media apps and social groups, all accessed from their phone.

Whether all of these types of interactions fulfill the same needs is uncertain. Whereas social connections are as necessary for survival as the more basic needs, some researchers have noted that true social connection has withered as technology use has grown. In this age of connectivity, young people can be disconnected from real friendships; they are unconnected in an always connected world. They may have thousands of friends on social media, but no one to share their innermost thoughts or activities with, no one who truly knows them.

Jean Twenge states that despite the promise of social media to connect us to friends, teens today are a lonely generation. Those who use social media daily but see their friends less frequently report the greatest feelings of loneliness. Twenge is shocked by the steady climb in rates of reported loneliness and depression among teens, a rise coinciding with the mass adoption of the smartphone, which has changed how teens interact socially. One trend in teen social life that Twenge finds particularly detrimental to mental health is increased awareness of being left out. This is not a new concern for teens; however, when today's teens do get together, they extensively document their experience on social media, leaving those not invited more aware than ever of being left out. Twenge finds this to be most true for females. Between 2010 and 2015, the number of girls reporting that they often felt left out increased by 48%.[27]

For young adults, social media use undermines social connection in much the same way. Facebook use among young adults has been associated with negative emotions and lower life satisfaction. More frequent social media use over time translates into steeper declines in overall mood and life satisfaction.[28] Lack of comments, likes, and feedback leaves social media users frustrated and lonely, but envy also plays a role in these negative emotional outcomes. Viewing images of others' travel and leisure activities and personal achievements can trigger envy.[29] Having superficial connections and idealizing others' lives do little to improve mental health. Despite technology that enables incessant contact and the potential to make new friends with little effort, the need to be intimately known is not being met through social media contact. The protective relationships that once allowed young people to explore while also remaining connected are endangered.

Loneliness is more likely to occur when sense of self is lacking. In contrast, a stronger sense of self can enable a person to tolerate aloneness, perhaps to even appreciate this time away from others to connect with and enjoy the self. The less connection a person has to their innermost true self, the greater their likelihood of suffering painful loneliness. When feeling empty and disconnected from inner life, people are more likely to seek attention and affirmation from others to validate their existence. Extreme desire for external validation arises from dissociation of inner thoughts, feelings, and values, but most social media users feel pressure to post content that will reap approval from others rather than content that authentically depicts who they are. Idealized versions of oneself do little to aid in the discovery of identity, which develops within both the social arena and the inner processes of self-exploration and growth. Finding balance between these domains can be challenging, especially for those who depend on others for validation. In the always-on realm of social media, many today have limited tolerance for the solitude that is necessary for development of sense of self.

Phone apps designed for anonymity have also appeared in recent years, in what technology developers believe is a backlash against the individuality-based social media outlets, such as Instagram and Facebook. Newer apps, such as Secret and After School, allow users to share their innermost thoughts with friends without revealing their identity. This supposedly allows users to be more emotionally vulnerable than they would be on other sites. These apps may provide the most accurate portrayal of relationship dynamics in an age where anonymity is necessary to allow self-awareness and vulnerability with friends. For those struggling with eating disorders, the mass culture of large groups and limited intimacy that epitomizes social media can be a minefield.

EATING DISORDERS AND CONNECTION

Eating disorders are typified by isolation and loss of connection to self and others. Sara was living a double life; trying to fit in with her crowd at school, while struggling in private with an eating disorder. Before coming to see me, she had lost 20 pounds over the past four months by doing what she calls "clean eating," cutting dairy and carbohydrates in an attempt to reshape her body to fit with how she viewed the other girls in her crowd. As an athlete, she was initially able to pass this behavior off as an attempt to boost her performance in sports. In the final weeks of her weight decline, Sara's parents began to express their concern to other family members and decided to seek treatment, an uncomfortable choice for a family that believes problems should stay within the family. When Sara's mother brought her to my office the first time, Sara said she was annoyed at her mother for making such a big deal because she is just trying to be healthy. It was only in the next few sessions, when Sara's mother was no longer present, that she shared her struggles with food, her body image, and her middle school social life.

In the social media age, group membership requires that a young person be ever present online, a taxing endeavor for a young person wrestling with body image distortions and a frequent desire to go unnoticed. A client may want to associate with like-minded individuals who are also engaging in disordered eating, while remaining secretive about the eating disorder with other peer groups. Walking a fine line to keep these parts of their life separate can further isolate the young person who needs a sense of congruence between who they really are and who they allow others to see.

Because social media groups overlap with one another and are more public than face-to-face groups, there is always the danger of information being leaked from one group to another. Most notably, young people today attempt to keep their peer group separate from family on social media by using different platforms. For example, they may have a Facebook account but no longer interact with friends through this site because they are connected there with adults as well. Instead they will use other platforms for posts that expressly target specific peer groups. This can backfire if information from one social group leaks into another. Sara's social groups consist of her long-term friends from elementary school, the cheer squad, and the sports teams to which she belongs. There is some overlap between these groups, but they follow one another on Instagram and use other apps for group chats. As she experimented with anorexic behaviors, she sought to identify with others on social media who shared the same desire for control and body perfection. On pro-ana sites, Sara gained a sense of comradery and found inspiration and advice, as well as emotional support for what she now called a lifestyle choice. She not only intensified her food restriction, she also began to identify as anorexic as she strove to win acceptance from this online community. Before long, she could no longer control her obsession with not eating. She spent most of her time scrolling through the profiles of those she followed and joining in these group conversations using a pseudonym to protect her identity.

Belonging to such groups can inspire extreme compliance with the norms and expectations of the group. Analyses of pro-ana sites shows that these sites promote group membership by defining how physical bodies are discussed. According to the authors of one study, "instead of being freed from the social meanings and constraints associated with physical bodies, much of the freedom gained in online interactions is the freedom to redefine selves and bodies in terms of prevailing norms around the culturally ideal body."[30] The thin ideal norm reinforces eating disorder related identities by espousing low body weight as a marker of success. As group identity in these types of settings become more important, other aspects of identity tend to decrease.[31] This put Sara in a bind; she was increasingly drawn to the pro-ana sites, but in spending more time interacting anonymously, she became more isolated from her school crowd. Exposed to pro-ED content, she also began to experiment with purging to compensate when she feels she has taken in too many calories. She feared she would never be able to attain the physical appearance she desired.

As we know, most social media interactions are conducted via visual images, thus bombarding Sara with carefully crafted images that overwhelm the fragile sensibilities of a person at war with her own body. What she sees when viewing these images originates from her own perceptions and, as such, reflects her own inner map for organizing and understanding self, the world, and others. Misinterpretations permeate the social media world in which Sara lives, and this barrage of images creates unrealistic ideals. Clients' reactions to viewed images relate to interpersonal processes and open the door to examining self in relation to others, a necessary process in the quest for identity.

REFERENCES

1. Anderson, S. M., & Chen, S. (2002). The relational self: An interpersonal social-cognitive theory. *Psychological Review, 109*(4), 619–645.

2. Swann, W. B., Jr., & Bosson, J. K. (2010). Self and identity. In S. T. Fiske, D. T. Gilbert & G. Lindzey (Eds.), *Handbook of social psychology* (pp. 589–628), Hoboken, NJ: John Wiley & Sons.

3. Hood, B. (2012). *The self illusion: How the social brain creates identity.* New York, NY: Oxford University Press.

4. Social Media Fact Sheet. (2019). Pew Research Center, Washington, D.C. Retrieved from https://www.pewinternet.org/fact-sheet/social-media/

5. Social Media Use in 2018. (2018). Pew Research Center, Washington, D.C. Retrieved from https://www.pewinternet.org/2018/03/01/social-media-use-in-2018/

6. Teens, Social Media, and Technology. (2018). Pew Research Center, Washington, D.C. Retrieved from https://www.pewinternet.org/2018/05/31/teens-social-media-technology-2018/

7. Steiner-Adair, C. (2013). *The big disconnect: Protecting childhood and family relationships in the digital age.* New York, NY: HarperCollins Publishers.

8. Boyd, D. (2014). *It's complicated: The social lives of networked teens.* New Haven, CT: Yale University Press.

9. Broderick, P. C., & Blewit, P. (2015). *The life span: Human development for helping professionals* (4th ed.). Upper Saddle River, NJ: Pearson.

10. Brown, B. B., Herman, M., Hamm, J. V., & Heck, D. J. (2008). Ethnicity and image: Correlates of crowd affiliation among ethnic minority youth. *Child Development, 79*(3), 529–546.

11. Burke, P. J., & Stets, J. E. (2009). *Identity theory.* New York, NY: Oxford University Press.

12. Lawler, S. (2014). *Identity: Sociological perspectives* (2nd ed.). Cambridge, UK: Polity Press.

13. van Dijck, J. (2008). Digital photography: Communication, identity, memory (p.63). *Visual Communication, 7*(1), 57–76.

14. Doster, L. (2013). Millennial teens design and redesign themselves in online social networks (p. 277). *Journal of Consumer Behaviour, 12*(4), 267–279.

15. Twenge, J. (2017). *iGen: Why today's super-connected kids are growing up less rebellious, more tolerant, less happy and completely unprepared for adulthood and what that means for the rest of us.* New York, NY: Atria Books.

16. Teens, Technology and Friendships. (2015). Pew Research Center, Washington, D.C. Retrieved

from https://www.pewinternet.org/2015/08/06/teens-technology-and-friendships/

17. Glass, I. (2017, December 14). 573: Status Update. This American Life. Podcast retrieved from https://www.thisamericanlife.org/573/transcript

18. Swann, W. B., Jr., & Pelham, B. W. (2002). Who wants out when the going gets good: Psychological investment and preferences for self-verifying college roommates. *Self and Identity, 1*(3), 219–233.

19. Burke, P. J., & Stets, J. E. (2009). *Identity theory*. New York, NY: Oxford University Press.

20. Stets, J. E., & Burke, P. J. (2000). Identity theory and social identity theory. *Social Psychology Quarterly, 63*(3), 224–237.

21. Whillans, A. V., Christie, C. D., Cheung, S., Jordan, A. H., & Chen, F. S. (2017). From misperception to social connection: Correlates and consequences of overestimating others' social connectedness. *Personality and Social Psychology Bulletin, 43*(12), 1696–1711.

22. Simple Fact (November 9, 2017). Sean Parker on Mark Zuckerberg and Facebook: You're exploiting vulnerability in human psychology. Interview retrieved from https://www.youtube.com/watch?v=D5-X915iKTc

23. Sherman, L. E., Payton, A. A., Hernandez, L. M., Greenfield, P. M., & Dapretto, M. (2016). The power of the like in adolescence: Effects of peer influence on neural and behavioral responses to social media. *Psychological Science, 27*(7), 1027–1035.

24. Prinstein, M. (2017). *Popular: The power of likability in a status-obsessed world*. New York, NY: Viking.

25. Alter, A. (2017). *Irresistible: The rise of addictive technology and the business of keeping us hooked*. New York, NY: Penguin Press.

26. 16- to 24-year-olds are the loneliest age group according to new BBC Radio 4 survey. (2018, January 10). Retrieved from https://www.bbc.co.uk/mediacentre/latestnews/2018/loneliest-age-group-radio-4
New Cigna Study Reveals Loneliness at Epidemic Levels in America. (2018, May 1). https://www.multivu.com/players/English/8294451-cigna-us-loneliness-survey/

27. Twenge, J. (2017). *iGen: Why today's super-connected kids are growing up less rebellious, more tolerant, less happy and completely unprepared for adulthood and what that means for the rest of us*. New York, NY, Atria Books.

28. Kross E., Verduyn P., Demiralp E., Park J., Lee D. S., Lin N., . . . Ybarra, O. (2013). Facebook use predicts declines in subjective well-being in young adults. *PLoS ONE, 8*(8): e69841. doi:10.1371/journal.pone.0069841

29. Krasnova, H., Wenniger, H., Widjaja, T., & Buxmann, P. (2013, February 27-March 1). *Envy on Facebook: A hidden threat to users' life satisfaction*. Paper presented at 11th International Conference on Wirtschaftsinformatik, Leipzig, Germany.

30. Riley, S., Rodham, K., & Gavin, J. (2009). Doing weight: Pro-ana and recovery identities in cyberspace (p. 349). *Journal of Community and Applied Social Psychology, 19*(5), 348–359.

31. Swann, W. B., Jr., & Bosson, J. K. (2010). Self and identity. In S. T. Fiske, D. T. Gilbert, & G. Lindzey (Eds.), *Handbook of social psychology* (pp. 589–628), Hoboken, NJ: John Wiley & Sons.

Chapter 10

BALANCING SOCIAL LIVES: USING VIEWED IMAGES FOR IDENTITY FORMATION

Fitting in is about assessing a situation and becoming who you need to be to be accepted. Belonging, on the other hand, doesn't require us to change who we are; it requires us to be who we are.

—Brené Brown

Feeling a sense of belonging while also establishing oneself as a separate and unique individual are central tasks of identity formation during adolescence and young adulthood. Authentic adulthood rests on self-differentiation, the interplay between autonomy and connection, wherein a young person is able to experience intimacy, connection, and belonging without losing a sense of who they are as an individual.[1] As you may recall, Sara was in the midst of her self-differentiation journey as she transitioned from middle school to high school while battling an eating disorder. With a social life that took place primarily on social media, Sara had to navigate a visual world that poisoned her search for identity.

Sara was nervous about therapy, so she requested that her mother be present in our first session; she seemed stifled by her mother's presence and only offered basic information about her school activities and friends. Sara's mother provided information about the family, which also includes Sara's two younger sisters, her father, and her large extended family. Sara clearly did not want to talk about her ongoing food restriction and the sole explanation she offered was that she was trying to avoid processed food to improve her performance in sports. She denied that her goal of clean eating was an issue and became tearful when her mother used the term *anorexic* to describe her, though she clearly met the criteria for that diagnosis. In a large study of 14- and 15-year-olds, those who practiced extreme food restriction similar to Sara's clean eating behaviors were 18 times more likely to develop an eating disorder than their peers who didn't diet.[2] The term *orthorexia* has been coined to describe an obsession with healthy eating that often leads a person to restrict foods deemed unhealthy, but orthorexia is not considered a formal diagnosis at this time.

When Sara came alone to her session the following week, she was more open about family pressure to excel in sports, at cheerleading, and at meeting her own self-imposed standards for perfection and food restriction. Sara expressed guilt for eating and a desire to lose weight because she thought she was bigger than her friends and a boy she liked. She hated the changes in her body had gone through since puberty and saw little reason to nourish "this ugly body." By describing her busy schedule of sports and cheer practice, she demonstrated that there was little time for anything else, but she said she liked it that way because she found it easier to control her eating when she was busy. When she arrived home in the evening, most of her time was spent in her room on social media. She was eager to show me some of the people she followed on Instagram, people who post about clean eating and working out. It is no wonder that she was consumed with body perfection, swimsuits, and defined abs.

Sara was prone to developing an eating disorder and to social media misuse. At times she was frustrated to the point of tears as she tried to express her thoughts and emotions with words, which did not come easily. She was not pleased to be in therapy nor that her family thought she had an eating disorder. Coming to therapy made her feel flawed and incompetent. Her perfectionism and desire for control led to conflict with her family over her refusal to eat, especially with her father, who thought her food rules were simply her way to control the family. If they went out to eat, Sara wanted to choose the restaurant. This dynamic was not new—since early childhood, Sara liked to follow a plan and would get upset when she made a mistake or when things did not go as she planned. Childhood traits like these are more common in those who later develop eating disorders:[3] up to 69% of those with anorexia and 33% of those with bulimia also have a diagnosis of obsessive–compulsive disorder.[4] Sara's parents expressed openness to exploring their family patterns once they recognized that Sara's need for order was in direct opposition to their own more laid back, even chaotic, style. Adolescence was a new parenting experience for Sara's very concerned parents, so we had frequent conversations about how they could support Sara's recovery.

One of the first changes that were made in Sara's home involved her social media use. In recent months, she began eating dinner alone in her room while using social media to connect online. She was allowed to skip family dinners because she was tired from her long days at school and she often did not want to eat what the rest of the family was having for dinner anyway. Unsurprisingly, Sara rarely ate the food she took into her room, preferring to dispose of it after her family went to bed. Her parents decided that she would return to the family dinner table so her food intake could be monitored. It turned out that Sara was not spending her evenings only with school friends on social media but also in anonymous interactions on an array of pro-ana sites. Although she was initially reluctant to change this behavior, she agreed to work with her viewed images from these sites to learn more about herself. Reactions to viewed images relate to both intrapersonal and interpersonal processes and thus provide an opportunity to examine oneself in relation to others. Photo therapy can be a potent means for helping a young person explore their own unique identity and their connection with others.

Changing unhealthy social media practices and giving up eating disorder behaviors are goals of therapy. Clients must explore alternative ways of being and be able to see for themselves that change is possible before they will commit to new ways of behaving. By exploring viewed images for hidden meaning, clients engage in the process of reframing values and beliefs to precipitate change. Those with eating disorders know that social media exerts a powerful influence on how they view themselves, yet ambivalence about change and fear of being left-out leads them to avoid confronting the behavior directly. The inner discord that arises from silencing this knowledge can be revealed when clients become aware of visual symbolic language that is repeatedly represented in the material they are choosing to view. Once the hidden meaning is decoded and brought to consciousness, images can be contemplated to learn what they are telling the client.[5] Bringing meaning out into the open exposes that which has been unconsciously censored.

PRO-EATING DISORDER IMAGES

Overt pro–eating disorder (pro-ED) sites on the Internet are now a thing of the past, yet newer manifestations of these models are now found on popular social media platforms that are easily accessed on a smartphone. Some sites, such as Instagram, have taken measures in recent years to curb pro-ED content, adding health warnings and making some terms unsearchable on its platform by banning hashtags such as #bulimia or #anorexia. But hashtags are a fluid creation, subject to the use of creative spellings, such as #thynspiration instead of #thinspiration or #thyghgapp instead of #thighgap, to evade attempts at moderation.[6] Social media sites insist that they are taking a stronger stance by including alternative spellings, but the issue is more complex.

A 2018 study found that users can evade hashtag policing by locating pro-ED content through other search methods, and site developers continually devise new ways to signal pro-ED content.[7] Many mainstream wellness communities contain pro-ED content that endorses extreme restriction even though the content may include seemingly healthy titles, such as clean eating, or various trendy diet plans, such as keto and paleo diets. Weight loss and the importance of being thin is the secret message many wellness communities communicate even if they no longer identify as pro-ED. In some ways, discerning the intent is more difficult than ever because what we eat has become a feature of identity on social media. Messages that what you eat and how you look reflect who you are abound on all social media platforms and intensify the identity formation process for those with the propensity toward disordered eating.

USING VIEWED IMAGES FOR INSIGHT

To learn more about a client's perspective, we must control our desire to convey our expert opinions on the dangers of pro-ED sites; we must allow them to show us what they are viewing without the fear of being wrong or judged. Asking the client to clarify what we are viewing together allows for deeper probing of the topic. I began this process with Sara by asking her questions about these sites from a beginner's viewpoint, that of an unenlightened adult. I asked her to explain the rules for interacting on these sites: who can post, how she found the people she follows, whether people can be blocked or denied access, and whether people use their real names. She immediately responded to these questions, becoming my tour guide to her social media, which then transitioned into her seeing the content from my perspective as well.

I asked her to describe what she was seeing as she looked at a particular image on her phone that I couldn't see sitting across from her. Sara described a post from a twenty-something woman who listed her food intake for the day and, more importantly to Sara, included an image of herself in a sports bra and shorts. I asked Sara to tell me a story about the person in this image, about her life and who she is. She began by telling me that she followed this person because she was beautiful and posted good workout plans. Obviously infatuated with the lifestyle that this young woman had created on social media, Sara told me that her life seemed perfect because she had worked hard to look the ways she does and now gets to enjoy the benefits. She said that this person was happy and had a great life.

Wanting to continue my unenlightened stance so Sara would continue to guide me through her social media world, I asked her if I could look at the image, and then I asked her where she was finding clues in the image that told her about this person's satisfaction. Sara described he woman's defined abs and artfully posed workout images as indicators that she has attained happiness. When I shared that I perceived this person differently, perhaps as someone who feels lonely due to her sole focus on goal attainment, and noted the lack of images that demonstrate connection, Sara had a surprising reaction. She tearfully shared that she did not feel close to anyone, not her friends nor her family. Not wanting to elaborate further, Sara stated that she didn't want to talk about this anymore. While this is a rather nonthreatening approach to broadening a client's view of reality, Sara was at an age when differences can seem insurmountable, and she likely felt some guilt about not feeling connected to her family. I affirmed her right to change the topic and offered her the chance to choose the topic.

At this invitation, Sara unexpectantly shared that she had started reducing her food intake to try to reverse or at least slow down all the changes in her body. Her breasts did indeed get smaller but then her stomach seemed to stick out further. She had difficulty identifying feelings directly, but she talked of her desire to taste food and to eat all she wants. The only time Sara felt calm and in control was when she restricted food, and she loved the head rush and feelings of being detached that she would get when she didn't eat. Sara's restricting usually followed a time of feeling swamped, often by social situations that occurred online. We discussed the codes, or rules, for social media and how she responds to viewing images. Increasing the client's awareness of the impact of viewing social media is foundational to altering its influence. Even though Sara has not committed to changing the disordered eating patterns at this point, she desired relief from anxiety, so my goal was to heighten her curiosity about the unconscious triggers for emotional avoidance that ensue when she has no words for her pain.

As clients learn to explore anxiety rather than shutting down and running from the discomfort, they are able to develop the ability to counterbalance the desire to escape. Putting feelings into words, coupled with relaxation training, stimulates neural integration, engendering increased affect tolerance and regulation so that as therapy progresses, the new narrative can be created.[8] Recovery requires a shift in the client's narrative from an eating disorder identity and their perceived membership in an elite group of those who are able to resist hunger to a broader conception of identity and belonging.

When Sara arrived at the next session she was noticeably calmer and more able to talk about the messages she receives on social media as well as her own food obsessions. She said that she keeps this part of her life secret from her friends, so she goes on healthy eating sites to interact with people who are like her. They regularly chat about how much weight they've lost by following a particular eating plan. She admitted that she tries to control her eating because it is the only thing she believes she can control, and then she explained why she was so upset when her mother called her anorexic: Sara began binging and purging shortly before beginning this treatment, and she felt like she failed at anorexia. In her eyes, learning to purge was a solution to loss of control with eating. By purging, she could get rid of calories when she overate, but she was distressed that she could no longer control her food intake. Although she was still severely underweight and wanted to continue clean eating, she also craved sweets and other denied foods. Because she feared that she wouldn't be able to stop eating if she started, she would not give herself permission to eat until her hunger overrode her ability to control her eating.

A few weeks after this session, Sara unexpectedly revealed to her parents that she wanted to start a YouTube channel where she could share fashion and makeup videos. When her mother frantically called to consult on this issue, we discussed the risks not only of creating the videos but also the potential for receiving damaging comments in response to her posts, and thankfully her parents rejected this idea; they were now savvier about the effects of social media on Sara's mental health. Later Sara agreed that looking at these types of sites trigger her body concerns, but she was only able to acknowledge this after she cooled down from not getting her way with her parents.

VIEWED IMAGES AND SELF-DIFFERENTIATION

As Sara's treatments continued, the photo therapy work with viewed images was interspersed with other therapeutic methods to address her eating disorder behaviors directly. For treatment to be effective, Sara needed a greater sense of self-differentiation, a term emanating from the family systems approach. Self-differentiation is the ability to balance closeness with others and autonomy, or individuality, to be able to distinguish one's own experience without undue outside influence.[9] As a primary aspect of identity development, the desire for self-differentiation surges in adolescence. Predictably, many people with eating disorders fear that in losing the eating disorder identity, they will no longer be set apart from others, but the eating disorder identity essentially signifies a lack of individuality, as it is characterized by conformity to prescribed cultural standards.

How people represent their individuality and social connection is evident in the images that result when people are instructed to take photographs that answer the question *Who are you?* Those who emphasize their personal identity produce images that exhibit greater individuality, self-directed values, and maturity, whereas those with low individuality produce images that reflect conformity to expected norms. Optimal human development occurs when individuality and connection are in balance.[10] Neither should be emphasized at the expense of the other. Self-differentiation within the context of relationship offers an experience of individuality and connectedness, separateness within nurturing relationship.

Social media does facilitate contact with others. Yet filtering the true self to create an online curated version does little to foster self-differentiation. With omnipresent camera phones, images are the new language for social interaction, and they have an unlimited potential to express individuality and creativity. Instead banal images that defy individuality by bowing to conformity have emerged. We see more and more of the same clichéd poses, appearances, and settings, and as these become more prevalent on social media, they define and shape how we see ourselves and others. Safety seems to lie in conforming to the expected images, so as not to be threatening, while also trying to set oneself only slightly apart or above to gain approval. A positive sense of self requires the autonomy to be who one is and the belief that one's individuality is valued.[11]

The images Sara viewed included the typical fare: those she followed in the wellness community, along with images from her social crowd. The content of these types of images is remarkably similar: young women posting images that signify status and attainment of physical perfection. While we viewed the images, I used questions to increase Sara's awareness of how the images were being perceived and interpreted. A later session with Sara, occurring in the fall after she started high school, illustrates this process. I asked her a series of questions as she scrolled through an endless stream of images of her social crowd.

What themes do you see repeated in these images? "Everyone wants to be the center of attention. They post selfies so everyone else will say all these nice things about them. The girls are talking about this banquet we're having. They're all obsessed with what dress to buy and who's going together. They're joking around about it, and all, but I think some of them are nervous about it too. They just don't want to show that part. You can't talk about being scared because you don't want to look like a baby or give people something to talk about."

What are the feelings shown in the images? "On the outside it's all fun and acting like everything is okay, but I think maybe that's just the way you have to be, like you feel more secure than you really are. I know some of my closer friends are worrying about how things are going to go. Guys are so immature— they say rude things, and everyone starts rumors, so you're afraid to say or do anything that might give everyone something to talk about. I don't know if my friends feel this way, but all this banquet stuff just makes me self-conscious about how I look. I want to eat healthy until then, so my stomach won't stick out in my dress."

What reactions are you having right now as you look at these images? "I don't feel too good about the way I look. A lot of my friends are really skinny, like this one here, so they look perfect in anything they wear. I like fashion, to put together outfits, but it all just doesn't fit for me."

How so? "Well, I don't look like they do no matter how hard I try. I hate that fact that I have all this fat."

Like most adolescents who want to fit in with peers, Sara had difficulty appreciating her uniqueness and was extremely hard on herself for not attaining her preconceived ideal weight, although she was still underweight. The self-conscious behaviors she described, typical as they are for this age, were driven by comparisons with others.

Conversations about viewed images naturally lead to working with clients to resist comparisons. Young people need to know that their own experiences have value and that when they enter into the comparison game, they are relinquishing the chance to gain knowledge of themselves as a distinctive individual. Cultivating an inner indicator of their own value necessitates a shift in social media habits. Likes and retweets are not the equivalent of worth, and profile browsing and following does little more than raise feelings of social anxiety. Peer comparison stems from feelings of inferiority and insecurity as perfect online lives are contrasted with a person's own imperfect real life. If a person chooses to respond by uploading their own carefully curated images in hopes of validation, the feedback loop of social anxiety is set in motion—cycling between seeking external validation and comparing self with others. As if this were not enough cause for social anxiety, they know that every pose and comment could become a permanent record on social media, there for all to see.

SELF-DIFFERENTIATION AND CONNECTION

Sara believed that she cannot be herself with her friends out of fear that they would negatively judge her for binging and purging, more shameful behaviors in her eyes than restricting, another measure for comparison among some of her peers.

How would you know if your friends were sharing some of these same feelings? "We talk about all the drama in our group, but I don't talk about trying to lose weight and would never want them to know I throw up. It's too embarrassing."

Nonetheless, Sara told me that her friendships were fine. She only saw a few friends at school due to differing schedules, and she expressed feeling let down by what she thought high school would be like. She said that the predominant types of social interaction are fake and dramatic. To Sara, everyone else seemed to be having fun, but she felt a sense of disconnection. Unless she initiated an activity outside of school, her friends seemed content to interact only on social media. This style of communication was evidently not fulfilling Sara's need for deep connection and engagement. If others didn't reciprocate her attempts to plan activities, Sara questioned her value in her peer group. The level of loneliness Sara was experiencing exacerbated her eating disorder, depression, and anxiety as she turned her attention to social media groups that reinforce harmful standards of female appearance.

Addressing loneliness is a paramount mental health intervention in our always connected, yet socially disconnected society. Loneliness is typified by the feelings of distress that arise when a person perceives that their social needs are not being met, especially the quality of social relationships.[12] As a social risk factor, loneliness is linked with stress, anxiety, anger, depression, and even suicide. These risks emanate from the sense of personal threat that loneliness engenders. Lonely people perceive the social world as unsafe, so they become hyper vigilant in social interactions, expecting that the exchanges will be negative. They pay more attention to negative signals from others and perceive rejection where it is not intended, thus decreasing the likelihood that they will attempt to or be able to meaningfully connect with others.[13]

Sara became less confident in her social abilities as she distanced from her friends. She interpreted their self-obsessed behavior to mean they did not find her fun or interesting to be around. In reality, she was experiencing the changing nature of social interactions in the current age. It was no wonder that her struggle for sense of self was heightened, "a perceived sense of social connectedness serves as a scaffold for the self—damage the scaffold, and the rest of the self begins to crumble."[14] Social connection poses unique challenges for individuals with eating disorders, whose relationships are hampered by an inability to express emotions and build connections.

According to Margo Maine, a clinical psychologist and author who specializes in treating eating disorders, those with eating disorders desire relationships but use their eating disorder symptoms to maintain emotional safety by using the relationship with the eating disorder as a replacement for less predictable interpersonal relationships.[15] Eating disorders are thought to be "disease(s) of disconnection,"[16] typified not only by disconnection from others, but also from the self. Unable to access thoughts, feelings, and needs, the person is unable to know or represent their authentic self, a major hindrance to feeling connected with others. For Sara, managing her eating disorder distracted her and disconnected her from the relational pain she experienced in her family and peer group. Relational connections are key to building capacity for self-differentiation within the context of mutually sustaining relationships,[17] the foundation of sense of self. Sara and I used her social media images to explore her use of eating disorder symptoms to protect her from relational challenges.

Increasing Sara's awareness of over-attention to negative social information that enhances her feelings of loneliness was addressed through helping her sort through automatic perceptions and thoughts that lead to disconnection from self and others. Together we examined the images Sara was viewing on her social media, and I asked her questions to help her identify perceptions, emotions, and thoughts while viewing such images. Beginning with concrete questions helped her identify emotions she views in the images.

Images of Missed Connection

Regarding an image of a group of her friends from the previous evening, *What emotions do you see demonstrated in this image?* "Everyone seems to be having fun, they're happy and want everyone else to know how much fun they're having." *How can you tell?* "It's obvious, they're all smiling and leaning in together, like they are all best friends." *What do you imagine are the reasons or expectations for taking and posting this image?* "There's a whole bunch posted by different people, so I guess they all want to show how much fun they had. Maybe also to make other people jealous, and like wish they were there or were friends with them." *How might you title it?* "Look what you missed out on." *What feelings come up for you as you view this image?* "Left out—but I didn't really want to go, even though they're my friends. I could've been there, but I just didn't feel like hanging out. Then when everyone started posting pictures, I regretted not going. *When you regret not going, what feelings come up for you?* "Umm [very quietly], I guess mostly anger."

Sara went on to explain her feelings of anger at herself for wasting her time moping around in her room and missing out on the fun, but she also recalled feeling hurt and angry that none of her friends reached out to encourage her to go out. Instead she stayed in her room all evening and purged the dinner she ate with her family. She felt she had overeaten because she ate the meal and dessert.

This small segment of using images in therapy initiated much deeper work on recognition and expression of emotions, self-regulation and control, and use of eating disorder symptoms to disconnect. Sometimes I ask clients to elaborate, using question such as *In what other ways are you disconnected from yourself? How do you disconnect from your thoughts/emotional experiences?* Sara expressed anger and sadness in her responses to these questions. It is often difficult for girls like Sara to admit they are angry if they have learned that these types of emotions are not acceptable to others. While Sara's family did not intend to discourage her from expressing herself, they did unknowingly communicate to her that as a female she should be quiet and agreeable. This message suppressed a number of emotions including many that could be utilized in asserting herself. Emotions cannot be selectively chosen for awareness. When we shut down the difficult feelings, we also distance from the positive ones.

One's ability to self-regulate depends on one's emotional awareness, which is dampened by vigilance to social threat and loneliness,[18] so finding evidence to disconfirm Sara's belief that her friends do not care whether she is present reframed her perceptions of belonging. Sara's use of eating disorder behaviors as a strategy for disconnection may temporarily bring relief from the anxiety of engaging with others, but this strategy also prevented her from developing relational skills. If a person doesn't know what they are feeling, they will be unable to know what others feel or even that feelings matter.

Because online interactions do not replace the type of connection that prevents feelings of isolation, we must also invest in face-to-face relationships. Technology revolutionized how social lives are managed, and more and more people have difficulty with social connection and identity formation. This technological revolution has made it possible for people to curate a sense of self in an online platform that does not require users to be genuine, nor does it provide experiences that build close relationships. The resulting paucity of relational practice has created a generation with social deficits stemming from an inability to understand the self or others. Online interactions may be filled with photographic images or emojis that represent emotions, but this type of interaction does little to create meaningful connection because it lacks depth. Sherry Turkle, a researcher of relationships and technology, asserts that the value of person-to-person conversation must be reclaimed if we are to combat the epidemic of loneliness and lost empathy.[19] Conversations with others builds our awareness of a our own inner dialogue and of what others are going through.

Images of Comparison

Further exploration of Sara's relationships through her viewed images allowed her to examine her relational images in a safe context. She showed me an image of one of her closest friends who recently made a careless comment in front of other friends about the amount of food Sara ate a restaurant one evening. This friend was unaware of Sara's eating disorder, as the disorder was a closely guarded family secret, per Sara's request. As she viewed this friend's selfie, Sara expressed previously unrecognized feelings of jealousy toward this girl, who Sara viewed as more popular and more socially skilled. The girl in this selfie is highly made up and posed and appears older than Sara. When I inquire about this discrepancy, Sara affirmed that this friend is her age, but appears older due to her skill in applying makeup. She told me that this girl's parents are much more lenient than Sara's and that she is engaging in some risky behaviors. This image provided an opening to help Sara explore her feelings and frequent comparisons with this friend.

Why might she have wanted to take this picture of herself in the first place? "I don't know—she wants to be this really edgy girl, especially since we're just freshmen, the youngest ones in school. She wears some pretty crazy clothes and has an older guy she's talking to. Guess she thinks she's more mature than the rest of us. I feel like she puts pictures up to show off. We all do really, but I don't post pictures of myself very often, only when I'm with friends."

Imagine that this friend is now looking at you. If this image could talk, what do you think it would say? "[Laughs] I have no idea. Let's see, probably that I shouldn't be so shy, or I should quit worrying about what everyone thinks."

Okay, what's the message that you think might be behind her words? "Now that I think about it, she might worry just as much as I do about what people think. I just hide in my room and she puts herself out there for attention. I don't think she feels that good about herself either, I mean, with everything she's gone through in her life, but she can be pretty mean sometimes, so it's hard to remember that."

What questions would you want to ask her? "Well first, why does she say embarrassing things in front of other people?"

Any clue as to what she would say? "I don't think she means to. She just wants to be funny, so she says something about my eating. It's not her fault. She doesn't know that eating is so hard for me. But she also makes comments sometimes about me being a Mexican, and that hurts my feelings. She wouldn't understand why saying things like that makes me feel bad. My parents want me to be proud of where we come from, but I wish it didn't have to be a big deal with some people. I try to act like things don't bother me because I feel like I have to always be in a good mood, really happy. Sometimes it's easier to just be alone than having to act like everything's great or that things don't bother me."

Other questions adapted from the work of Weiser[20] are used when assisting clients to work with the social media images they view in the context of developing empathy and relationship skills:

- *What has happened in her life that has brought her take this photograph?*
- *If you could climb into the photograph to be with this person, how would you pose the two of you together?*
- *What does the image see when looking at you?*
- *What questions might the image want to ask you?*
- *Could this person be having the same type of experiences or feelings you are?*
- *How can you tell these things?*
- *How does the image communicate this information to you?*

Images for Connection

A therapeutic opportunity is present when the client feels the desire to disconnect rather than remain in connection. Developing and practicing new relational strategies for remaining in connection decreases reliance on the eating disorder as a coping mechanism. A relational approach to exploring strategies of disconnection that occur in response to interpersonal challenges can be facilitated by asking the client to answer questions such as:

- *What situations in my relationships lead me to disconnect from others?*
- *What emotions am I feeling when I am most likely to disconnect?*
- *What emotions lead me to connect with others?*
- *How do I disconnect from others?*
- *How do I use the eating disorder to disconnect from others? What happens when this occurs?*
- *Do I ever use the eating disorder to connect with others? What is the result?*[21]

I wanted Sara to continue to share parts of her life with her parents as appropriate to her stage of development. Her recognition of their role in her life was highlighted in contrast to Sara's friend who was likely given too much freedom and too little support from her parents. Sara and I discussed pressure from her family to talk about her struggles when they sense she is struggling. She knew it is important to have a safe place to process her emotions, but she preferred to do that only in therapy for now. Several positive changes came from this exchange.

Sara realized her family was uncertain about how to help her and she could have input into when and how they interact with her. We devised a plan for her parents to give her space when she desires it, but to be available if she asks for help. She was most comfortable talking to her mother, and together they agreed on a simple technique of Sarah asking to do something together when she needs additional support, a way of using connection as a coping strategy when she wants to restrict, binge, or purge.

A few months later, Sara opened up to a few of her closest friends about her struggles with food and body image and realized that she did not have to put on a happy front with her friends. When Sara separated how she felt on the inside from the outward manifestation of who she was and what she was feeling, it was at great cost to her feelings of connection with her true self and with others. Although her pattern was to minimize her heritage, it was also important that Sara explore her ethnicity to gain a better sense of identity as "strategies of disconnection frequently arise around shame and a sense of unworthiness."[22] Shame plays a role in identity development, especially for minority populations. By examining her strategies for disconnection, Sara became more connected with others and with herself. She recognized her use of eating disorder behaviors to disconnect from her emotions and herself when she felt she did not fit in or was slighted by others.

Images to Externalize the Eating Disorder

Separating the self from the eating disorder is a crucial step in recovery. Externalizing the eating disorder from self reduces blame, guilt, and shame and increases self-compassion and capacity for change.[23] One well-known externalizing technique relies on asking the client to write a letter to the eating disorder (ED), draw a picture of it, or give it a descriptive name to reinforce the separation between the eating disorder identity and other aspects of self. Letters to and conversations with the ED fortify this distinction by prompting the client to express the negative impact of the ED on their healthier self.[24] With continued growth and strengthening of the healthy aspects of a person, the eating disorder identity can be dismantled.

Adapting this technique to the social media age requires few changes. I asked Sara to take a photo or imagine how ED would look, to create a hashtag that would likely accompany the online image, and to compose posts she would like to write if she saw the online image of ED. Intrigued by this idea, she readily engaged in the assignment. She created ED as an unwanted stalker who continues to send her messages despite her unresponsiveness, reflecting her relationship with her eating disorder at that point: an on-again, off-again relationship that represented her ambivalence to ending it once and for all. She s able to articulate ways to respond to unwanted comments and her own thoughts, much needed practice to challenge the eating disorder identity.

SELF-DIFFERENTIATION AND SOLITUDE

As Sara gained greater insight into her use of the eating disorder to disconnect from difficult emotions and experiences, she began a shift toward desiring recovery. She developed new coping strategies and spent less time alone in her room. Sara no longer isolated to engage in eating disorder behaviors, but during those times when she was not with her friends or on her phone she didn't know how to spend her time. Sara needed to connect with her interests, thoughts, and feelings without the distraction of outside influences. Discovering who one is occurs in the company of others, but also in times of solitude, when one can reflect on experiences. Belonging and solitude exist in relation to one another, with each individual needing varying degrees of both for optimal health. Some find solitude peaceful and restorative, whereas others find it miserable.

Self-differentiation transpires within the context of relationships as well as in alone-time, contemplating and integrating information about the self. To self-differentiate from others requires a balance of connection to others and to one's own inner experience. If everyone is constantly connected, how is a young person to differentiate between what others think and their own thoughts? Young people often crave constant social interaction, but they also need alone time to process the events of their lives. Some view solitude as a problem that can be solved by technology, yet time alone without the distraction of others is necessary for development of self. Understanding and accepting oneself must occur before a person can have healthy connections with others. Comfort with the self allows a person to be authentic in their relationships with others.

Because identity encompasses both social identity and personal identity, identity formation may more accurately described as seeking to define who one is as an individual residing within their relational matrix. All relationships begin with the self. The quality of relationships and the quality of the time spent alone depend on how well individuals know themselves and how they feel about themselves. Allowing oneself the space to develop and become acquainted with oneself can be challenging for clients whose early relationships did not meet their emotional needs. Early relationships that provide a calm, soothing milieu facilitate the neural integration necessary to build an internal sense of self and to give the individual assurance that they can be alone with their internal processes. Those who have repeatedly experienced this sense of emotional safety are able to notice their internal state and develop the competence to manage their emotions.[25]

Clients with eating disorders often have deficits in the capacity to manage their emotions due to their early relationship environment. "Eating disorders are one of a subset of externalizing disorders, with a primary etiology being the failure of early attachment relationships to teach sufficient self-regulation and co-regulation capabilities."[26] Food-seeking and food-avoidance behaviors are used as external regulators when internal means of emotional regulation are undeveloped. Those with eating disorders may create a constant stream of social interactions to distract them from emotions, or they may isolate from others to engage in eating disorder rituals in an attempt to numb themselves to overwhelming emotions. For these clients, solitude can be difficult because, in the quiet times of being alone, emotions arise that the client does not yet have the capacity to manage.

MANAGING SOCIAL MEDIA

Sara is now more aware of the impact of social media on her perceptions of herself. After she opened up to her aunt about her growing awareness, her aunt suggested that Sara have a phone without Internet access, but Sara and her mother agreed that Sara won't learn to handle social media later on if she doesn't gain those skills now. For a generation who has lived a considerable proportion of their waking hours online, there is a certain reliance on phones to fill spaces of boredom and soothe anxiety. We discussed the need for her to become more aware of the time she spent reflexively looking at her phone to fill her alone times. She set a goal to be more present in the moment, not looking at her screen, and to choose to be with others and spend time outside. She is calmed by playing with her dog, so she set aside time each day to play games with him. Sara was optimistic that her generation will find ways to manage social media, because they also see the benefits it offers. She already knew that technology moderation is essential to mental health, and she is learning that she must carefully choose to use social media only in ways that are meaningful to her.

Choosing to break the habitual use of technology is exceedingly difficult when so much of life is mediated through devices. Additionally, there are powerful reward systems in the brain that are activated when we receive a text or notification, which is a primary force behind obsession with social media. Recreating positive feelings is a primary driving force behind social media. Turning off automatic notifications breaks this particular reward path, making it more likely that technology use can be consciously monitored. Sara is aware that checking her social media gives her some positive feelings but also has a downside. Identifying the need she is trying to fulfill helps her to become more aware of her media use. Most often she is bored, wants to feel connected, or wants affirmation from others. Self-awareness led to some behavior changes, such as unfollowing some people whose posts trigger her eating disorder thoughts, leaving her phone in her room when she is spending time outside or with her family, and moving some of the apps on her phone so they are less visible.

These strategies brought up some strong emotions for Sara at times, but she was determined to have the choice of using her phone when it is beneficial to her and she understands the value of learning to be present with her inner experience. With a growing ability to discuss her feelings without being overwhelmed, Sara talked about the shame she felt regarding her body. She admitted that she gets anxious of weight gain when she notices her breasts are getting larger and noted that models and athletes are small-breasted. Her talents and interests in fashion and athletics both include an excessive focus on the body, which reinforced her confusion as she attempted to integrate her physical self into her identity. Body image disturbance plays a prominent role for those with eating disorders, and it is only through voicing the concerns in other areas of their lives that resolution, given time, can occur.[27] Issues of control, autonomy, and feelings of powerlessness, expressed through restriction and food rituals, are gradually resolved as clients learn to convey their emotions and declare their pain in words.

As her treatment progressed Sara noted her emotions on a regular basis, which enables her to make conscious choices regarding how she will respond. Food restriction occurred only occasionally, and she rarely binged or purged. Now that she is less engaged on social media, she feels free from the belief that she must wear makeup and look a certain way each day. More of her focus is on who she is, not what she should look like. There is a sense of authenticity about

Sara that is evident in how she presents herself when she comes to my office, on social media, and by her own reports of her interactions with peers. Identity theorists define authenticity as "the feeling that one is being one's true self. . . . Not feeling authentic is a negative state. . . . it has to do with what might be called the core self; who one is as a person across situations, across time, and across relationships."[28] Sara reflected back on her journey thus far and realized that she tried to present various identities she thought would secure acceptance from friends, but none of those identities were really her. By sharing images of herself dressed in a certain style and interacting in ways she thought fit the part, she was trying on preconceived identities.

BALANCING SOCIAL LIVES

How well one knows oneself determines the quality of the time spent alone. Sara's comfort with being alone is paying off; she feels less dependent on others for affirmation and can choose whether to be with other people. Having a rich inner life, which is enriched by connections with others yet is not dependent on being with someone else to feel whole, gives her confidence that she can meet some of her own needs. With a sense of self-differentiation, she can balance autonomy with connection. Solitude is no longer a frightening state that she must distract herself from.

Using images from Sara's social media for her photo therapy treatment was instrumental to effectively treating her eating disorder, for it is through this medium that she initially gained awareness of the messages she was taking in each day. To thrive in today's digital culture, we all need to understand how social media has been, and continues to be, engineered to keep us constantly connected and to understand the impact of social comparison. Because digital saturation has hampered social development, most young people also need to know how to build true connections based on mutual openness. I wonder if true social connection is still possible in a world in which face-to-face contact is diminishing. Before technology enabled constant connection, we knew what it was like to be out of contact with loved ones and we valued human contact. Clients like Sara reassure me that this generation will find ways to harness the power of technology in ways that augment, not replace, human contact, because the need and desire for connection remains written into our DNA.

Social media technology can facilitate or hamper the building of mutually sustaining relationships that are vital to our humanness. Social media can be used to schedule times of face-to-face connection with friends and family. When being there in person truly isn't possible, video conferencing technology, such as FaceTime or Skype, may be a way to maintain the bonds that were created in person. The ubiquitous camera has opened a world of possibilities for social bonding and affirmation of personhood. To connect authentically, social media must be used intentionally to create social networks where meaningful interactions take place. Rather than posting images to garner likes or meaningless affirmations, it can be used to connect on a deeper level.

Due to the immediate accessibility and gratification of social media, we may find it difficult to break our habits of checking social media, but with repeated practice in resisting the temptation to fill our needs with online activity, social media use can become more intentional. When a young person has a full life and ample skills to soothe difficult emotions, technology will take its rightful place as an adjunct to meaningful relationships.

REFERENCES

1. Kerr, M. E., & Bowen, M. (1988). *Family evaluation: An approach based on Bowen theory*. New York, NY: W. W. Norton & Company.
2. Golden, N. H., Schneider, M., & Wood, C. (2016). Preventing obesity and eating Disorders in adolescents. *Pediatrics, 138*(3). doi:10.1542/peds.2016-1649
3. Tagay, S., Schlottbohm, E., Reyes-Rodriguez, M. L., Repic, N., & Senf, W. *(2014)*. Eating Disorders, trauma, PTSD, and psychosocial resources. *Eating Disorders, 22*(1), 33–49.
4. The National Center on Addiction and Substance Abuse (CASA) at Columbia University. (2003). *Food for Thought: Substance Abuse and Eating Disorders*. The National Center on Addiction and Substance Abuse (CASA). New York, NY: Columbia University.
5. Weiser, J. (1999). *PhotoTherapy techniques: Exploring the secrets of personal snapshots and family albums*. Vancouver, BC: Judy Weiser and PhotoTherapy Centre Publishers.
6. Chancellor, S., Pater, J., Clear, T., Gilbert, E., & De Choudhury, M. (2016). #thyghgapp: Instagram Content Moderation and Lexical Variation in Pro-Eating Disorder Communities. Paper presented at the 19th ACM Conference on Computer-Supported Cooperative Work and Social Computing. Retrieved from http://www.munmund.net/pubs/cscw16_thyghgapp.pdf
7. Gerrard, Y. (2018). Beyond the hashtag: Circumventing content moderation on social media. *New Media and Society, 20*(12), 4492–4511.
8. Cozolino, L. (2017). *The neuroscience of psychotherapy: Healing the social brain* (3rd ed.). New York, NY: W. W. Norton & Company.
9. Kerr, M. E., & Bowen, M. (1988). *Family evaluation: An approach based on Bowen theory*. New York, NY: W. W. Norton & Company.

10. Dollinger, S. J., Preston, L. A., O'Brien, S. P., & DiLalla, D. L. (1996). Individuality and relatedness of the self: An autophotographic study. *Journal of Personality and Social Psychology, 71*(6), 1268–1278.

Dollinger, S. J., & Clancy Dollinger, S. M. (2003). Individuality in young and middle adulthood: An autophotographic study. *Journal of Adult Development, 10*, 227–237.

11. Swann, W. B., Jr., & Bosson, J. K. (2010). Self and identity. In S. T. Fiske, D. T. Gilbert & G. Lindzey (Eds.), *Handbook of social psychology* (pp. 589–628), Hoboken, NJ: John Wiley & Sons.

12. Peplau, L. A., & Perlman, D. (1982). Perspectives on loneliness. In L. A. Peplau & D. Perlman (Eds.), *Loneliness: A sourcebook of current theory, research and therapy* (pp. 1–18). New York: John Wiley & Sons.

13. Cacioppo, J. (2009). *Loneliness: Human nature and the need for social connection.* New York, NY: W. W. Norton & Company.

14. Hawkley, L. C., & Cacioppo, J. T. (2010). Loneliness matters: A theoretical and empirical review of consequences and mechanisms (p. 220). *Annals of Behavioral Medicine, 40*(2), 218–227.

15. Maine, M., & McGilley, B. H. (2019, February). *Evidence based practice and practice based evidence: Truths and consequences of eating disorders and their treatment.* Proceedings from the Annual Symposium of the International Association of Eating Disorders Professionals. Palm Springs, CA.

16. Tantillo, M. (2006). A relational approach to eating disorders multi-family therapy group: Moving from difference and disconnection to mutual connection (p. 86). *Families, Systems, & Health, 24*, 82–102.

17. Tantillo, M. (2006). A relational approach to eating disorders multi- family therapy group: Moving from difference and disconnection to mutual connection (p. 86). *Families, Systems, & Health, 24*, 82–102.

Tantillo, M., & Sanftner, J. L. (2010). Mutuality and motivation: Connecting with patients and families for change in the treatment of eating disorders. In M. Maine, D. Bunnell, & B. McGilley (Eds.), *Treatment of eating disorders: Bridging the gap between research and practice* (pp. 319–334). London, UK: Elsevier.

Trepal, H. C., Boie, I., & Kress, V. E. (2012). A relational cultural approach to working with clients with eating disorders. *Journal of Counseling and Development, 90*(3), 346–356.

18. Tice D. M., & Bratslavsky, E. (2000). Giving in to feel good: The place of emotion regulation in the context of general self-control. *Psychological Inquiry, 11*(3), 149–159.

19. Turkle, S. (2016). *Reclaiming conversation: The power of talk in a digital age.* New York, NY: Penguin Books.

20. Weiser, J. (1999). *PhotoTherapy techniques: Exploring the secrets of personal snapshots and family albums.* Vancouver, BC: Judy Weiser and PhotoTherapy Centre Publishers.

21. Koehn, C. V. (2010). A relational approach to counseling women with alcohol and other drug problems. *Alcoholism Treatment Quarterly, 28*, 38–51.

22. Jordan, J. V. (2010). *Relational-cultural therapy* (p. 29). Washington, DC: American Psychological Association.

23. Hoffman, R., & Kress, V. E. (2008). Narrative therapy and non- suicidal-self-injurious behavior: Externalizing the problem and internalizing personal agency. *Journal of Humanistic Counseling, Education and Development, 47*(2), 157–171.

24. Shaefer, J., & Rutledge, T. (2003). *Life without Ed: How one woman declared independence from her eating disorder and how you can too.* New York, NY: McGraw-Hill Education.

25. Cozolino, L. (2017). *The neuroscience of psychotherapy: Healing the social brain* (3rd ed.). New York, NY: W. W. Norton & Company.

26. Lapides, F. M. (2010). Neuroscience: Contributions to the understanding and treatment of eating disorders (p. 39). In M. Maine, B. Hartman McGilley, & D. Bunnell (Eds.), *Treatment of eating disorders: Bridging the research practice gap* (pp. 37–52). San Diego, CA: Academic Press.

27. Zerbe, K. J. (1995). *The body betrayed: A deeper understanding of women, eating disorders, and treatment.* Carlsbad, CA: Gürze Books.

28. Burke, P. J., & Stets, J. E. (2009). *Identity theory* (p. 125). New York, NY: Oxford University Press.

Chapter 11

DAMAGING IMAGES

*The challenge of recovery is to reestablish ownership of your body and your mind—
of your self. This means feeling free to know what you know and to feel what you
feel without becoming overwhelmed, enraged, ashamed, or collapsed.*

—Bessel van der Kolk

Social media is a platform for sharing and connecting, offering new opportunities for self-expression and self-exploration. Despite these benefits, there are inherent dangers when information and images are readily shared online, without the subject's consent. Others' images of us provide a glimpse into how they perceive us, and the images can impose unwanted expectations or qualities, thus they are imbued with power. The use of the phrase "take a picture" is fitting, as the images that others take of us are usually made for their reasons rather than our own. Allowing oneself to be photographed requires some level of trust in the photographer. If the photographer is unwisely trusted, the image they construct may be dehumanizing.

PUBLIC IMAGES

Claire, whose case will be discussed in detail later in the chapter, is a young adult who contacted me after her ex-boyfriend shared his private images of her online. When she ended their relationship, he circulated intimate images of her on social media, a behavior known as revenge porn. Claire was not the first client to tell me of experiences with loss of privacy on social media. Sixteen-year-old Haley cried uncontrollably as she told me how she got drunk at a party and then saw photos of her first sexual encounter on social media the following day. Haley decided it was not safe to go to parties because the older boys try to take advantage of the younger girls there. Lauren, a first-year college student, lost control of images that were taken during her encounter with another college student while on spring break. She participated in a sexual act with this young man while under the influence of alcohol and a deep desire for attention from him. Later, she had a vague recollection of taking a selfie with the young man, and she became obsessed with the possibility that he would circulate the photo. Stories like these bring the topics of objectification and power dynamics into therapy sessions.

The male gaze, a concept originating from feminist film theory, defines the way women's bodies are objectified and treated as commodities to be sold by advertising, pornography, and even by women themselves. Sociologist Ben Agger frames the selfie trend as "male gaze gone viral,"[1] to describe how females self-objectify themselves when they post selfies that conform to sexualized stereotypes. These are the selfies in which females adopt the poses, settings, and attire reminiscent of pornography. This puts females in a double bind because they know there are double standards for men and women, yet they succumb to the desire to exhibit their sexuality, knowing that they can also be punished for this act. They believe they are taking control of their sexuality, only to find they have stepped into a long history of objectification. For young women in the throes of developing their sexual identity, this is a time of confusion and great vulnerability.

We see this clearly when what were intended to be private, intimate images are shared online after a relationship goes sour. Images taken to be shared by the couple can suddenly become public pornography when jilted partners share revenge porn. Losing control of an image that is circulated without the individual's consent leads to feelings of disempowerment. Gone are the days when a person could simply ask someone to return the negative and all copies of a photograph and thus possess some confidence that compromising images would not be shared. Females are the primary targets for revenge porn because they have the most to lose in a society that offers mixed messages regarding female sexuality; but males, likewise, can be objectified or objectify themselves when images reduce them to a stereotype. One such stereotype is of effortless masculinity in which they must appear naturally muscled and self-possessed. Males, like females, willingly engage this in act, yet when sexually explicit images are shared, males typically have less to lose socially than females do.

Not all damaging images have a sexualized nature. Some images are more benign but still feel too intimate to be shared publicly. It is like we are peering in through a portal of someone's life that should be viewed only by their closest relations. Our comfort with this new technology has eclipsed the signals that we have entered a sacred or private place. We pass an image off as just a facile, expected image, one that we see hundreds of times each day, while technology unquestionably blurs the line between private and public domains. Further complicating the private/public dichotomy, social media platforms make content "public by default, private through effort."[2] Only through effort is the visibility of shared online content made private.

To understand the nature of image circulation, we need an awareness of how images are transmitted on the Internet. The term "grabbing" explains the unique way in which social media viewers consume and share visual material. Grabbing operates on multiple levels: the images we take to share, those we grab to keep on our phone or computer, those images we grab to circulate on social networks, those grabbed when someone hacks our accounts or gains illicit use of our phone, and forwarded images of something shared privately. Another level is the data grabbed from any image on the Internet that is sold to marketers or used for social research projects like Selfiecity.[3] The grab means that once an image is shared, control of that image is forfeited forever.[4] This is one reason that online content is so enduring; copying, sharing, and saving are simple processes that encourage distribution of content.

Unfortunately, we are living in a time epitomized by incivility and polarized thinking. The impact of hurtful, unsolicited responses to online sharing can be devastating for anyone, but especially so for a young person seeking affirmation of who they are. If someone reacts negatively to a photograph, it can feel like an attack on the person, as the line between the visual depiction and the actual person is often blurred. When images are shared and gossip begins to circulate, stopping the spread of the content is impossible. Human are curious by nature, but their less benign tendencies increase the visibility and potential harm of gossip, spreading it as quickly as possible. Once an image, video, or any form of communication is shared, it cannot be retrieved. With the advent of search engines, almost anything can be located by entering a few key words.

PRIVACY

Concerns over privacy violations dominate the discourse on social media, with companies like Facebook and Twitter reportedly collecting data about users through tracking, facial recognition software, and profiling. Some users have deleted their social media accounts in an effort to regain privacy, but most people seem willing to sacrifice privacy for convenience. Removing oneself from social media is unlikely to restore privacy. It seems that social media companies are now building profiles on nonusers by collecting information shared by friends, so friends' posts can also compromise a person's privacy.[5] Technologies like social media necessitate a greater understanding of the function and value of privacy.

Privacy is necessary for identity development. In an article titled "What Privacy Is For" in the *Harvard Law Review*, Georgetown University law professor Julie E. Cohen reviews privacy from a legal and societal standpoint while also articulating the indispensable nature of privacy for the individual. She states that privacy is a barrier to the scrutiny and judgment of society. Privacy provides room to develop identity, "creating spaces for play and the work of self-[development]" and "lack of privacy means reduced scope for self-making."[6] In a nod to how the self relates to the larger world, she asserts that privacy "enables individuals both to maintain relational ties and to develop critical perspectives on the world around them."[7] Without privacy, the boundary between self and other is blurred, and the self-exploration required for creating the self-narrative is stifled by societal and cultural pressures.

TRAUMA IN THE NARRATIVE

A rather tall, stately brunette, Claire, whom we met at the beginning of the chapter, looks the part of a fitness instructor in her athletic wear and sleek ponytail, yet she is also wearing a heavy coat of foundation and a thick application of eyeliner. Physically, she appears to have invested a great deal of sweat equity in her toned muscles, leaving me to wonder how her makeup will weather the workout session she looks forward to after each of her therapy sessions. With rapid-fire speech that betrayed no emotion, she relayed the basics of why she came. She brushed past what she referred to as a string of boyfriends, beginning in early adolescence, to her most recent relationship.

After two years of dating Tanner, she decided she was no longer attracted to him and abruptly ended their relationship. He tried several times to reunite, but she was not interested in talking to him nor in reconsidering their relationship. In hindsight, she wishes the breakup had been mutual and less of a surprise to him because he reacted by sharing intimate photos and personal information online, leading to harassment and humiliation. Claire recounted this incident without emotion, and when I pointed this out, she stated that she probably deserved what he did on some level because she treated him harshly throughout their relationship and then ended it with little notice. She stated that this is her pattern: At first, she is intensely interested in getting to know a man, but soon she becomes disillusioned with him and begins to treat him poorly.

In an abrupt topic shift, Claire related that her mother was mean to her throughout her childhood. From an early age, Claire was told that she was fat. When she began menstruating at age thirteen her mother said that only fat girls start their periods this early. Parents who body-shame their children most likely have body image disturbances themselves. Children who experience this shaming incorporate the body image disturbance of the parent. Claire's father belittled her attempts to gain his attention. Although he was rarely home, when he was home, she hid in her room to avoid his harsh words. As if justifying for the way she was treated, Claire explained that both of her parents drank and used drugs early on. Her mother continues to use multiple drugs, while her father now only drinks. Although she has few memories of her life before leaving home for college, there were incidents of being locked in her room when her mother did not want to deal with her and of finding her mother passed out when she came home from elementary school. Often there was no food in the house, so when it was available, she ate all she could get her hands on. Like many children who are not receiving care and attention from their parents, Claire recalls craving attention from her teachers and other adults.

Unresolved trauma impedes the creation of a meaningful life story and leaves a person susceptible to retraumatization. Like many who have experienced trauma, Claire's life story and her identity center on her childhood trauma and her current difficulties. Although Claire was unaware of the association, Tanner's betrayal after their breakup triggered her to relive her unresolved trauma and to seek treatment for the first time. She had engaged in a series of eating disordered behaviors since childhood. Eating disorders are not uncommon to trauma survivors, who, in their attempts to escape from trauma reactions, lose touch with what they feel and who they are. Treatment is thus complicated because the early trauma and the resultant damage to identity must be resolved before the eating disorder can abate. As I worked with Claire, a quote I read years ago kept coming into my thoughts. "To have one's identity disrupted is to travel without a compass."[8] Claire's difficulties when she first came to see me personified identity disruption as she strived to navigate the complex social world of a young adult in the social media age.

Nurturing parents present children with experiences that provide them with emotional connection and safety, laying the foundation for future functioning. Siegel's groundbreaking synthesis of interpersonal neurobiology research shows that human connections impact the neural connections that shape all aspects of human functioning.[9] Through their attunement to the child's needs, parents play a vital role in setting the stage for their child to develop the ability to regulate emotions. As the child matures, dyadic regulation, in which the adult and child are in attunement, gradually paves the way for the child to self-regulate autonomously.[10] Hence, development of emotional regulation is dependent on social interactions. The dysregulation of emotion seen in many clients impairs their ability to respond adaptively to their experiences in the world.

Not receiving the necessary emotional attunement to develop emotional resources or a stable foundation to build a sense of self is a large part of Claire's story. She was often the target of her parent's anger and was left to manage her emotions without the resources to do so. Claire's father was a functioning alcoholic with a highly prestigious career that enabled them to live in an upscale neighborhood and send her to private schools. She quickly learned to separate how she felt on the inside from the way she appeared on the outside. Some parents, who had suspicions of her family's dysfunctions, would not allow their children to visit Claire's house, which was fine with Claire because her mother's behavior was unpredictable and caused more than one embarrassing incident. Claire worked hard to present a carefree attitude around others, but inside she experienced difficulty relating to those who had not experienced similar issues. The disparity between how she felt on the inside and how she appeared on the outside had exacted considerable costs, including loss of self, loss of genuine relationships, and intense internal conflict.

With parents who cannot attune to who she is or how she feels due to their substance addiction, Claire is no one's precious child. A child who is given the message that she is special and valued will carry that belief forward through life. If she is later treated poorly by another, she will know that this treatment doesn't feel right and will not allow others to mistreat her. The developmental deficits resulting from trauma make it more likely that an individual will be unable to accurately read another's intent, increasing the likelihood that future relationships will repeat these dysfunctional dynamics.

Bessel van der Kolk, a leading authority on trauma, recognizes the importance of attuned caregiving and suggests that developmental trauma underlies the symptoms of emotional dysregulation as well as difficulties with identity and competence.[11] Clients like Claire come to our offices with symptoms of nightmares, insomnia, and flashbacks, along with limited ability to recall childhood events. These clients are often highly anxious, controlling, and avoidant of emotions. Also common are an array of negative cognitions such as self-blame, expectations that others will harm or disappoint them, and critical beliefs about themself. Trauma disorganizes neural development with far reaching consequences. Memory—"the foundation for both the implicit reality (behavioral responses, emotional reactions, perceptual categorizations, schemata of the self and others in the world, and possibly bodily memories) and explicit recollections of facts and of the self across time"[12]—is subject to the disorganizing effects of trauma.

Memory enables children to narrate their lives and create a sense of self through interactions with others—a process of narrative co-construction that occurs as knowledge, feelings, and behaviors are explored and thereby experiences are integrated into a coherent story. Autobiographical memory, the basis of narrative, is constructed from the external events and internal experiences of daily existence. "The organization of autobiographical memory that includes input from multiple neural networks enhances self-awareness and increases the ability to solve problems, cope with stress, and regulate affect."[13] Trauma interrupts the plot of the narrative that is necessary for emotional regulation, setting patterns of behavior, and self-organization.

TRAUMA AND EATING DISORDERS

Eating disorder symptoms started in early childhood for Claire; she recalls worrying whether there would be anything for dinner and being out of control with food when it was available. By early adolescence she was experimenting with a range of behaviors including restriction, binging, and purging. Contemporary research implicates trauma in the development of eating disorders,[14] and unresolved trauma is a perpetuating factor in the continuation of eating disorder symptoms.[15] This association transcends age and gender. Children, adolescents, and adults, as well as individuals of both genders, show a link between trauma history and disordered eating.[16] Individuals with eating disorders have a significantly higher occurrence of trauma than individuals without eating disorders, and some studies have found that the highest incidence of lifetime post-traumatic stress disorder (PTSD) occur in populations that exhibit bulimia and binge eating.[17] A Swedish study found no significant differences in traumatic exposure between specific eating disorder diagnoses, but did link trauma history to the severity of eating disorder symptoms.[18] The U.S. National Comorbidity Survey Replication study found that virtually all men and women with anorexia, bulimia, and binge eating disorders had a history of at least one potentially traumatic event in their lifetime.[19]

Both eating disorders and trauma commonly include extreme disconnection from the body, a deficit that leaves a person cut off from sensing the inner states of the body. A person must sense what is going on in their body to experience the full range of emotions and sensations of humanness. The foundation for the self relies on self-awareness of the physical sensations that convey the inner states of the body.[20] Individuals with eating disorders are notoriously disconnected from body sensations, such as hunger and satiety, causing them to have trouble taking care of physical needs. If body sensations are muted, a person is numbed from the difficult emotions of living, but also from the pleasures of being alive. In one study, over eighty percent of clients with anorexia and sixty-five percent with bulimia also suffered from alexithymia,[21] a Greek term meaning *no words for emotions*. Alexithymia, characterized by difficulties with identifying, describing, and communicating feelings, is also pervasive in trauma survivors. For example, when I asked Claire how she felt when Tanner shared the photos he had taken of her online, she told me that she went running for the rest of the evening. Unable to experience the intense emotions of betrayal and embarrassment, Claire relied on the only method she knew to deal with the emotions she didn't know she was having.

COMPLEX TRAUMA

Claire's negative experiences in her family of origin, like many clients with eating disorders and trauma, were more extensive than post-traumatic stress disorder resulting from a single event. Complex trauma exposure refers either to a series of occurrences or one prolonged occurrence of child maltreatment such as long-term emotional abuse and neglect, physical abuse, sexual abuse, and witnessing domestic violence.[22] Claire likely experienced most or all of these events during her childhood—extreme emotional and physical neglect from her parents, physical abuse at the hands of her father and older brother, and witnessing of her parents frequent physical altercations. Later in her treatment, Claire wondered if there was other abuse when she was very young, but she could not recall any clear memories to corroborate her suspicions. Profound neglect or abuse that occurs in the caregiving relationship is acutely devastating to child development and sense of self because it occurs within the social environment that is supposed provide to safety and stability.

Healthy childhood development is dependent on a caregiver providing an environment that includes scaffolding for the growth of many developmental competencies. In the absence of this support, the effects of trauma can go beyond the symptoms associated with typical PTSD. A 2003 paper from the National Child Traumatic Stress Network Complex Trauma Task Force[23] brings together extensive research on the physical, emotional, cognitive, and relational effects of childhood abuse that represent impairment to neurobiological development. When Claire first began treatment, her array of difficulties extended into multiple domains of impairment including: self-awareness (emotion, body sensations), self-regulation (food, sleep, emotions, exercise), affective (anxiety, depression), cognitive (obsessive–compulsive thoughts, negative self-worth, distraction), coping (increased susceptibility to stress, intense reactions and/or numbing), relational (avoidance, lack of affiliation, and connection), and revictimization.

Similar to the ways in which drugs and alcohol are used to self-medicate, eating disorders serve to distract, sooth, or numb from the symptoms associated with trauma. In an early childhood environment where emotions are frightening or intolerable, children come to believe that their emotions are bad and should be avoided. Therefore, when emotions are unavoidably experienced, the individual feels shame and disgust. Eating disorder behaviors are often used in an attempt to avoid or numb the emotions. The eating disorder is a flight mechanism used to escape the pain of the trauma.[24] When these strategies are used, the traumatic experiences are not resolved and their destructive effects continue to cause difficulties.[25]

Claire began her eating disorder journey by binge eating whenever food was available, a common behavior in children with unreliable food sources. Later, she learned to purge as she attempted to negate the effects of binging. Because her father was in the medical field and had a bias against therapy, the only treatment she received for her eating disorder was from a psychiatrist who put her on stimulant medication to control her binges. In our first session, Claire proudly reported that she no longer binged, however, in this discussion it became clear that she was engaging in extreme control of her food intake and had obsessive thoughts regarding control. She ate the same breakfast and lunch each day and had three or four "safe" dinner options to choose from each night. She gradually opened up about the extreme exercise habits that filled her evenings and admitted that she runs more frequently when she feels overwhelmed. Deviating from this routine resulted in increased anxiety and obsessive thoughts. This rigid type of control is frequently a strategy to counteract intense feelings of helplessness and lack of power.

EXERCISE ADDICTION

Exercise addiction is of growing concern in our fitness-obsessed age and often goes hand in hand with an eating disorder.[26] It is common for those diagnosed with an eating disorder to also engage in extreme physical fitness to control weight.[27] Now viewed as a compensatory behavior, like purging or laxative use, extreme exercise can have equally deleterious effects. One survey found that almost two-thirds of fitness professionals have encountered a client who may have anorexia.[28] This is likely a conservative estimate because anorexia is more easily identified than other eating disorders due to the characteristic low weight of these individuals. Those with bulimia or binge eating are unlikely to be as readily identified. Claire was extremely physically fit, and although she hovered above the weight that would classify her as having anorexia, she engaged in an array of disordered behaviors relating to food and exercise, and considering these behaviors is a much more accurate way to assess a client for the presence of an eating disorder.

I noticed that Claire, like many of my clients today, had embedded technology in all aspects of her life. Wearable technology is a type of clothing or accessory, usually a watch, used to track movement and give instant updates on fitness metrics. This technology introduces several elements that increase the likelihood that it will foster behavioral addiction, but the presence of only one element is sufficient to raise the risk for addiction.[29] First, fitness trackers set goals that are just beyond reach; the most common is the arbitrary ten thousand steps, which is a default goal on many devices. Another element is the reinforcing feedback of the dings or beeps that sound when goals are met. Two other contributing elements are an acknowledgement of incremental progress and setting tasks that slowly become more difficult over time, both of which are inherent in exercise goals. But what happens when those goals are met? For many, the desire to reach higher levels, to go well beyond ten thousand steps, is exacerbated by the numerical counting inherent to wearable technology.

Constant monitoring of numbers disconnects clients from the experience of being in tune with bodily sensations, creating a mindlessness that detracts from noticing how the body is reacting to exercise. It makes exercise mindless and fosters obsession with progressing to the next goal, heightening the likelihood of injury or overuse of joints and muscles. Exercise addiction experts liken the use of wearable technology to calorie counting; both make us less intuitive about what our body needs.[30] By obsessing over numerical targets, food is restricted even when the body signals a need for nourishment, and signs that the body has had enough physical activity are ignored. The last element in wearable technology that raises the risk for behavioral addiction is the powerful force of social connection. Wearable technology enables individuals to sync fitness goals with others and report progress, thereby heightening the risks associated with social behaviors such as competition and attempts to fit in with others.

Technology is designed to reinforce behaviors that lead to widespread adoption; it is designed to lead us to believe that we cannot live without these products and their platforms that connect us, making it difficult to break the cycle of behavioral addiction. Individuals with eating disorders may be especially prone to addiction and to having difficulties managing technology use. They are vulnerable to the relentless visual images and messages in peer interactions and advertising on social media, and because they are responsive to body image disturbance, they perceive content differently from others.[31] Researchers are now beginning to show a relationship between technology addiction and eating disorders,[32] which is not surprising given the use of technology to monitor, control, and manage weight.[33] But technology use is often ignored in eating disorder treatment. In one study, about half of healthcare professionals working with clients with eating disorders indicated that technology-related topics were irrelevant to treatment goals, instead preferring to focus on eating disorder symptoms, past history, and family and personal relationships.[34]

Traumatic experiences of parental neglect and emotional abuse have long ranging effects on a person's susceptibility to the addictive process. Traumatized individuals are highly vulnerable to visual content and to potential subsequent trauma exposure through visual content. Conscious and subconscious information is directly transmitted along visual pathways to brain structures involved in emotional memory,[35] and haunting visual images related to a trauma experience continue to elicit an alarm response in the visual context long after the danger has passed.[36]

IDENTIFYING WITH THE DAMAGED IDENTITY

According to van der Kolk,[37] one of the most insidious effects of trauma lies in the disruption of the ability to correctly read social behaviors in other people. Traumatized individuals feel unsafe in their bodies. To cope with overwhelming emotions, trauma survivors learn to ignore internal signals and become experts at numbing themselves to feelings. Likewise, to engage in eating disorder behaviors, a person must disconnect from body sensations, either ignoring signals that they are eating beyond a level of comfort or bodily needs for nutrition. They are often acutely vulnerable to adversity and stress.[38] Since body sensations and emotions are intricately entwined, failure to be tuned-in to the body negates the visceral reactions that are necessary for reading others' intentions. Trauma survivors may not pick up on cues that signal danger in relationships, making them highly susceptible to entering relationships in which they are again traumatized, or they may exhibit such heightened sensitivity that they may misperceive danger where there is none, leaving them prone to avoiding connection with others. Both responses indicate an inability to read others and internal cues within their body that could guide self-protective behaviors.

Claire's relationship history illustrates her confusion about connecting with others and her difficulty assessing the safety of relationship partners. During the ongoing trauma in her childhood, Claire sought the care and attention of other adults for her physical ailments. She spent a great deal of time in the school nurse's office and recalled her desire for touch. Throughout these years, she did not confide in these adults about what was going on in her home. She wanted connection but did not trust that they were safe to confide in. In later years, she shared some of her background with a couple of boyfriends, but when they didn't know how to respond, she distanced herself and treated them poorly until the relationships ended. It was only when Claire met Tanner that she finally thought she had found someone who wanted to hear her story and could truly understand what she had been through. He, too, had had a difficult childhood, so she felt she could tell him everything she had always wanted to share. Her only friend Jennifer did not care much for Tanner, but Claire refused to listen to her comments about his selfishness and temper. Even though Claire considered Jennifer a friend, she could not bring herself to allow Jennifer to provide support and a more balanced view of her relationship with Tanner. Her own emotional dysregulation led her to isolate herself and engage more fervently in her eating disorder. Like many people with early childhood trauma, Claire did not have good intuition about harmful situations or relationships. Her sense of self did not expect, nor think she deserved, to be treated with respect.

As Claire lost interest in her relationship with Tanner, he demanded more and more of her time. She retreated to the gym after work, where she ran on the treadmill for a few hours. At that point, Claire was disconnected from herself and from Tanner, so she was in no way prepared for his response to her breaking off their relationship. During their relationship she had allowed Tanner to take some photos of her with the spoken agreement that he would never show them to anyone else. To say that Claire was unprepared for him to share them on social media is an understatement. Her reaction ranged from rage to despair to suicidal thoughts. When she finally contacted an aunt, whom she had not seen in several years, it was clear that she needed professional help.

Claire deeply identified with a damaged identity that relies on self-contempt, deprivation, and attempts at body perfection to manage emotions she was not equipped to handle. Claire had no sense of herself outside of her fitness identity and felt that her efforts never seem to be enough. She tried to get away from replaying the few events she remembered from her childhood, but she found that she was distracted and impatient with the day-to-day events of her life as well. By shutting off from the frightening sensations, she had also lost her ability to feel alive in the present. Feeling uncomfortable in her own skin and that she somehow did not belong to the human race, she cycled between feeling shame and feeling numb. Suicidal thoughts after having her personal life exposed on social media prompted her to contact her estranged aunt and to seek help for the first time. Sexualized images posted on social media, without a person's consent, may trigger emotional reactions akin to those experienced in response to earlier trauma, pushing them to seek relief.

We must first help clients to move out of the fight, flight, or freeze state and facilitate the therapeutic relationship, because they will work for change only if they feel safe. In *The Neuroscience of Psychotherapy*, Louis Cozolino states that psychotherapy is a neurobiological intervention based on healing through social connection. It offers the chance to rebuild neural structures and thus create healing, even from great difficulty and trauma. "Putting feelings into words and constructing narratives about experiences are integral to emotion regulation, the interweaving of neural networks of emotion and cognition, and the experience of a coherent sense of self."[39] When therapy offers emotional attunement, affect regulation, and the co-construction of narratives, it promotes the neural connections that enable the client to enter the healing process.

For Claire to find herself, that is, to develop her identity, she must discover what she knows to be the truth—her truth. The adaptive response to trauma is to separate parts from the self, an action that induces alexithymia, not being able to sense and communicate one's feelings. To separate from painful experiences, erasing knowledge and acting as if everything is fine can be adaptive at the time, but over time, the loss of self erodes one's trust in feelings and memories. Self-awareness grows from observing and naming what is going on internally and in the environment. Regaining sense of self can occur only when there is also awareness of the body, because the visceral connection with the self relies on the body to communicate what a person feels. This connection helps clients separate truth from untruth and know whom and what can be trusted.[40] For those with eating disorder symptomology complicated by trauma, treatment must address both conditions using a trauma-informed approach. As Claire reflected on her past, she expressed concern about her ability to tolerate the feelings that will arise. The following passage from van der Kolk's *The Body Keeps the Score*[41] sums her dilemma succinctly:

> *Traumatized people are often afraid of feeling. It is not so much the perpetrators (who, hopefully, are no longer around to hurt them) but their own physical sensations that now are the enemy. Apprehension about being hijacked by uncomfortable sensations keeps the body frozen and the mind shut. Even though the trauma is a thing of the past, the emotional brain*

keeps generating sensations that make the sufferer feel scared and helpless. It's not surprising that so many trauma survivors are compulsive eaters and drinkers, fear making love, and avoid many social activities: Their sensory world is largely off limits. (p. 210)

Claire has spent a lifetime cultivating strategies to avoid feeling. She has deep trauma wounds that impact her sense of self and her ability to trust others. When Claire first came to treatment her days were filled with work and her evenings and weekends were filled with solitary time at the gym until she returned home to sleep. She needed to first gain physical awareness so she could reclaim her body and self. A review of studies on clients with eating disorders and alexithymia found that treatment focusing on identifying and describing emotions decreases alexithymia scores and eating disorder symptoms.[42] Before Claire could tolerate directly addressing her trauma, she needed to increase her capacity to notice sensations in her body and use this information to identify emotions. To tolerate affect Claire learned breathing strategies and mindfulness for calming her hyperaroused emotional system. We continued this work in the context of the trauma treatment, but she needed to have basic calming skills to prepare for the work ahead. As she gained greater awareness of her internal state and was able to calm from emotional arousal, we moved on to the work of trauma resolution and construction of her new narrative, which is the topic of the following chapter.

REFERENCES

1. Agger, B. (2012). *Oversharing: Presentations of self in the internet Age.* New York, NY: Routledge.
2. Boyd, D. (2014). *It's complicated,* (p. 12). New Haven, CT: Yale Press.
3. Selfiecity: Investigating the style of self-portraits (selfies) in five cities across the world. Retrieved from http://selfiecity.net
4. Senft, T. M., & Baym, N. K. (2015). What does the selfie say? Investigating a global phenomenon. *International Journal of Communication, 9,* 1588–1606.
5. Lindsey. N. (2019, February 3). New research shows that social media privacy might not be possible. Retrieved from https://www.cpomagazine.com/data-privacy/new-research-study -shows-that-social-media-privacy-might-not-be-possible/,
6. Cohen, J. E. (2013). What privacy is for (p. 1911). *Harvard Law Review, 126,* 1904–1933.
7. Cohen, J. E. (2013). What privacy is for (p. 1906). *Harvard Law Review, 126,* 1904–1933.
8. Young, M. B. (1988). Understanding identity disruption and intimacy: One aspect of post-traumatic stress (p. 32). *Contemporary Family Therapy, 10,* 30–43.

9. Siegel, D. J. (2012). *The developing mind: How relationships and the brain interact to shape who we are* (2nd ed.). New York, NY: Guilford Press.

10. Hofer, M. A. (1994). Hidden regulators in attachment, separation and loss. *Monographs of the Society for Research in Child Development, 59*(2-3), 192-207.

11. van der Kolk, B. (2014). *The body keeps the score: Brain, mind, and body in the healing of trauma.* New York, NY: Penguin Books.

12. Siegel, D. J. (2012). *The developing mind: How relationships and the brain interact to shape who we are* (2nd ed., pp. 83–84). New York, NY: Guilford Press.

13. Cozolino, L. (2017). *The Neuroscience of psychotherapy: Healing the social brain* (3rd ed., p. 231). New York, NY: W. W. Norton & Company.

14. Brewerton, T. D. (2004). *Clinical handbook of eating disorders.* New York, NY: Dekker.

Feldman, M. B., & Meyer, I. H. (2007). Childhood abuse and eating disorders in gay and bisexual men. *International Journal of Eating Disorders, 40*(5), 418–423.

Mitchell, K. S., Mazzeo, S. E., Schlesinger, M. R., Brewerton, T. D., & Smith, B. N. (2012). Comorbidity of partial and subthreshold PTSD among men and women with eating disorders in the National Comorbidity Survey-Replication Study. *International Journal of Eating Disorders, 45*(3), 307–315.

Reyes-Rodriquez, M., Von Holle, A., Ulman, T. F., Thorton, L. M., Klump, K. L., Brandt, H., . . . Bulik, C. M. (2011). Posttraumatic stress disorder in anorexia nervosa. *Psychosomatic Medicine, 73*(6), 491–497.

Tasca, G. A. Ritchie, K., Zachariades, F., Proulx. G., Trinneer, A., Balfour, L., . . . Bissada, H. (2013). Attachment insecurity mediates the relationship between childhood trauma and eating disorder psychopathology in a clinical sample: A structural equation model. *Child Abuse and Neglect, 37*(11), 926–933.

Wonderlich, S. A., Crosby, J. E., Mitchell, J. E., Thompson, K. M., Redlin, J., Demuth, G., . . . Haseltine, B. (2001). Eating disturbance and sexual trauma in childhood and adulthood. *International Journal of Eating Disorders, 30*(4), 401–412.

15. Brewerton, T. D. (2007). Eating disorders, trauma, and comorbidity: Focus on PTSD. *Eating Disorders, 15*(4), 285–304.

16. Brewerton, T. D. (2007). Eating disorders, trauma, and comorbidity: Focus on PTSD. *Eating Disorders, 15*(4), 285–304.

Briere, J., & Scott, C. (2007). Assessment of trauma symptoms in eating-disordered populations. *Eating Disorders, 15*(4), 347–358.

17. Brewerton, T. D. (2007). Eating disorders, trauma, and comorbidity: Focus on PTSD. *Eating Disorders, 15*(4), 285–304.

Dansky, B. S., Brewerton, T. D., O'Neil, P. M., & Kilpatrick, D. G. (1997). The National Womens Study: Relationship of victimization and posttraumatic stress disorder to bulimia nervosa. International Journal of Eating Disorders, 21(3), 213–228.

18. Backholm, K., Isomaa, R., & Birgegård, A. (2013). The prevalence and impact of trauma history in eating disorder patients. *European Journal of Psychotraumatology, 4.* doi:10.3402/ejpt. v4i0.22482

19. Mitchell, K. S., Mazzeo, S. E., Schlesinger, M. R., Brewerton, T. D., & Smith, B. N. (2012). Comorbidity of partial and subthreshold PTSD among men and women with eating disor-

ders in the National Comorbidity Survey-Replication Study. *International Journal of Eating Disorders, 45*(3), 307–315.

20. Damasio, A. (2012). *Self comes to mind: Constructing the conscious brain.* New York, NY: Vintage. Books.

21. Beales, D., & Dolton, R. (2000). Eating disordered patients: Personality, alexithymia, and implications for primary care. *British Journal of General Practice, 50*(450), 21–26.

22. Cook, A., Blaustein, M., Spinazzola, J., & van der Kolk, B. (Eds.) (2003). *Complex trauma in children and adolescents* (White paper). Retrieved from the National Child Traumatic Stress Network Complex Trauma Task Force, Substance Abuse and Mental Health Services Administration (SAMSA) U.S. Department of Health and Human Services. https://www.nctsn.org/what-is-child-trauma/trauma-types/complex-trauma/nctsn-resources?search=&resource_type=16&trauma_type=3&language=All&audience=All&other=All

23. Substance Abuse and Mental Health Services Administration (SAMSA) U.S. Department of Health and Human Services. (2003). *Complex trauma in children and adolescents* (White paper) retrieved from the National Child Traumatic Stress Network Complex Trauma Task Force https://www.nctsn.org/what-is-child-trauma/trauma-types/complex-trauma/nctsn-resources?search=&resource_type=16&trauma_type=3&language=All&audience=All&other=All

24. Fisher, J. (2017). *Healing the fragmented selves of trauma survivors.* New York, NY: Routledge.

25. Brewerton, T. D. (2007). Eating disorders, trauma, and comorbidity: Focus on PTSD. *Eating Disorders, 15*(4), 285–304.

26. Berczik, K., Szabo, A., Griffiths, M., Kurimay, T., Kun, B., Urban R., & Demetrovics, Z. (2012). Exercise addiction: Symptoms, diagnosis, epidemiology, and etiology. *Substance Use & Misuse, 47*(4), 403–417.

27. Holtkamp, K., Hebebrand, J., & Herpetz-Dahlmann, B. (2004). The contribution of anxiety and food restriction on physical activity levels in acute anorexia nervosa. *The International Journal of Eating Disorders, 36*(2), 163–171.

Sussman, S., Lisha, N., & Griffiths, M. D. (2011). Prevalence of the addictions: A problem of the majority or the minority? *Evaluation and the Health Professions, 34*(1), 3–56.

28. Wojtowicz, A. E., Alberga, A. S., Parsons, C. G., & von Ranson, K. M. (2015). Perspectives of Canadian fitness professionals on exercise and possible anorexia nervosa. *Journal of Eating Disorders, 3*(40), 1–10.

29. Alter, A. (2017). *Irresistible: The rise of addictive technology and the business of keeping us hooked.* New York, NY Penguin Press.

30. Schreiber, K., & Hausenblas, H. A. (2015). *The truth about exercise addiction: Understanding the dark side of thinspiration.* New York, NY: Bowman & Littlefield Publishers.

31. Perloff, R. M. (2014). Social media effects on young women's body image concerns: Theoretical perspectives and an agenda for research. *Sex Roles: A Journal of Research, 71*(11-12), 363–377.

32. Tao, Z. (2013). The relationship between Internet addiction and bulimia in a sample of Chinese college students: Depression as partial mediator between Internet addiction and bulimia. *Eating and Weight Disorders, 18*(3). doi:10.1007/s40519-013-0025-z

33. Šmahel, D., Macháčková, H., Šmahelová, M., Čevelíček, M., Almenara, C. A., & Holubčíková, J. (2018). *Digital technology, eating behaviors, and eating disorders.* Cham, Switzerland: Springer.

34. Čevelíček, M., Šmahelová, M., & Šmahel, D. (2018). Professionals' reflections about the impact of digital technologies on eating disorders. *Basic and Applied Social Psychology, 40*(3), 125–135.

35. Bayle, D. J., Henaff, M. A., & Krolak-Salmon, P. (2009). Unconsciously perceived fear in peripheral vision alerts the limbic system: A MEG study. *PLoS ONE, 4*(12), e8207.

36. van der Kolk, B. (2014). *The body keeps the score: Brain, mind, and body in the healing of trauma.* New York, NY: Penguin Books.

37. van der Kolk, B. (2014). *The body keeps the score: Brain, mind, and body in the healing of trauma.* New York, NY: Penguin Books.

38. Brewerton, T. D., & Dennis, A. B. (2016). Perpetuating factors in severe and enduring anorexia nervosa. In S. Touyz, P. Hay, D. Le Grange, & J. H. Lacey (Eds.), *Managing severe and enduring anorexia nervosa: A clinician's guide.* New York, NY: Routledge.

39. Cozolino, L. (2017). *The neuroscience of psychotherapy: Healing the social brain* (3rd ed., p. 362). New York, NY: W. W. Norton & Company.

40. van der Kolk, B. (2014). *The body keeps the score: Brain, mind, and body in the healing of trauma.* New York, NY: Penguin Books.

41. van der Kolk, B. (2014). *The body keeps the score: Brain, mind, and body in the healing of trauma.* New York, NY: Penguin Books.

42. Nowakowski, M. E., McFarlane, T., & Cassin, S. (2013). Alexithymia and eating disorders: A critical review of the literature. *Journal of Eating Disorders, 1*(1), 1–21.

Chapter 12

NARRATIVES FOR SELF-REALIZATION: COUNTERING DAMAGING IMAGES

A well-thought-out story doesn't need to resemble real life. Life itself tries with all its might to resemble a well-crafted story.

—Isaac Babel

Storytelling is a natural process of the human mind; we are both captivated by stories and deeply desire to tell them. A person's life narrative, the story the mind creates to make sense of or characterize the self, includes events, both trivial and important, and stories, both big and small. It is through the organizing of these events and stories into a meaningful life narrative that the sense of self is created. Narratives have the power to create and the power to heal. For healing to occur, the life narrative must incorporate an adaptive identity, one without eating disorder or trauma identities. At times, there is great resistance to letting go of a maladaptive identity that has provided a sense of safety or control in the midst of chaos.

Anyone who has been on the receiving end of a young child's story knows that the sequencing of events and culmination of their story may not follow what we consider proper storytelling structure. Practice hones the ability to sequence, to work through steps to solve problems, and to use story content to manage emotions. An emerging ability to characterize the self in abstract terms during adolescence and young adulthood fosters the organization that is necessary for drawing themes together to develop sense of self. Making meaning of these stories enables self-realization, the fulfillment of the client's potential, a therapeutic goal that may be impossible to achieve without the resolution of underlying trauma. Physical, cognitive, and emotional difficulties reside within a matrix of damage that impairs day-to-day functioning in traumatized individuals and limits their ability to organize stories into a coherent narrative. Until trauma is treated, there is little hope that the incoherent stories can coalesce into a narrative of self-realization.

INTEGRATION OF NARRATIVES

The therapist's role in the integration of client narratives is, first and foremost, to create and maintain a connection that allows the client to feel heard, seen, and safe in the presence of another. Allowing this connection can be daunting for a trauma survivor who has been betrayed by those who should have offered protection, thus therapist attunement during trauma work is crucial. Because the brain is a social organ, deeply responsive to significant relationships like psychotherapy, the co-construction of narratives in therapy is "capable of resculpting the brain's neural networks. Constructing and editing autobiographical memory can bridge processing from previously dissociated neural networks into a more cohesive story of the self."[1] Neural integration develops through conscious awareness of experiences, thoughts, emotions, sensations, and behaviors.

Narratives are based on memories retrieved from the past along with the modifications that arise when meaning is made in the telling of the story. The unending potential for rewriting of the narrative arises from the fact that neural networks of the brain are capable of continual modification. When clients enrich their story by incorporating new meaning, they can become editors and authors of new, more empowering stories. They can try on new ways of being and interacting in the world. Constructing a positive self-narrative can emphasize agency and redemption and is associated with better mental health across time.[2] Conscious awareness of the present shapes emotional experiencing, which, when coupled with meaning-making, promotes insight.

Trauma, however, keeps an individual locked in the past, replaying the same old stories and scenarios. Bessel van der Kolk describes this as a difficulty of memory, body awareness, identity, and capacity to move forward in life. "In order to know who we are—to have an identity—we must know (or at least feel that we know) what is and what was 'real.' We must observe what we see around us and label it correctly; we must also be able to trust our memories and be able to tell them apart from our imagination."[3] To do this, clients must directly address and resolve trauma. Many individuals, like Claire, must deal with the cumulative effects of multiple traumas. These clients may not recall specific traumatic content or be able to make a connection between current difficulties and their traumatic experiences; they are, nevertheless, severely hampered by the residual effects.

Goals of therapy for complex trauma are to increase the client's ability to: (1) feel safe (both physically and emotionally), (2) calm emotional reactions, (3) maintain calm in response to images, thoughts, and other sensations that remind them of the past, (4) engage in relationships while remaining fully present, (5) recognize the losses that surround relational trauma and make meaning of the traumatic events that keep them locked into negative patterns, and (6) develop adaptive views of themselves in the present and future.[4] Regardless of which treatment modality is chosen, these goals must be kept in mind. Complex trauma has poorer treatment outcomes than more basic forms of PTSD that result from a single traumatic event do, but complex trauma can be effectively treated with phase-oriented and multimodal modalities.[5] In the previous chapter, I introduced the initial treatment strategies used with Claire to help her begin to identify her emotions and calm from the storm of dysregulation. In this chapter, Claire's case is used to illustrate the phase-oriented treatment, which is based on the adaptive information processing model (AIP)[6] originally developed by Francine Shapiro to treat trauma. This model posits that trauma arises from dysfunctional stored memories, which are amenable to change when the memories are processed within larger adaptive networks.

Shapiro's therapeutic approach, Eye Movement Desensitization and Reprocessing (EMDR),[7] is a comprehensive approach with standardized protocols, including features of psychodynamic, interpersonal, cognitive behavioral, experiential, and body-focused therapy methods. While extensive review of the mechanisms of change initiated by EMDR are beyond the scope of this book, experts in the emerging field of neurobiology have offered explanations based on the modification of neural networks.[8] The EMDR processing protocol involves focusing attention on internal experiences such as memories, self-beliefs, emotions, and body sensations along with a bilateral, sensory stimulus that guides perceptual attention to external cues. The bilateral stimulation (BLS) may be administered through eye movements (the origin of "eye movement" in the name), audio tones, or through physical taps. The procedural components of

EMDR, including the dual attention stimuli, are thought to facilitate adaptive information processing of traumatic material.

Creation of new neural circuits and neural integration appear to be the primary objectives of EMDR, whether it be integration of affect with cognition, sensation, and behavior, or integration of traumatic memories into normal information processing.[9] The goal is to update the memory network to bring about resolution of emotional learning that has caused negative core beliefs about the self. Due to neuroplasticity, the brain can unlock the synapses of targeted emotional learning to allow modification of an existing memory on the basis of new information accessed in the therapeutic process.[10] The reconsolidation process is inherent in the brain's continual cycle of recalling memories and returning them, the same or altered, to long-term storage, but intentionally using the reconsolidation process to modify memories increases the efficacy of the therapeutic process.

Three steps toward therapeutically affecting memory reconsolidation are: (1) evoke target knowledge by presenting salient cues; (2) facilitate perceptions that pointedly differ from what is expected, which unlocks the original memory; and (3) present a new learning experience that contradicts or supplements the prior knowledge.[11] The steps of the reconsolidation process that are required for the brain to unlearn problematic existing knowledge are present in the EMDR protocol. After reconsolidation, emotional reactions to traumatic memories or cues are no longer activated, and symptoms of behavior, emotion, and thoughts related to the emotional reaction cease to occur. This suggests that when negative memories are reactivated in a safe, therapeutic environment, firmly grounded in the present, they can be reconsolidated without the negative affect that was stored with the original memory.[12] Using EMDR on dysfunctional memories, lessens their emotional intensity by prompting their reconsolidation within a safe environment.

TRAUMA REVISITED: ADAPTIVE INFORMATION PROCESSING

Despite the difficulties in treating clients with complex trauma, there is growing evidence that EMDR is effective with this population.[13] Still, resolution of trauma symptoms within a few sessions is unlikely to be a realistic goal when working with clients with a complex array of symptoms. EMDR fits within the phase-oriented model that has been shown to be effective with complex trauma.

Therapy dropout rates are high for those with complex trauma, but EMDR can offer relief to these clients without the recounting of details or even the sharing of memory content at all, allowing a client to process difficult material that cannot easily be articulated or that brings up core issues of shame or defectiveness. Detailed explanations of the EMDR theory, process, and supporting research can be obtained from EMDR resources listed at the end this chapter. One should not implement any EMDR protocol without first acquiring the required training; therapists working with clients with eating disorders and trauma would do well to become trained in the EMDR technique.

Therapeutic Resource Development

The first phase of EMDR treatment consists of stabilization, which includes development of trust in the therapeutic relationship and of resources and strategies the client can use to increase their affect tolerance and their capacity to observe internal and external experiences without becoming overwhelmed. Front-loading affect management enables the client to remain present to do the subsequent reprocessing work.[14] Without this preparation and attention to dyadic attunement during EMDR, trauma processing can potentially retraumatize the client. Multiple resources are reinforced throughout treatment—it is important that clients practice state change and containment strategies for managing difficult emotions or memories that may arise in the processing and between sessions. This phase also includes psychoeducation about negative memory networks that have become hardwired in the brain over the years and the use of EMDR to clean out and rewire these networks. Explaining what the process will entail gives the client a sense of control over the therapy.

In the first months of Claire's treatment we focused on affect tolerance as she slowly demonstrated trust in our relationship by revealing more about her past. Additional resource development was necessary to prepare her to calm strong emotions that can arise during and between EMDR sessions. Therapeutically reconsolidating a memory requires the memory be brought to mind without the client being so emotionally overpowered that the memory cannot be considered in the perspective of the safety of the present moment. In the AIP model, therapeutic resource development utilizes BLS to help the client adaptively change their emotional state by accessing core resources for tolerating and regulating strong affect.

Inquiring about symbolic, imaginal, or relational resources, along with experiences of success or mastery, is a starting point for identifying additional resources. The resources may rely on images, stories, metaphors, or humor. For clients with attachment difficulties, it is vital to identify positive attachment experiences, or, if these experiences are not available, to build resources signifying nurturing and safety. Claire had difficulty coming up with resources initially, but when asked to go inside for a moment in a calm state, she told a story of being asked by a childhood dance teacher to demonstrate an arabesque to the class. As she narrated this tale, her face lit up and she began to tear up as she described how she felt at that moment: light and content. I asked Claire to name this nurturing resource because the client's identification of the resource provides a shortcut to the calming effects now and during future processing. To foster a vivid association between Claire's chosen word, arabesque, and the calming feeling, Claire focused on the image in her memory and the word arabesque, along with her emotions and body sensations, during short sets of BLS to strengthen the resource.

Claire had a great deal of fear regarding what she might remember during processing, so I taught her the Two-Hand Interweave[15] to overcome her ambivalence to experiencing potentially disturbing mental content. By mentally placing the part of her that uses exercise to avoid her feelings in one hand and the part of her that wants to end this self-abuse in the other hand, she alternately opened and closes each hand to stimulate BLS, and this helped her feel more confident in handling information that might come up in processing. Despite her fears, she applied herself to developing and practicing these resource strategies.

Claire was ready to move to the next phase, trauma processing, once she could access memories without numbing or becoming overwhelmed by her emotions. She had learned to maintain the dual awareness of safety in the present moment and in another's presence while accessing difficult emotions and traumatic memories. The dual awareness she developed gave her the capacity to stay present in her body in the face of strong emotion and memory activation: she could feel safe in knowing that the traumatic events belong to the past

Treatment for complex trauma must be customized to the client's needs and guided by the client responses. Processing past, present, and future targets, along with reevaluation across treatment, form the basis of EMDR treatment. The following section on trauma processing is an overview of two EMDR sessions with Claire in which images that others had taken of her were used to facilitate memory processing of past and present targets. The images that other people take of us symbolize the version of us that they have constructed, and these may in some ways denote ownership or how they want us to be. Examining these images allows us to compare others' visual representations of the client with the client's own perspectives, thus facilitating self-knowledge and the opportunity to reimage oneself in more authentic ways. These sessions were selected for their ability to illustrate the power of images to facilitate EMDR processing; they do not represent the entire EMDR protocol used with Claire.

Trauma Processing

After clients have been well-prepared to manage the associated affect, trauma processing takes precedence over processing of current triggers for eating disorder behaviors because trauma is foundational driver for these behaviors.[16] The primary goal of this phase of treatment is to process the traumatic memories that keep the client locked into dysfunctional trauma-related beliefs and behaviors. Resolution of these patterns results from working directly with traumatic memories and triggers.[17] Creating a hierarchy of potential targets at the start of treatment, and keeping in mind that the sequence of targets is likely to shift as processing proceeds, is the first order of business. Once trauma is processed, clients are empowered to eliminate the remaining eating disorder symptoms.

Claire had a number of potential targets on her list: childhood emotional neglect and experiences of extreme loneliness; unmet needs for attachment and connection; emotional and physical abuse; her parent's addictions and divorce; episodes of binging, starving, and exercise; and, most recently, the traumatization of having intimate photographs of her shared online. Due to the developmental nature of Claire's numerous experiences of neglect and her difficulty in recalling much of her childhood, she stated that the most recent betrayal by her boyfriend stands out as the biggest trigger of her urge to restrict. Claire's response highlights the importance of flexibility in sequencing targets for processing. Ignoring or minimizing early neglect and abuse, which underlie current behaviors, is not unusual for clients with eating disorders. By processing the more recent trauma first, there is a high likelihood that earlier traumatic events will be brought into the process and will be resolved. Symptoms of trauma exposure for those with both childhood and adult trauma have been shown to be effectively reduced when EMDR targets the adult trauma that is obviously linked with the current symptoms.[18] Therefore, beginning with this trigger had the potential to impact Claire in a positive manner, and, as expected, her most recent trauma linked back to earlier trauma, thus enabling her to access and process earlier memories concurrently.

EMDR relies on the client's ability to access internal images for processing in session. When asked to recall an image that represents the worst part of the intimate photo event, Claire blankly stared across the room and stated that nothing came to mind. She told me she felt disconnected, like it had happened to someone else. Stories contain visual imagery because our minds fill in the picture with rich detail based on our inner perceptions, but perhaps Claire blocked these images to protect herself. Sometimes, "forgetting into the unconscious" is the only way to endure a situation at the time of traumatization. Images associated with the trauma can allow retrieval of self when the past is reclaimed by accessing privileged knowledge of the self.[19] The use of others' images of a client can be a launching point for examining identity across time and creating new stories of identity.

As we talked about the images her boyfriend took of her, Claire realized that she was so overcome upon seeing what he had done that she only glanced at them before reporting that they had been posted without her consent. The images were quickly removed from social media, but she saved them on her phone, although she was not sure why. As an indication of her desire to move forward, she stated that she was ready to face seeing them now. I asked her to choose one that brought up a strong response for her. It matters not whether the therapist can see the images, only that the client can use them as a bridge to the thoughts, emotions, and sensations brought up by viewing them. Claire flushed as she first flipped through the images and then chose one to focus on. As her eyes clouded with tears, she said that she was ashamed that she let Tanner take these photos.

Using the standard EMDR protocol, Claire was prompted to *Identify the negative belief about yourself this memory brings up.* "I don't deserve to be loved." Claire relayed that the image is huge in her mind, like on a movie screen. Clients can shrink the size of an image or allow it to go black and white if they feel inundated in the moment. I asked Claire to notice the image and belief, along with the emotions and sensations she was experiencing in her body, while staying present as sets of BLS were applied, which initiated the processing. At the end of the first set, Claire gave a brief account of the evening these images were taken. "I didn't want Tanner to take any photos of me, but he promised that the images would be our special secret and no one else would see them. Now when I see these images all I can remember is how uncomfortable I felt allowing him to take those pictures. When I see them now, it's like I'm still giving him all the power—so he wouldn't get mad or get his feelings hurt, but then I was the one who got mad that I had to do what he wanted. I didn't respond to any of his messages for a few days, and he was texting me constantly to answer him. I'm still mad at myself for giving in to him." *What do you notice now?* "I'm totally exhausted." The next set of BLS was initiated and she was guided to notice those sensations.

Over the next several sets of BLS, Claire was encouraged to continue her discovery by returning to the original image. After sets, I asked her questions like *What do you get now?* I would also remind her to notice the memory while staying here with me. She initially focused on her belief that none of her boyfriends cared enough about her to try and understand what she had been through, but then she amended this to they couldn't understand what she has been through. She realized she chose these men because she thought each of them would give her the care she didn't get from her family. *That's a heavy burden for a high school boy.*

Through the next several sets Claire continued to stay in the same loop, describing her current relationship difficulties. "I don't let anyone in enough to really know me or be there for me. It's safer to keep one foot in and one foot out the door." And she wondered if she doesn't get too close to anyone so she can keep her options open. "About two months into a new relationship, I become really distant and mean so they will leave and I won't have to breakup with them." Then she described a weekend getaway with Tanner in the mountains a few months back when she was more wracked with obsessive thoughts about eating than usual and wasn't able to work out, so she purged several times to relieve the tension. She ruined the weekend for both of them, but when he didn't leave, as she expected, she ended the relationship.

Cognitive looping occurs when clients are stuck in the same negative thoughts and continue to have a high level of disturbance through sets of BLS. When this occurs, a cognitive interweave, a more proactive EMDR technique, can be used to introduce new information or a new perspective, instead of depending on the client to provide it. Interweaves occur when the therapist offers a statement or question to "therapeutically weave together the appropriate neural networks and associations."[20] This is similar to the strategy in photo therapy of asking questions to explore an image, especially if the image portrays something that is profoundly different from the client's perception of the actual moment, thus creating a cognitive struggle.[21] While photo therapy protocol might ask, *What's under this?* I use less direct questions in these situations to introduce interweaves that elicit thoughts and imagery related to more adaptive perspectives.

The cognitive interweave question, *What would someone not know about you from looking at this photograph?* followed by additional BLS sets brought up information that Claire was previously unaware of. As Claire moved through several sets of processing, there were gradual shifts, indicating the processing of a block. She began by recalling a car wreck her father was involved in when she was in third grade. Even though it was uncertain whether he would survive his injuries, she remembers smiling when she was told of the accident. Claire continues to feel guilty that she reacted this way. While continuing the processing, her heartbeat rose as she recalled walking in on her father and a woman other than her mother in bed. She recalled her father threatening to send her off to live with her aunt if she told anyone. "I was afraid of him, that he would lose his temper and throw me against the wall, so I didn't tell anyone." She didn't know whether her mother knew about this affair, but she believed her father encouraged her mother to overuse prescription drugs because it allowed him to do what he wanted.

When Claire's breathing or other nonverbal behaviors indicated something was emotionally significant, I guided her to notice any sensations in her body and where the sensations were located as I initiated another set of BLS. She recalled childhood memories of being in unsafe situations with her father and feeling confused when he made suggestive comments to her and teased her in sexually inappropriate ways while also making her keep his sexual secrets. She linked this back to the original image we began with and to Tanner sharing the nude images of her. I asked her another cognitive interweave question to draw out the meaning she makes of that image: *How much of this image is representative of yourself, and how much is Tanner's definition of you?* "Tanner tried to take the pictures and make them look the way he wanted me to be, like I'm his property," and by posting them on social media, he affirmed his belief that the photos were his property, too.

Mixed messages on the taboo topic of sexuality was the norm in Claire's family. She was to tolerate her father's inappropriate remarks and to cover up his sexual exploits while he teased her about her own sexuality. Claire learned that she had to play by others' rules: males can be sexual, and she needs to please them, but she should be ashamed of her own sexuality. She was humiliated by Tanner, and she reacted by taking her feelings out on herself. Claire stated her anger at not being allowed to be as sexual as guys and her resolve to not allow someone else to control her sexuality. These expressions showed that Claire was constructing a new story around these images as she claimed that she has a right to privacy and to be sexual.

As the processing continued, Claire expressed self-blame for her attraction to men who are similar to her father. I ask, *Who is responsible for your learning to choose men like him?* This helped Claire recognize that her parents didn't protect her but also that she does not have to put herself in the same situation. She does not have to be with unsafe men to avoid being alone, and she does not have to sabotage relationships by shutting off from her emotions or who she is. Claire's insight from this session was significant: she learned that she is not responsible for what her father did or taught her, but she must start making better choices if she wants to break her patterns with men.

Using cognitive interweaves on topics of responsibility, safety, and choice accelerates processing of early trauma to resolve negative cognitions, such as beliefs that one does not deserve to be loved. A person who experiences the early trauma of threatened abandonment or the trauma of abandonment by parents who were unable to care for them due to addiction may be capable of initiating relationships, but growing intimacy in the relationship may trigger fear of again being abandoned and unhealthy relationship behaviors.[22] After the distress behind the negative cognition is resolved, BLS is used to strengthen the positive cognition "I deserve to be loved," and a body scan is performed to identify any remaining tension that would indicate a need for additional work on this target. For a client who did not witness positive relationships in their family, it is important to discuss the characteristics of and strategies for healthy relationships in future sessions.

The second EMDR session with Claire, described next, also began with a current trigger for her eating disorder symptoms, Claire's repetitive focus on her weight. Disruptive eating disorder behaviors are adaptive in the sense that they serve to manage affect. Eating disordered behaviors sometimes become the sole focus of treatment when the clinician is distracted from addressing the root cause of the client's need for affect management. Indeed, the client desires relief from overwhelming affect, and affect management strategies are imperative to symptom management, but the underlying trauma will remain and continue to trigger strong affect unless it is directly addressed. Symptom-focused EMDR can effectively identify memories rooted in early trauma that are activated and germane to present symptoms.[23] Individuals with eating disorders are exceptionally adept at exiling shame, emptiness, and misery to their bodies so they don't have to experience these crushing emotions. Bridging neural networks that hold the disparate components of the memories underlying these feelings while in the safe, dual awareness of EMDR, facilitates processing of the trauma. The AIP model suggests that insight and integration arise when the neural networks are bridged.

Negative beliefs about physical appearance underlie eating disorder thoughts and behaviors; extreme body dissatisfaction initiates and reinforces the dysfunctional behaviors. Clients cannot be talked out of negative beliefs nor otherwise convinced of their falsity Until the material at the core of the negative belief is addressed, clients will continue to believe they are overweight despite evidence to the contrary. Similarly to many other eating disorder clients, Claire spoke of being overweight across her entire life as if it was an indisputable fact, so I asked her to bring some childhood photos to our next session, which she readily agreed to do. When I saw the images she brought, I didn't see the chubby child she perceived herself to have been, but my opinion was irrelevant to her deeply engrained belief about herself. I asked basic questions about the images for context, *Who took this image?* "My mom. There aren't that many photos of my childhood, but she was the only one who took any pictures at all, other than school pictures." *What do you remember about the day this image was taken?* "Nothing really. I remember not liking to have my picture taken, but I don't remember anything in particular about this day. My mom would say mean things about my pictures, like make fun of my hair or say I looked fat in them." Rather than continuing with additional questions, as would be the course in photo therapy, these images can be used as a path for Claire to explore the source of her body dissatisfaction by processing the related, though currently unconscious, content associated with them through EMDR.

Claire viewed these images through another person's constructed version of her, made for their own reasons and captured at the moment of their choosing. *What negative belief comes up for you when you view these images?* "I'm fat and ugly." Accessing early memories associated with Claire's body hatred was initiated with an EMDR float-back technique,[24] which began by guiding her with the prompt: *Allow your mind float back to an earlier time when you felt fat and ugly, and tell me the image that comes to mind.* The first image that Claire recalled spurred her to recount an earlier story, one she told me the day we met, when her mother implied she was fat and told her that fat girls start their periods early. In this session, she added to the original story, recalling other times her mother criticized her body and that she was also repeatedly told that she had pimples because she ate fattening foods. Claire was encouraged to notice a particular aspect of this content and her sensations while experiencing a series of BLS sets. She then drifted back to earlier memories that she had previously been unable to recall. Several memories evoked the terror she felt when locked in her room by her mother and the loneliness and despair she experienced upon finding her mother passed out in bed in the afternoon when she returned from school. She was able to process through these disturbing memories by using previously established resources.

Claire walked through her childhood home in her mind and cried in desolation as she felt stuck in various rooms. I suggested she observe her memories as if she were a passenger on a train, merely observing the scene, and despite her distress, she was able to continue processing these painful memories. The kitchen had particularly disturbing associations—she realized that her mother was angry at her for wanting and needing to be fed. These words express her dilemma: "I want her to get up and make dinner or take care of me. She would sometimes wake up and get really mad at me for bothering her. Then it was worse. She still didn't make dinner, just screamed at me until I ran upstairs and hid. I still feel guilty when I'm hungry, just like I did then. The less I eat, the less guilty I feel. I hate needing so much. I can't make my mom happy or make her quit using drugs, but at least I can have a body she won't criticize if I work hard enough."

Food symbolizes many aspects of the mother–child relationship. In infancy, feeding time is a bonding experience, and food soothes the discomfort of hunger. In many ways, how food and feeding is handled is the child's first introduction to the function of food and the child's right to have needs, both physically and emotionally. Shame at having physical needs, having a body that needs nourishment, puts a person in a problematic predicament. Giving into needs results in shame and guilt. Not giving into needs is less shameful but destroys the body. Unless this is resolved, clients will always feel too big and too needy. It's no wonder Claire freaked out if she gained a pound and relished compliments for losing weight.

For the next set, I asked Claire, *What comes to mind when you think of feeling guilty for needing a mother?* "When I look at that picture of me as a little girl, I don't' see the chubby kid my mother said I was. I wanted so much for her to act like she loved me and take care of me [crying]. *Stay there and focus on what you feel in your body* [with another set of BLS]. Claire continued to cry as she described feeling small and helpless. *Is there anyone who can be there for you?* "My aunt, Jen. She would have helped if she knew what was going on. She is telling me that she is sorry she was not there for me. I remember that she gave me that shirt I'm wearing in the picture for my birthday. I didn't get to see her much. I don't think my mom liked her to show me attention. Yeah, I think she would have been there for me." *Is there a message in that photo?* Claire knew immediately. "I want to accept myself and not let my mom or how she treats me define who I am." *How do you feel about this?* "I'm sad I have no one. I'm so alone. I wasn't living all those years, I'm not really living now either. I realize I have to let go of trying to control everything."

The last processing set in this session resulted in Claire viewing her aunt as a potential support. It is helpful to end sessions with a focus on resources, such as the safe/calm place, to provide grounding and a sense of closure. Claire selected her aunt as a resource, which is a good choice as her aunt has demonstrated a desire to be more involved in her life and is the person who helped Claire seek treatment. BLS was used to strengthen her ability to access positive thoughts, feelings, and imagery related to her aunt.

Both of these EMDR sessions illustrate how powerful others' images of us can be, whether they are kept in family collections or put on social media for public consumption. Many inner processes are censored from our awareness until a new way of perceiving an image sheds light on relationship dynamics between us and another.[25] Bringing the unconscious into awareness can be empowering.

At the next session, Claire reported that she was initially quite upset after the previous week's session, but that she successfully used self-tapping to strengthen her resources and to calm herself. She said she thought she had accepted the fact that her parents are still not really in her life, but that she still felt some anger and disappointment that they won't get their lives together. She was also very sad about not getting the care she needed from them, especially from her mother, but she knew she was making progress because she was not overwhelmed by these feelings. She recalled a dream she had a few nights earlier of telling her mother off for being selfish and then turning around and seeing other family members there confirming her statements. Through dreams such as this, clients report continued processing as their mind continues to transform the material brought up in EMDR sessions.

Claire gained a new awareness of the roots of her eating disorder behaviors as well as the roots of other behaviors that impacted her negatively—not reaching out to others, not asking for help, and allowing abusive people into her life. Her early strategy of showing her neediness did not get her addicted mother to respond to her needs, so Claire learned to be manipulative and controlling. When this, too, did not produce the response she wanted, she knew of no other means to protect herself than to distance herself from everyone. Resolving her difficulties connecting with others, which were acquired when various strategies failed to work in the past, reduced her need for control and perfectionism and to create a false self. Reconnecting to and processing the pain of early abandonment allowed Claire to mourn the losses and develop a healthy self, free from body obsession and the need to hide behind heavy makeup and a perfect appearance.

Shame can be replaced by self-compassion and a newly created narrative. Claire's erratic childhood with addicted parents hindered the creation of a life story from which she could form a healthy identity. The clinician's role is to facilitate the processing of the trauma so that narratives from the past can be edited based on new information and perceptions. "The overall goal is combining emotion with conscious awareness and rewriting the story of the self. These processes, when successful, enhance growth, integration, and flexibility of neural networks and human experience."[26] Once past traumas are processed, the therapist and client move to the final stage of EMDR treatment, which addresses future behaviors.

Linking Past Experiences with Future Expectations

The final stage of EMDR treatment aims to equip the client with the ability to take updated information, learned in processing, into future situations and encounters. The future protocol consists of EMDR targeting along with education, modeling, and imagining a future.[27] Trauma robs one of their future by inhibiting a person's ability to imagine. It is only through reconsolidating memories to resolve trauma that the client can hope to escape the unrelenting symptoms that keep them locked in the past. With resolution comes the opportunity to create a coherent narrative and form a healthy self-identity.

Coherent narratives depend on one's ability to order life experiences sequentially. By integrating multiple neural networks, the narrative organizes autobiographical memories to enhance self-awareness and self-regulation. "To serve their important role in emotion regulation, narratives need to have a brief summary or hook that can be held in mind in the present moment."[28] This hook reminds the client instantly of the beginning, middle, and end of the narrative. Similar to resource development prior to trauma processing, a hook can be an image, word, or phrase that instantly calls to mind the message of the narrative. Reinforcing this resource with BLS further integrates the positive narrative. Claire chose an internal image of herself standing on the edge of the Grand Canyon, a place she hopes to one day visit. To her, this image signifies "vast hope." Whether this image remains in her mind or becomes another file on her phone, it signifies an imagining of her future.

In many ways, the goal of trauma treatment is to free clients to realize their full potential. This seems to align with purpose, the need in all humans to have a reason for existence. Referring to Pavlov's assertion that the "Reflex of Purpose" is the most important factor in life, Bessel van der Kolk believes that one the most destructive effects of trauma is damage to the "Reflex of Purpose." By inhibiting the effective use of the emotions that motivate people to develop themselves to the fullest, trauma impairs the drive and capacity to hope for something better.[29] We must have a comfortable connection with our inner sensations to access our emotions and to know that desire lives within us. If clients can trust their emotions to give them accurate information, they can regain the energy to strive for self-realization and a sense of purpose. Effective trauma treatment activates the brain's natural neuroplasticity through the multiple modalities of body awareness, emotion regulation, connection with others, trauma processing, and rewriting the narrative.

EMDR RESOURCES

Chen, R., Gillespie, A., Zhao, Y., Xi, Y., Ren, Y., & McLean, L. (2018). The efficacy of eye movement desensitization and reprocessing in children and adults who have experienced complex childhood trauma: A systematic review of randomized controlled trials. *Frontiers in Psychology, 9*(534). doi:10.3389/fpsyg.2018.00534.

Cooke, L. J., & Grand, C. (2009). The neurobiology of eating disorders, affect regulation skills and EMDR in the treatment of eating disorders. In R. Shapiro (Ed.), *EMDR solutions II: For depression, eating disorders, performance and more* (pp. 129–150). New York, NY: W. W. Norton & Company.

Cozolino, L. (2017). *The neuroscience of psychotherapy: Healing the social brain.* (3rd ed.) New York, NY: W. W. Norton & Company.

Ecker, B., Ticic, R., & Hulley, L. (2012). Unlocking the emotional brain: Eliminating symptoms at their roots using memory reconsolidation. New York, NY: Routledge.

Korn, D. L. (2009). EMDR and the treatment of complex PTSD: A review. *Journal of EMDR Practice and Research, 3*(4), 264–278.

Panksepp, J., & Biven, L. (2012). The archaeology of mind: Neuroevolutionary origins of human emotions. New York, NY: W. W. Norton & Company.

Parnell, L. (2008). *Tapping in: A step-by-step guide to activating your healing resources through bilateral stimulation.* Boulder, CO: Sounds True, Inc.

Scholom, J. (2009). Integrating eating disorders treatment into the early phases of the EMDR protocol. In R. Shapiro (Ed.). *EMDR solutions II: For depression, eating disorders, performance and more* (pp. 114–128). New York, NY: W. W. Norton & Company.

Shapiro F. (2001). *Eye movement desensitization and reprocessing: Basic principles, protocols, and procedures.* New York, NY: Guilford.

Shapiro, F. (Ed.) (2002). *EMDR as an integrative psychotherapy approach: Experts of diverse orientations explore the paradigm prism.* Washington, DC: American Psychological Association.

Shapiro, F., & Forrest, M. (2016). *EMDR: The breakthrough therapy for overcoming anxiety, stress, and trauma.* New Your, NY: Basic Books.

Shapiro, R. (Ed.) (2005). *EMDR solutions: Pathways to healing.* New York, NY: W. W. Norton & Company.

Shapiro, R. (Ed.) (2009). *EMDR solutions II: For depression, eating disorders, performance and more.* New York, NY: W. W. Norton & Company.

Solomon, R. M., & Shapiro F. (2008). EMDR and the Adaptive Information Processing Model: Potential mechanisms of change. *Journal of EMDR Practice and Research, 2*(4), 315–325.

van der Kolk, B. A., Spinazzola, J., Blaustein, M. E., Hopper, J. W., Hopper, E. K., Korn, D. L., & Simpson, W. B. (2007). A randomized clinical trial of eye movement desensitization and reprocessing (EMDR), fluoxetine, and pill placebo in the treatment of posttraumatic stress disorder: treatment effects and long-term maintenance. *Journal of Clinical Psychiatry, 68*(1), 37–46.

van der Kolk, B. (2014). *The body keeps the score: Brain, mind, and body in the healing of trauma.* New York, NY: Penguin Books.

REFERENCES

1. Cozolino, L. (2017). *The neuroscience of psychotherapy: Healing the social brain* (3rd ed., p. 399). New York, NY: W. W. Norton & Company.
2. Adler, J. M., Turner, A. F., Brookshier, K. M., Monahan, C., Walder-Biesanz, I., Harmeling, L. H. . . . Oltmanns, T. F. (2015). Variation in narrative identity is associated with trajectories of mental health over several years. *Journal of Personality and Social Psychology, 108*(3), 476–496.
3. van der Kolk, B. (2014). *The body keeps the score: Brain, mind, and body in the healing of trauma* (p. 136). New York, NY: Penguin Books.
4. Substance Abuse and Mental Health Services Administration (SAMSA) U.S. Department of Health and Human Services. (2003). *Complex trauma in children and adolescents* (White paper)

retrieved from the National Child Traumatic Stress Network Complex Trauma Task Force) https://www.nctsn.org/what-is-child-trauma/trauma-types/complex-trauma/nctsn-resources ?search=&resource_type=16&trauma_type=3&language=All&audience=All&other=All

5. Korn, D. L. (2009). EMDR and the treatment of complex PTSD: A review. *Journal of EMDR Practice and Research, 3*(4), 264–278.

6. Solomon, R. M., & Shapiro F. (2008). EMDR and the Adaptive Information Processing Model: Potential mechanisms of change. *Journal of EMDR Practice and Research, 2*(4), 315–325.

7. Shapiro F. (2001). *Eye movement desensitization and reprocessing: Basic principles, protocols, and procedures.* New York, NY: Guilford.

   Shapiro, R. (Ed.) (2005). *EMDR solutions: Pathways to healing.* New York, NY: W. W. Norton & Company.

8. Ecker, B., Ticic, R., & Hulley, L. (2012). Unlocking the emotional brain: Eliminating symptoms at their roots using memory reconsolidation. New York, NY: Routledge.

   Panksepp, J., & Biven, L. (2012). The archaeology of mind: Neuroevolutionary origins of human emotions. New York, NY: W. W. Norton & Company.

9. Cozolino, L. (2017). *The neuroscience of psychotherapy: Healing the social brain* (3rd ed.). New York, NY: W. W. Norton & Company.

10. Ecker, B., Ticic, R., & Hulley, L. (2012). Unlocking the emotional brain: Eliminating symptoms at their roots using memory reconsolidation. New York, NY: Routledge.

11. Ecker, B., Ticic, R., & Hulley, L. (2012). Unlocking the emotional brain: Eliminating symptoms at their roots using memory reconsolidation. New York, NY: Routledge.

12. Panksepp, J., & Biven, L. (2012). The archaeology of mind: Neuroevolutionary origins of human emotions. New York, NY: W. W. Norton & Company.

13. Chen, R., Gillespie, A., Zhao, Y., Xi, Y., Ren, Y., & McLean, L. (2018). The efficacy of eye movement desensitization and reprocessing in children and adults who have experienced complex childhood trauma: A systematic review of randomized controlled trials. *Frontiers in Psychology, 9*(534). doi:10.3389/fpsyg.2018.00534.

14. Shapiro, R. (Ed.) (2009). *EMDR solutions II: For depression, eating disorders, performance and more.* New York, NY: W. W. Norton & Company.

15. Cooke, L. J., & Grand, C. (2009). The neurobiology of eating disorders, affect regulation skills and EMDR in the treatment of eating disorders. In R. Shapiro (Ed.), *EMDR solutions II: For depression, eating disorders, performance and more* (pp. 129–150). New York, NY: W. W. Norton & Company.

16. Scholom, J. (2009). Integrating eating disorders treatment into the early phases of the EMDR protocol. In R. Shapiro (Ed.). *EMDR solutions II: For depression, eating disorders, performance and more* (pp. 114–128). New York, NY: W. W. Norton & Company.

17. Shapiro F. (2001). *Eye movement desensitization and reprocessing: Basic principles, protocols, and procedures.* New York, NY: Guilford.

18. van der Kolk, B. A., Spinazzola, J., Blaustein, M. E., Hopper, J. W., Hopper, E. K., Korn, D. L., & Simpson, W. B. (2007). A randomized clinical trial of eye movement desensitization and reprocessing (EMDR), fluoxetine, and pill placebo in the treatment of posttraumatic stress diorder: treatment effects and long-term maintenance. *Journal of Clinical Psychiatry, 68*(1), 37–46.

19. Weiser, J. (1999). *Photo Therapy techniques: Exploring the secrets of personal snapshots and family albums* (p. 307). Vancouver, BC: Judy Weiser and PhotoTherapy Centre Publishers.

20. Shapiro F. (2001). *Eye movement desensitization and reprocessing: Basic principles, protocols, and procedures* (p. 249). New York, NY: Guilford.

21. Weiser, J. (1999). *Photo Therapy techniques: Exploring the secrets of personal snapshots and family albums* (p. 307). Vancouver, BC: Judy Weiser and PhotoTherapy Centre Publishers.

22. Koukkou, M., & Lehmann, D. (2006). Experience-dependent brain plasticity: A key concept for studying nonconscious decisions. *International Congress Series, 1286,* 45–52.

23. Korn, D. L. (2009). EMDR and the treatment of complex PTSD: A review. *Journal of EMDR Practice and Research, 3*(4), 264–278.

24. Shapiro F. (2001). *Eye movement desensitization and reprocessing: Basic principles, protocols, and procedures.* New York, NY: Guilford.

25. Weiser, J. (1999). *Photo Therapy techniques: Exploring the secrets of personal snapshots and family albums* (p. 307). Vancouver, BC: Judy Weiser and PhotoTherapy Centre Publishers.

26. Cozolino, L. (2017). *The neuroscience of psychotherapy: Healing the social brain* (3rd ed., p. 38). New York, NY: W. W. Norton & Company.

27. Shapiro F. (2001). *Eye movement desensitization and reprocessing: Basic principles, protocols, and procedures.* New York, NY: Guilford.

28. Cozolino, L. (2017). *The neuroscience of psychotherapy: Healing the social brain* (3rd ed., p. 191–192). New York, NY: W. W. Norton & Company.

29. van der Kolk, B. (2014). *The body keeps the score: Brain, mind, and body in the healing of trauma* (p. 78). New York, NY: Penguin Books.

Chapter 13

AUTHENTIC IDENTITY IN A SOCIAL MEDIA AGE

For a long time, we assume we know who we are, until the moment we fully realize who that is; in that moment, identity is no longer predictable, but rather takes the form of a truth that, like any other, can become a sentence with no more than a change of perspective.

—Sergio Chejfec

Most of us do not easily embrace change. We look to our past and realize that much has shifted in our lifetimes, but we have a harder time predicting the future. Maybe we want to believe that we ourselves and the lives we live now will remain stable, that the continuous vicissitudes of life will settle into a state of constancy. The imagination cannot begin to foresee or comprehend the technological advances of the next twenty years any easier than it could predict the impact of smartphones and social media on daily life today. Young people must now grapple with issues of identity, privacy, and social dynamics in a world that holds little semblance to the one in which previous generations came of age. New innovations such as virtual reality and artificial intelligence are likely to present further challenges, as the line between digital and physical realities is further blurred in the coming decades.

In the media a steady stream of reports present evidence of the fragility of those currently coming of age. Generation snowflake is a particularly apt moniker for this generation that appears less resilient and more sensitive than previous generations. Their reports of mental health difficulties are reducing the stigma of mental illness, but at the same time indicate alarming trends: at least 30 million people in the United States suffer from eating disorders,[1] college campuses cannot keep up with the demand for mental health care, and many young people feel incapable of entering the workforce. Therapists are obliged to continually learn new skills and adapt to changing cultural forces to remain relevant agents of change for a generation raised in the public arena of social media.

In past generations, the achievement and timing of marker events signaled entry into adulthood. By their mid-twenties, most young people of the last century had attained a formal education, left home, entered the work force, married, and become parents.[2] Massive cultural changes, many driven by technological advances, have caused youths to delay their entry into adulthood and altered the very nature of the phase between childhood and adulthood, as well as the criteria used to assess whether one has attained adulthood. An extended period that begins after adolescence, emerging adulthood,[3] is now characterized by tasks that were previously thought to occur in adolescence. Primary among these tasks is identity formation, a task that takes on new meaning in an era of mass consumerism, globalization, and enlarged social networks. It is within this changing landscape that therapists meet clients, one now dominated by visual images and a 24/7 online presence.

The overarching aim of this book is to illustrate therapeutic means to aid identity formation within the social media context in which the search for self now occurs. Eating disorders are identity thieves that steal the authentic self by diverting attention away from the true feelings, reactions, and values of a person. Eating disorders take over a person's life until they define themself only by how closely they are able to adhere to the rules of the eating disorder. Eating disorder treatment is exceptionally challenging in the social media age because clients are acutely sensitive to visual images and are reinforced for adhering to unrealistic standards of appearance. Effective treatment strategies must acknowledge the centrality of photographs to sense of self in this population. Successful therapies initiate neurobiological change; hence, we choose methods and interventions that cultivate neuroplasticity. *Cultivate* is a fitting term for what we, as therapists, do to nurture and stimulate neural growth and integration. With an emphasis on relationships and narrative construction—the foundation upon which identity formation progresses—the treatment excerpts in this book illustrate how these concepts fit with the self-oriented processes of compassion, reflection, awareness, differentiation, and realization to cultivate neurobiological enrichment.

Client-centered experiential photo therapy techniques fit within a model of neural enhancement based on extensive connections between the visual and emotional systems in the brain. The personal nature of the images used in photo therapy and the relational context of the model permit therapists to meet clients where they are in the social media age—online and immersed in visuals. Adapting treatment to the unique demands of young people who are struggling with identity formation requires therapeutic interventions that cultivate skills in social media literacy, relational engagement, rewriting narratives, and the self-oriented processes of compassion, reflection, awareness, differentiation, and realization that enable clients to experience a sense of self.

CULTIVATING SOCIAL MEDIA LITERACY

With mass adoption of digital technology and social media, visual images have come to exert enormous influence on how we perceive and interact with ourselves and others. Imagine for a moment a social media feed without images, just lines and lines of text. Would these platforms have the same appeal without the visual images that bring the content alive? Probably not, for most of us, as we have become accustomed to the language of visual images, and we expect to be entertained and educated by a continuous stream of images. As the preferred means of expression, images saturate and bring immediacy to all aspects of life. Images have unmatched facility to speak symbolically, to unlock underlying meaning, and to reach suppressed emotions.

The freedom to express all parts of the self, including parts that are often hidden in order to gain acceptance and approval, is necessary to form an authentic identity. It can be exceedingly difficult to unify what one feels on the inside with one's outer expression of self, especially on social media. But not feeling authentic is a negative state. Being one's true self is the basis for self-worth and feelings of authenticity.[4] In contrast, creating an online persona for others to like or follow flattens and narrows the self into a self-brand that centers on self-promotion and inauthenticity. Self becomes a product, and there is always a loss of self in the transactional nature of selling the self.

When it is impossible to know or voice what one feels, thinks, wants, or needs, one's true self remains buried beneath a false persona that relies on approval from others. Overdependence on affirmation from others constrains all aspects of life. Accordingly, identity formation in the public forum of social media is fraught with potential difficulties. Social media users self-censor when they worry about how much to share and what others' will think of their posts. Have they disclosed too much, and do they come across as bragging? The gap between reality and the idealized narrative can make a person feel like a fraud. Without a reasonably steady sense of identity, a client is likely to cling to their eating disorder identity, unable to recognize harmful beliefs.

Photo therapy pays homage to the significance of visual images to young people today, and the techniques described in this book are accessible to practitioners regardless of whether they have expertise in photography. Like art-based therapies, photo therapy allows interpretive freedom for client-directed exploration without, however, the imperative that the therapist be trained in art or photography. In fact, those with photographic training may find their attention diverted to issues of composition or exposure instead of adhering to the therapeutic processing of images as communicators of meaning and emotions. Although photo therapy is not a standalone treatment for eating disorders, photo therapy techniques offer additional therapeutic skills to the already-trained therapist that assist in processing visual content. The techniques are most effective when creatively combined to fit the unique needs of each client.[5] The techniques can be incorporated into other treatment modalities and creatively combined to address each client's particular social media difficulties. Photo therapy emphasizes client choice and personal interpretation, empowering the young person who is in the midst of identity formation.

Through therapeutic conversations around images, whether they be client-produced or taken by others, clients acquire the discernment to interact with social media in ways that empower them to resist unhealthy cultural messages and to live more of life offline. Understanding why social media draws people in and how images distort the truth are essential to cultivating social media literacy. Similarly to the open-ended questions used in motivational interviewing, photo therapy questions allow clients to explore their experiences with images and consider their readiness for change. While photo therapy techniques have been used in a variety of therapeutic settings, application to social media practices make it more relevant than ever.

CULTIVATING RELATIONSHIPS

In the social media age not only are young people marrying later, they are also, as a general rule, less connected to others. Owing to the superficial nature of online life and limited face-to-face relationships, young people may view relationships as exceedingly important or perilously undependable. With marriage no longer a marker event for reaching adulthood, one's subjective sense of independence and autonomy may be a more relevant measure than the timing or accomplishment of marker events.[6] In an era typified by lack of empathy and alarming levels of loneliness, autonomy brings forth new challenges for young people, for autonomy itself is buttressed by social relationships, and it is within relationship that identity is solidified. The relational aspects of health cannot be underestimated. Virtually all modern psychotherapies acknowledge the importance of the client–therapist relationship to successful therapy outcomes. The neurobiological basis for the healing potential of relationships is based on the premise that the human brain is hardwired to connect. From our very first relationships, our brains are wired through interaction with others. It is in this context that neural complexity develops, and it is in relationships of attunement, empathy, and resonance that the brain heals.[7]

Eating disorders, however, are diseases of disconnection, often beginning as a means to deal with pain and to self-protect when relationships are challenged. Eating disorder symptoms provide emotional safety, but at the same time compete with and even replace relational opportunities to the detriment of connection. Healing from an eating disorder takes place in and through relational connections, both with the therapist and with others; however, social media does not inherently provide the type of relational connections that foster growth and healing.

Face-to-face conversations with another person bring forth a full sensory encounter as we make eye contact, hear the voice, and perhaps touch and even note a distinct smell associated with the experience. These interactions trigger neurochemical responses that regulate and connect relational participants to one another. Online exchanges are not in and of themselves harmful, but they do not provide the same level of connection as, and they do little to alleviate the human need for, face-to-face contact with others. While technology will continue to push the boundaries of online interactions, humans will not outgrow the need for direct human connection.

To develop the skills we need to interact in a face-to-face context, we must practice reading others and responding in the moment. Online relationships do little to foster these skills because asynchronous texting and posting don't mimic real time interactions. Therefore, many young people lack the skills to develop a social life or meaningful relationships. Development of these skills then becomes one of the goals of therapy, and the therapeutic relationship begins the process in which clients can meaningfully connect with another and practice newly acquired skills. Conversations may focus on identifying needs that the client is trying to meet through social media and ways to connect with others that will reliably meet those needs. Surprisingly, because they have interacted primarily online, many young clients do not know how to initiate or maintain friendships outside of structured activities. There is no simple cure for loneliness, but developing relationships is a foundational piece.

CULTIVATING NARRATIVES

Identity is always a work in progress, not a one-time discovery. A person doesn't grow up, form an identity, and retain that static sense of self for the rest of their life. Instead, the mind is continually constructing and modifying the self-narrative through repeated activation of neural networks that modify existing mental patterns and memories. The narrative story is the format through which we make sense of implicit autobiographical memories that may remain outside of conscious awareness but that, nevertheless, impact identity. Self-narratives are the principle means by which we communicate, to ourselves and others, who we are; they ebb and flow over time as identity is expanded and reworked in response to experiences. When an incoherent or missing narrative is rewritten, there is potential for healing.

As visual messages have come to dominate social media, young people seek to boil down their identity communication into images, icons, and symbols (emojis, avatars, and memes) to be shared and understood rapidly on social media. By accessing these images and their corresponding stories, young people are brought into therapeutic conversations that offer valuable perspectives on the hidden emotional content of their lives. Through these activities, new neuronal linkages are created and integrated to broaden the ingrained mental states that have produced inflexible and incoherent narratives.[8] The narrative process involves complex layers of brain integration as it links countless forms of representation, including memories of touch, sounds, smells, and visual images along with the emotions they arouse. According to Dan Siegel, a coherent narrative occurs through interhemispheric integration, which represents the "drive to make sense of the mind."[9] While the right hemisphere's retrieval of autobiographical representations creates the imagery and symbolic themes of the narrative, the left hemisphere makes sense of or interprets cause–effect relationships in the narrative and enables linguistic processing of the representations. Impaired bilateral integration is evident in eating disordered individuals when they are unable to access internal emotional reactions and bodily states.

Blending of left- and right-hemispheric processes is necessary for a coherent narrative and is an outcome of photo therapy techniques. For instance, recall the symbolic supremacy of images to represent emotional and autobiographical processes, which enabled individuals, whose stories were shared in preceding chapters, to experience and understand the thoughts and sensations of themselves and others. This integration is necessary for an individual to relate to others, for it is only through emotional awareness that true relatedness to others can occur. Emotional awareness, in combination with interpretive left-hemispheric processes that make sense of this content by the telling of the tale, makes for a coherent life story, one that organizes the sense of self and prepares a client to share their narrative with others. The narrative process integrates multiple layers of neural circuits throughout the brain and between brains,[10] making the act of storytelling a powerful experience for both the narrator and audience. The value of sharing our narrative with another should not be underestimated, for sharing of our life story creates relational bonds. Coherent narratives reconsolidate memories so that the past, the present, and the future can exist in the same story. The narrative is much more than remembrances of past events, "our narrative identities are the stories we live by" in the future.[11] Making sense of the past and imagining the future build sense of self and empower a person to live a life of intention and choice.

CULTIVATING SELF-ORIENTED PROCESSES

The self-oriented processes described in the case excerpts throughout this book serve multiple therapeutic purposes. Engaging in self-compassion, self-reflection, self-awareness, self-differentiation, and self-realization enables clients to experience a sense of self. Neural integration is cultivated through these processes when a client notices their reactions in mind and body as they respond to experiences and learn to express their thoughts and feelings.

Self-compassion, the first process (discussed in Chapter 4), is one of the most difficult to attain and is often not fully recognized until late in the course of therapy. For those struggling with eating disorders, there is often a surface level of shame around the eating disorder behaviors themselves, especially for binge eating and purging behaviors, which are judged as disgusting and out of control. There are also deeper levels of shame around the inability to eat normally or live up to societal expectations for the thin ideal. Deep roots of shame arise from abuse and neglect, as well as from not feeling accepted by family members or living up to their expectations. As we saw with Brandon, self-compassion can only grow when perspectives are broadened through insight into past experiences and a shift away from self-blame for things that were not his fault. Reviewing his family images opened the possibility for rewriting his identity narrative to focus on strengths and resilience rather than shame and negative evaluations. This therapeutic experience updates a client's identity to garner greater self-compassion.

Self-reflection is an essential method for knowing the self. By directing attention inward, self-reflection offers an opening into unconscious aspects of the self and an awareness of thoughts and emotional states. Critical, internalized voices may be brought into awareness, along with behaviors that cause or impede recovery. For clients like Tia, images trigger eating disorder thoughts and behaviors, but their own images may be used as a portal into unconscious aspects of the self that they have previously been unable to access. Self-reflection is about observing, listening, and learning what one's inner voice is saying. Because it may bring up strong emotions, self-reflection occurs only when the therapeutic relationship is comfortable and safe. Neural integration occurs when cognitive and emotional expression are experienced simultaneously. Self-reflection is foundational to self-regulation, self-soothing, and to gaining perspective on readiness for change.

Self-awareness builds from self-reflection as clients learn to detect the unconscious motives that drive their behavior. Macy, who you met in Chapter 7, gained self-awareness as she realized that she was aspiring to the wrong things for the wrong reasons. An overvaluation of peer acceptance was played out in excessive posting of selfies in hopes of affirmation from others and in difficulty setting boundaries with others. In viewing her selfies, she became more aware of her physical sensations, which told her she was experiencing strong emotional reactions to the images. Being able to perceive bodily reactions is the underpinning of emotional awareness. Self-awareness can exist only to the degree that conscious awareness of current body states can be experienced.[12] Macy must know what she is feeling to know herself. As she combined right-hemispheric emotional awareness with the verbal left-hemispheric processes of exploring her narrative story, she experimented with new ways of thinking and acting.

Macy's growing self-awareness allowed her to identify her own values without undue influence from her peers, which moved her to the next self-oriented process: self-differentiation—the interplay between autonomy and connection. Typically, the desire for self-differentiation surges during adolescence, but Macy was comfortable in her roles and relationships until she entered college, when she was faced with building new peer networks. She relied on her identity as an athlete until this was no longer an option. Transitions and stressful situations may bring identity struggles to the forefront, especially if identity is dependent on roles or external characteristics.

For a young adolescent like Sara, the self-differentiation journey may be more typical, but it may be a longer process, due to the time required for other developmental processes to co-occur. When I first began treating eating disorders, it was routinely estimated that length of treatment was eight to ten years. Unease with this statistic led to a deeper exploration and comprehension of the difficulty in treating anorexia in very young adolescents, who are simultaneously undergoing changes in cognitive, emotional, and physical realms. This excessively long treatment estimate demonstrates the difficulty of treating severe psychological disorders in the midst of a slow developmental process such as adolescence.

Self-differentiation is only one of the challenges as clients seek to balance autonomy and connection in a time when social media does little to foster individuality or enable meaningful connections. Sara and I first studied social media images to expand her awareness of pro-ED content. Individuals with body image disturbances project their general life concerns onto their bodies instead of dealing with their negative emotions. Sara's intense feelings were expressed through her eating disorder behaviors instead of through directly facing the strains of adolescence and relational challenges with her peers. Her reactions to social media images chronicled her self-differentiation journey as Sara contemplated connection, comparison, and the place of her eating disorder in her life. By reconnecting with offline experiences, Sara moved forward on her identity journey.

The final process, self-realization, comes to fruition when clients draw themes together in their narrative to make meaning of their life story and find a sense of purpose in their lives. For clients, like Claire, whose history includes childhood neglect and trauma as well as more recent trauma on social media, self-realization is impossible without resolution of the trauma that underlies the eating disorder symptoms. By addressing the trauma, assisted by the use of family images and social media images, Claire engaged in self-oriented processes to reconsolidate her memories in a new narrative that enables her to trust her emotions rather than numbing from them and avoiding her feelings through excessive exercise and restriction. A shift in perspective freed her from self-doubt and confusion. For many of our clients, social media mimics self-realization by providing a platform to purvey a false identity that is created to obtain acceptance and approval in an online culture, fixated on poisonous images. Cultivating self-realization imparts the freedom to show the true self, and it is the heart of authenticity

CULTIVATING IDENTITY

Despite the fact that the brain is constantly altering content and shifting memories with each recall event, identity contributes to a vital sense of permanence. The self feels continuous only once there is the neural complexity to bring together the past with the present and to unite thoughts with emotions into a coherent narrative. Imagine the brain collecting thousands and thousands of images and assembling them into the self-narrative, much like a movie consists of static frames that create the semblance of a continuous storyline when viewed as a continuous thread. The narrative process is about freeing clients to write the next chapter. These days, clients will more often use images as a visual device to supplement their narrative storyline. Images convey client experiences on a deeper emotional level than words alone. Through self-oriented processes, the brain is able to shift perspectives and build a healing narrative that organizes the seemingly chaotic experiences and overabundant images into a coherent identity.

REFERENCES

1. Hudson, J. I., Hiripi, E., Pope, H. G., & Kessler, R. C. (2007). The prevalence and correlates of eating disorders in the National Comorbidity Survey Replication. *Biological Psychiatry, 61*(3), 348–358.

   Le Grange, D., Swanson, S. A., Crow, S. J., & Merikangas, K. R. (2012). Eating disorder not otherwise specified presentation in the U.S. population. *International Journal of Eating Disorders, 45*(5), 711–718.

2. Rindfuss, R. R. (1991). The young adult years: Diversity, structural change, and fertility. *Demography, 28,* 493–512.

3. Arnett, J. J. (2000). Emerging adulthood: A theory of development from the late teens through the twenties, *American Psychologist, 55,* 469–480.

4. Burke, P. J., & Stets, J. E. (2009). *Identity theory.* New York, NY: Oxford University Press.

5. Weiser, J. (1999). *PhotoTherapy techniques: Exploring the secrets of personal snapshots and family albums* (p. 307). Vancouver, BC: Judy Weiser and PhotoTherapy Centre Publishers.

6. Broderick, P. C., & Blewitt, P. (2015). *The life span: Human development for helping professionals* (4th ed.). Upper Saddle River, NJ: Pearson.

7. Lapides, F. M. (2010). Neuroscience: Contributions to the understanding and treatment of eating disorders. In M. Maine, B. Hartman McGilley, & D. Bunnell (Eds.), *Treatment of eating disorders: Bridging the research-practice gap* (pp. 37–52). San Diego, CA: Academic Press.

8. Siegel, D. J. (2012). *The developing mind: How relationships and the brain interact to shape who we are* (2nd ed.). New York, NY: Guilford Press.

9. Siegel, D. J. (2012). *The developing mind: How relationships and the brain interact to shape who we are* (2nd ed., pp. 371–372). New York, NY: Guilford Press.

10. Siegel, D. J. (2012). *The developing mind: How relationships and the brain interact to shape who we are* (2nd ed., pp. 371–372). New York, NY: Guilford Press.

11. McAdams, D. P., Josselson, R., & Lieblich, A. (2006). Introduction. In D. P. McAdams, R. Josselson, & A. Lieblich (Eds.), *Identity and story: Creating self in narrative* (p. 4). Washington DC: American Psychological Association.

12. Damasio, A. (2000). *The feeling of what happens: Body and emotion in the making of consciousness.* New York, NY: Mariner Books.

APPENDIX A

PHOTO THERAPY QUESTIONS AND EXERCISES

This list of photo therapy questions and exercises is included to provide guidance for implementing photo therapy with images that clients are exposed to. The purpose of using these questions and activities is to assist clients to discover their meaning of the images.

USING THE FAMILY ALBUM

What photo shows the rules for how someone must be to be included in your family?

What does the selected photo say about this memory?

Is this family album a true picture of your childhood?

What do these images say?

What would you change to make the images more accurate?

What do these images say about your body?

Tell me about your favorite image of yourself.

Observe who is standing next to or touching whom in the non-posed images.

What's important for me to know about your family as I look at this image?

What would you like to tell the people in this photo?

USING IMAGES CREATED BY THE CLIENT

What do you notice about these images as you see them all together?

What were you hoping these images would capture emotionally?

Pick only one of the images that is most representative of you. How did you decide what would be in this image?,

How did you decide how much to include in the image?

Does this image have a message to give?

Where does this message come from?

Ask the image: what do you say about my own life?

Photo Narrative Assignment

Initial Assignment:

1. This assignment asks you to communicate with yourself about yourself.
2. Take 8 photographs to tell the story of you to yourself.
3. Your images can be of anything as long as they tell the story of yourself over time, including the future if you wish.
4. Create an eight- page book of your images.
5. You are the creator and the audience for the story you will tell through this photo narrative. This is your story that you show in images and we will view in the images.

Follow-up Assignment

1. Review the original photo narrative and ask yourself how you might retell the story.
2. Record your thinking by taking 8 more photographs that depict yourself as you now see yourself.
3. Include these photos in your revised book.
4. Like before, you are the creator and the audience for the story you will tell through this photo narrative. This is your story that you show in images and we will view in the images.

Externalizing the Eating Disorder Assignment

1. Take a photo or imagine how your eating disorder looks.
2. Create a hashtag that would likely accompany the online image.
3. Compose posts you would like to write if you saw the online image of your eating disorder.

USING SELFIES

What was it like to plan this selfie?

What did you caption it with?

How did you choose which version to post?

Did it come out like you wanted?

What do you like about this selfie?

Tell me a story about this person.

What's this selfie saying?

What does the person in this selfie want?

Where does that register in your body?

How is this selfie feeling?

What does this selfie want to be feeling?

What does this selfie bring up for you?

Questions for Today's Selfie Says Assignment

When you took this selfie, whom did you unconsciously take it for?

How did you want them to react to it?

What's the message in this selfie?

What would you want to ask this person in the selfie?

What do you like about this image?

Where in your body do you register the feelings you get in viewing this selfie?

Is this the real you in this selfie? If yes, how so?, or If not, how not?

What would this selfie say, if it could talk?

What would this selfie say to the first selfie you ever showed me?

What does this selfie not show?

Using Viewed Images

Tell me a story about the person in this image, about her life and who she is.

What themes do you see repeated in these images?

What are the feelings shown in the images?

What reactions are you having right now as you look at these images?

How would you know if your friends were sharing some of these same feelings?

What emotions do you see demonstrated in this image? How can you tell?

What do you imagine are the reasons or expectations for taking and posting this image?

How might you title it?

What feelings come up for you as you view this image?

Why might the photographer have wanted to take this picture of herself in the first place?

If this image could talk, what do you think it would say?

What's the message that you think might be behind these words?

What questions would you want to ask the image?

Any clue as to what it would say?

What has happened in the person's life that has brought her take this photograph?

If you could climb into the photograph to be with this person, how would you pose the two of you together?

What does the image see when looking at you?

What questions might the image want to ask you?

Could this person be having the same type of experiences or feelings you are? How can you tell these things? How does the image communicate this information to you?

USING OTHERS' IMAGES OF CLIENT

Who took this image?

What's under this image?

What do you remember about the day this image was taken?

What would someone not know about you from looking at this photograph?

How much of this image is representative of yourself, and how much is another's definition of you?

What negative belief comes up for you when you view these images?

Is there a message in that photo?

APPENDIX B

DATE & LENGTH OF TIME	VISUAL MEDIA (how and what you are viewing)	THOUGHTS (how you have been socialized to interact and the critical or supportive internal dialogue)

SENSATIONS EMOTIONS	BEHAVIORS (actions taken in response to what is viewed, thoughts, and emotions)

Index

Note: Italicized page locators refer to figures.

About the Author

Shauna Frisbie is a licensed professional counselor and approved supervisor for licensed professional counselors (LPC-S), a Certified Eating Disorders Specialist (CEDS), and a National Certified Counselor (NCC). She graduated from Texas Tech University in 1998 with a master's in Human Development and Family Studies and in 2001 with a doctorate in Counselor Education. Dr. Frisbie has taught psychology, family studies, and counseling at Lubbock Christian University since 2001 and is currently a professor of clinical mental health counseling. Her clinical work with children, adolescents, and adults has taken place in various settings including agencies, the Texas Tech Health Sciences Center, and private practice. She has been in private practice, specializing in eating disorders and trauma, since 2000.

An avid interest in photography and the role of photography in modern society, as well as extensive work with adolescents, led Dr. Frisbie to explore the impact of social media on mental health. As an eating disorder specialist, she seeks to expand treatment methods to address social media use in this population. In addition to working with eating disorders, Dr. Frisbie is currently involved in international research projects on the impact of trauma on children and adolescents. She lives on the high plains of Texas with her husband. Find out more about Dr. Frisbie at www.drfrisbie.com.